KREJCIR

KREJCIR

BUSINESS AS USUAL

Angelique Serrao

Angelique.

Jonathan Ball Publishers

Johannesburg & Cape Town

© Text Angelique Serrao 2016
© Published edition 2016 Jonathan Ball Publishers

Originally published in South Africa in 2016 by
JONATHAN BALL PUBLISHERS
A division of Media24 (Pty) Ltd
PO Box 33977
Jeppestown
2043

Reprinted in 2017

ISBN 978-1-86842-744-4
ebook ISBN 978-1-86842- 45-1

Twitter: www.twitter.com/JonathanBallPub
Facebook: www.facebook.com/JonathanBallPublishers
Blog: http://jonathanball.bookslive.co.za/

Cover design by Michiel Botha
Cover image of Radovan Krejcir at the Palm Ridge Magistrate's Court
courtesy of *The Star*, taken by Antoine de Ras
Design and typesetting by Triple M Design
Indexed by Sanet le Roux
Printed and bound by CTP Printers, Cape Town
Set in 10.5/15pt Sabon MT Pro

For my sunshine boys –
Even on days when the darkness in the world intrudes,
you show me that there is light.

Angelique Serrao

Contents

RADOVAN KREJCIR:
Timeline of key events

June 2005: Krejcir escapes from the Czech police and flees the country.

July–September 2005: Krejcir makes allegations against the Czech Government from his hideout in the Seychelles.

21 April 2007: Krejcir arrives in South Africa and is arrested.

4 June 2007: Krejcir is released on bail from the Kempton Park Magistrate's Court.

13 June 2007: Krejcir hands himself back to the police after his arrest warrant is reissued.

6 July 2007: Krejcir is released on bail after his second arrest one month earlier.

October 2008: Krejcir's application for asylum in South Africa is refused; he appeals to the Refugee Appeal Board.

1 December 2009: Banker Alekos Panayi makes a statement implicating Krejcir in a money-laundering scheme.

5 December 2009: Private investigator Kevin Trytsman is shot at his lawyer's offices.

8 February 2010: German national Uwe Gemballa arrives in South Africa and is reported as missing the next day.

3 May 2010: Strip-club owner Lolly Jackson is murdered.

September 2010: Krejcir's extradition case is reopened after a ruling that the magistrate in the previous proceedings was not impartial.

27 September 2010: Uwe Gemballa's body is found.

29 October 2010: First arrest takes place in Gemballa's murder.

21 March 2011: Gangland boss Cyril Beeka is murdered in Cape Town.

22 March 2011: The Hawks raid Krejcir's house.

25 March 2011: Krejcir hands himself over to the police.

28 March 2011: Krejcir appears in court over a case involving medical fraud.

17 April 2011: Lolly Jackson murder accused, George Louca, tells the media he did not kill Jackson.

20 September 2011: Ian Jordaan, Jackson's former lawyer, is murdered.

28 September 2011: Jackson's former business partner Mark Andrews is murdered.

10 October 2011: Drug dealer Chris Couremetis is gunned down by hit men.

12 February 2012: Krejcir is arrested for robbery.

26 March 2012: Louca is arrested in Cyprus.

16 April 2012: Fraud charges are dropped against Krejcir.

October 2012: Robbery charges against Krejcir are withdrawn.

24 July 2013: Automatic weapon attached to a car shoots at Krejcir; he escapes uninjured.

12 October 2013: Drug dealer Sam Issa is gunned down.

2 November 2013: Krejcir's accomplice Veselin Laganin is shot dead.

12 November 2013: A bomb explodes inside Moneypoint, Krejcir's front business.

22 November 2013: Krejcir is arrested for kidnapping, drug dealing and attempted murder.

25 November 2013: Krejcir appears in court.

February 2014: George Louca is extradited to South Africa from Cyprus.

May 2014: SARS seizes all of Krejcir's assets with a preservation order.

5 November 2014: George Louca signs five key affidavits.

6 February 2015: Krejcir is charged with Issa's murder.

21 April 2015: Louca reveals in court that Krejcir allegedly killed Jackson.

11 May 2015: Louca dies in prison.

26 September 2015: Krejcir tries to escape from jail.

12 November 2015: Three men found guilty of Uwe Gemballa's murder.

27 November 2015: Krejcir's Bedfordview and Bloemfontein houses are auctioned off by SARS.

December 2015: Krejcir is transferred to C-Max Prison, Kokstad.

23 February 2016: Krejcir is sentenced to 35 years in prison.

8 March 2016: Gemballa's convicted murderer, Kagiso Ledwaba, escapes from Palm Ridge Magistrate's Court.

20 April 2016: Krejcir loses appeal against his conviction and sentence.

CHAPTER 1

'WITH THE RIGHT CONNECTIONS, MONEY CAN BUY YOU ANYTHING'

These are the words of a dead man.

He was a petty criminal. A thug. A hit man. Someone you shouldn't trust. Even his identity wasn't something you could be sure of. He had multiple names: George Smith, George Louca, George Louka.

Take your pick. They are all right, and all wrong, depending on whom you speak to.

His words can never be proven – he is dead, after all, and he was not someone to trust. But, there his words are, in black and white, signed and stamped by a commissioner of oaths.

They were uttered in his dying days, in a jail cell, witnessed by his lawyer, who swore the man had transformed. Because Louca had nothing left to lose – the cancer that had started in his lungs had spread. It was now in his throat and he could barely talk. He was a shadow of the big brute of a man who had been terrorising Bedfordview before he fled the country in 2010. There was no hope for him. He would die, alone, in a jail cell, far from his family in Cyprus.

And, with death so close, he was no longer scared. He would write down a little of what he knew about the man whose very name instilled fear in those who heard it: Radovan Krejcir.

If you believed Louca, Krejcir was the man who had led him to this point of no return. Krejcir was a man so dangerous, it was only Louca's inevitable death that would make him spill the beans.

Most of Louca's words would never be heard in court, though. There would be no prosecutions. No one would pay for what had happened, for the blood that had been spilt. But Louca's words were there, written down, so that, one day, everyone would hear what he had said in his dying days.

That day has come ...

George Louca met Krejcir in April 2007. They shared a cell at the Kempton Park Magistrate's Court. Louca had been arrested on charges of theft. Krejcir was a fugitive from the Czech Republic. He was red-flagged and arrested as soon as he set foot in South Africa.

According to Louca,[1] 'Krejcir introduced himself as a businessman of considerable wealth and influence in Europe who had extensive international business experience. He advised that upon his release from custody he intended to establish businesses in South Africa.

'Over a period of several days Krejcir and I engaged in discussion. It became apparent that Krejcir was concerned by the fact that he knew almost no-one in this country; that his command of the English language was limited; that he had no prior experience of the South African business environment and there were issues around his immigration status. For these reasons he expressed interest in the possibility of using my services. I offered to assist him in exchange for the promise of financial reward.

'Krejcir and I were locked up in our cell at night but for most of the day we were free to walk about as we pleased. We had access to the fenced yard at the Kempton Park Magistrate's Court.

'One day a young girl, approximately 15 or 16 years of age, appeared at the gate of the yard and signalled for my attention.

'When I approached her she addressed me in English, asking whether I knew "Mr Radovan". Once it was confirmed that I knew Krejcir, the girl passed me a letter through the gate and instructed me to deliver it to Krejcir.

'Upon receipt of the letter, Krejcir commented that it was written in Czech but appeared, in his opinion, to have been written by someone using one of the free language translation software applications available on the internet.

'Krejcir said that he had been offered an opportunity to guarantee his release on bail in consideration for payment of a bribe.

'He was interested in exploring this opportunity and if possible to come to an arrangement which would ensure his release, but at the same time he was cautious and concerned as to whether the person (or people) making the approach could be trusted.

'As he explained it, Krejcir was expected to make telephone contact with a person whose number was supplied in the letter.

'For this reason, Krejcir asked me whether I could source a mobile phone which could be used for this purpose. I obtained a cell phone.

'He asked me to make the telephone call, on his behalf, to the person whose number appeared in the letter. He seemed concerned that with his limited English he might be at a disadvantage in communicating clearly and also be unable to assess whether the person or people he was dealing with could be trusted.

'I called the number provided in the letter and spoke to a woman.'

They came up with an arrangement that an upfront payment of R1 million would be made by Krejcir and, following his release, a further R3 million, which Krejcir allegedly later renegotiated to R500 000.

Louca was in charge of handing over the bag with the money. It was about 10 pm and dark outside. He was travelling with a woman called Ronell, who had helped source the cash through a loan.

They were in her Mercedes, just as they had planned, awaiting further instructions. The bag of money was in the car. Louca had opened it briefly and noted that it contained a substantial amount of cash.

The phone rang. It was the woman. She told them to drive onto the R21 highway towards Pretoria and stop at an Engen petrol station on the way. They stopped at the garage and waited. Another call came. They were told to get back onto the R21. They drove for a bit and were then instructed to pull over by the side of the road.

Louca was told to get out with the bag and walk a short distance away from the car. 'I did as I was instructed and though it was quite dark ... I could see the lights of a vehicle which had stopped at a distance behind the Mercedes.

'I walked about 10 or 12 metres from the rear of the Mercedes carrying the bag, before placing it on the side of the road. Then I returned to the Mercedes.

'Ronell and I waited briefly in order to ensure that the bag was collected. Looking behind us … I could see someone picking up the bag.

'… We drove off.'

Radovan Krejcir had just secured his freedom. South Africa, it seemed, was a country that spoke to his values, where he could, and would, do anything. This was the place for him – a place he could call home.

CHAPTER 2

BILLIONAIRE ON THE RUN

Radovan Krejcir was young, and he was rich – a Czech billionaire still in his thirties. The world was at his feet and he knew how to live large. He had a gorgeous bombshell of a wife, drove around in red Ferraris and could be spotted in the most fashionable districts of Prague. Over six feet tall and with a witty sense of humour, he was the kind of man who turned heads.

Back in the 1990s Krejcir wasn't yet known as an underworld kingpin. In the Eastern Bloc country, a part of the world that has gained a reputation for creating sinister mafia Dons, he was small fry, an unknown.

But that would change – and embarrassingly so for the police – in the European summer of 2005, when, overnight he became a household name.

Radovan Krejcir was born in Dolní Žukov, a village in the Czech Republic, on 4 November 1968. His mother, Nadezda Krejcirova, was a successful businesswoman and one of the wealthiest women in the country. His father, Lambert, was a member of the Communist Party during the socialist era.

Krejcir graduated from the University of Ostrava as an engineer. He married Katerina Krejcirova, a beauty with black hair and green eyes, who was eight years his junior. They had two children, Denis, who was born in 1992, and Damian, born in 2009.

By the time he was 21, Krejcir had a business selling food, drinks and cigarettes, and, allegedly, Smarties. Like his mother, he had entrepreneurial flair and his business flourished, developing into a network of companies trading in all sorts of goods, particularly fuel.

Krejcir had amassed a fortune by the time he was 30, most of it made during the wave of state-industry privatisation that followed the 1989 Velvet Revolution, which saw the overthrow of the communist government in the former Czechoslovakia.

He flashed his wealth around, acquiring numerous properties and luxury cars. His home was a villa near Prague, a luxury 2 000-square-metre estate partially carved into a hillside, estimated to have cost $15 million. There were squash and basketball courts, indoor and outdoor swimming pools, and an enclosure for a pet tiger. A giant aquarium sported reef sharks and a large moray eel.

It didn't take long before Krejcir was in trouble with the law. Slowly, the image of a successful young businessman became tarnished as it emerged that he had been infiltrating the Czech criminal underworld. Police investigations were opened against him for fraud, tax evasion and counterfeiting.

His company, which imported oil, mainly from Germany and Russia, was accused of not paying taxes and owed the state millions of Czech crowns. Krejcir was also accused of various financial crimes, such as transferring huge sums of money to the Virgin Islands to avoid paying tax.

He was first arrested in 2002 and spent seven months in jail before being released on a technicality. He was arrested again in September 2003 and spent a year in custody for loan fraud. He and his accomplices were suspected of stripping a company known as Technology Leasing of its assets.

In January 2011 the Municipal Court in Prague convicted Krejcir of breach of trust and sentenced him to eight years in jail. This was one of many crimes of which he was found guilty in his home country. He never served the sentences.

In 1996 Krejcir acquired possession and control of shares that he was contractually obliged to return to a company called Frymis. He failed to return the shares, causing damage of approximately 75 million Czech crowns (approximately R30 million). Much later he was eventually convicted on a charge of fraud relating to these shares, and sentenced to six and a half years in prison, which was later reduced on appeal to six years.

He was also alleged to have been one of the organisers of customs-duty evasion by a fuel importer registered in the Czech Republic. According to SARS investigators, on 3 December 2012 he was convicted for his involvement, *in absentia*, and sentenced to 11 years' imprisonment and a fine of 3 million Czech crowns.

Krejcir was also charged with having ordered and organised the abduction of a businessman, Jakub Konecny, who was allegedly forced to sign blank promissory notes, and other documents in Krejcir's presence. He was convicted and sentenced to six and a half years' imprisonment for blackmail.

The fraudulent activities were one thing, but the pile of dead bodies that started to accumulate around him was more concerning. A key witness in a tax-evasion case against Krejcir, Petr Sebesta, was found murdered with a cartridge in his hand, a typical warning from the Czech mafia.

Krecjir was arrested in 2002, when he spent a few months in jail before being released. He was found guilty of crimes in his home country years later, after he had fled the Czech Republic. During his first stint behind bars in 2002, his father, who owned a printing business, mysteriously disappeared. A well-known and influential football-club owner, Jaroslav Starka, was arrested in 2006 for the murder. Police believed Lambert had been kidnapped to force his son to pay up his business debts. Some believe Lambert had a heart attack when he was bundled into the trunk of the kidnapper's vehicle. His body was never found and Krejcir said he believed Czech state agents dissolved him in a vat of acid.

The football-club owner denied any involvement in the abduction, saying he and Krejcir were on good terms.

The so-called godfather of organised crime in the country, Frantisek Mrazek, was murdered in a professional hit in January 2006 when a sniper shot him outside his office building. Czech media pointed fingers at Krejcir, saying he blamed Mrazek for his father's death. South African writer and researcher Julian Rademeyer in 2010 said Krejcir laughed when asked if he had anything to do with the killing.[1] Krejcir pointed out he had been in the Seychelles at the time of the murder: 'Yes, I shot one bullet from the Seychelles and the bullet travelled all the way direct to his heart. I'm very good ... I saw this guy twice in my life. We never had a fight. It is the same situation as my father. They killed him and afterwards said it was my criminals. All the time it was the top government and secret service guys.'

Krejcir claimed that he was the victim of a political vendetta, spurred on by a prime minister whose ascent to power he had, ironically, helped fund. He admitted having funded the election campaign of the Czech Social Democratic Party candidate, Stanislav Gross, in a deal whereby Gross would hand Krejcir control of the state petroleum company, CEPRO, in the event that he was elected prime minister.

Krejcir claimed Gross had refused to honour the agreement and asked Krejcir to hand over the promissory note. Incensed, Krejcir refused and threatened to go to the media.

'During July 2002, I was arrested on trumped-up charges of fraud and detained for a period of seven months during which I was physically and psychologically tortured so as to reveal the whereabouts of the promissory note,' Krejcir is quoted as saying in *Lolly Jackson: When Fantasy Becomes Reality*.[2] 'During the period of my incarceration, my father was questioned as to the whereabouts of the promissory note. He was unable to supply any information ... and was abducted and eliminated as a result.'

Some years later, just before midnight on 18 June 2005, 20 balaclava-clad security police and state prosecutors entered Krejcir's villa. They were investigating a tip-off that there were plans to kill a customs official who was a witness in one of the fraud cases they were investigating against Krejcir.

The media reported that Krejcir watched them as they conducted the search operation, following the police as they searched his mansion. A few hours later, the police realised he was gone. It was widely reported that he had asked to go to the bathroom and escaped through a window. However, Krejcir later said that corrupt police officers had allowed him to leave. He told Rademeyer that there was no window in his bathroom.

'I don't know how you could escape from 20 guys with machine guns and masks on their faces.' He told Czech journalist Jiri Hynek[3] that the reason the police wanted to arrest him was that the Social Democrats did not want to repay him the money he had lent them.

He said the police asked him for money, telling him they would let him go. He then pretended to look for the cash, walked out the back door and didn't return.

According to Czech press reports, the morning of his escape he ate breakfast at a friend's house nearby and was spotted filling up a Lamborghini at a petrol station in Slovakia three days later.

A few weeks later, Krejcir emerged in Istanbul. He said later that he had stayed in the Czech Republic for a week. From Prague he went to South Bohemia and Moravia. From a mountainside cottage in Beskydy friends helped him flee the country by falsifying a passport, under the name of Tomiga. He entered Poland by bicycle, took a train to the Ukraine then flew to Istanbul.

By then, everyone in the Czech Republic knew who he was. His escape was a national embarrassment, and it cost police chief Jiri Kolar his job.

Searching his villa, the police had got a picture of everything Krejcir had allegedly been up to. The house contained a secret strongroom packed with weapons, jewellery, share certificates and classified police documents. A police officer later testified in court that they had also found a parliamentary ID card and DNA was found on skiing goggles that matched that of the entrepreneur who had vanished, Konecny. According to TV Nova,[4] Konecny had disappeared in March 2005.

The policeman also said they found a briefcase containing notes, diagrams and plans of criminal activities, and forged passports.

In a factory Krejcir owned they found billions of crowns in counterfeit currency. Mixed into the boxes of cash was 8 million crowns (about R3 million) in genuine currency. Krejcir told Rademeyer the boxes of cash were an elaborate birthday gift for a close friend.

From Istanbul, Krejcir flew to Dubai where he met up with his wife, who was facing complicity charges, and son. They flew to the Seychelles.

Ensconced in a five-star hotel overlooking the turquoise seas of the archipelago, Krejcir had escaped the clutches of the law. He was secure in the knowledge he could not be touched because the Czech Republic had no extradition agreement with the small island state, whose citizenship he purchased in 2006. He even felt bold enough to thumb his nose at the Czech authorities by giving regular interviews in the Czech media from his island retreat.

He was set to live out his days in tropical luxury. But, for the man who had become so used to wheeling and dealing, the slow pace of island life was not quite the paradise he had thought it would be.

Hynek, the Czech journalist, visited him and remarked that he did not think that Krejcir was satisfied in the Seychelles: 'It's a type of prison for him because he can't go anywhere.'

'It was so boring there, like being a prisoner in paradise,' Krejcir later told Rademeyer.[5]

Perhaps it was out of boredom, or an act of revenge after Czech police arrested five people believed to be his closest accomplices and declared that he was the ringleader of a dangerous gang, but, either way, Krejcir wrote a book, *Radovan Krejcir – Revealed*, in which he describes the Social Democrats' actions[6] as the country's equivalent of the Watergate scandal. Czech Finance Minister Bohuslav Sobotka said Krejcir had lied to get back at the party for breaking up his crime ring.

In the book he disclosed that he had lent money to the Social Democrats in return for special favours. 'I am certain that the present political leadership and the police knew I was beyond their reach the minute they heard I was in the Seychelles. All their media statements about trying to get me extradited were just a smoke screen for the public. I consider myself innocent.'[7]

People in the Seychelles didn't know who he was, until the Czech journalists started arriving. He wrote in his book how, after the journalists came, he would go to the pub and people were silent and looked at him with fear in their eyes.

Soon there was trouble in paradise. In February 2007, Czech authorities signed an extradition treaty with the Seychelles, which would come into effect six months later. It was time for Krejcir to move.

He applied for passports under the name Egbert Jules Savy for himself, Sandra Savy for his wife and Greg Savy for his son, which he received without difficulty.

Just as his departure from the Czech Republic had caused enormous embarrassment for the state, it was the same story when he left the Seychelles. *Le Nouveau Seychelles Weekly*[8] demanded that President James Michel explain how it was possible that Krejcir had been issued legitimate passports under a false name: 'The public is clamouring for an explanation as to how a legal passport could contain a false name.'[9]

A senior official from the Department of Immigration was allegedly behind the issuing of the passport. Krejcir regularly frequented the private offices of the civil servant at Independence House, the government offices, and he was a guest at the man's home. The passports were issued when a certain Michel Elizabeth, described in the local press as a 'diligent incorrupt-ible civil servant' was on holiday. He was apparently asked to take annual leave during that time.

Passports in hand, Krejcir left the island of Mahé aboard his yacht, offi-cially heading for the Amirante archipelago, where he boarded another vessel bound for Madagascar.

Seychelles media learnt that as soon as Krejcir had left Mahé, a letter was sent to the non-existent Egbert Jules Savy demanding that the passport be returned to the immigration authorities for cancellation.

Police in the Seychelles were informed and they issued a red alert to Interpol identifying Krejcir as the holder of an illegally obtained passport.

'Krejcir, it seems, had not endeared himself well with some senior mem-bers of the local police, even though Krejcir had provided foreign currencies to import new police vehicles,' wrote *Le Nouveau Seychelles Weekly*.[10]

There was speculation that the Seychelles authorities had allowed him to leave the country, and then alerted Interpol to get rid of him and make him someone else's problem.

In Madagascar Krejcir boarded a flight and on 27 April 2007 at 5.15 pm, he arrived in South Africa.

CHAPTER 3

FUGITIVE AT THE DOOR

The police were waiting. They knew who he was. His passport with a fake name, his beard and his glasses fooled no one. The Czech Republic's most wanted fugitive was at our door. He was arrested as soon as he set foot in Johannesburg.

The Czech authorities were ecstatic. Czech intelligence officers said they had been monitoring him for a long time and had been waiting to pounce. They said police from five countries cooperated on the case. Interior Minister Ivan Langer called a press conference and handed out photos of a detained Radovan Krejcir.

'He did not put up any resistance and was very surprised,' Langer said.[1]

The Czech Republic now had 40 days to lodge an extradition request with South Africa to bring Krejcir home.

'I anticipate that an extradition request will be processed in the coming days. We are waiting for word from our colleagues in South Africa as to whether they want any additional information. If they don't need any further data, then we will file our request and issue an arrest warrant,' said Justice Minister Jiri Pospisil.[2]

It looked like Krejcir's time on the run was up.

He appeared in the Kempton Park Magistrate's Court two days later and his case was immediately postponed. A special delegation from the Czech Republic arrived in South Africa in a bid to stop Krejcir from being released on bail. Johannesburg High Court Senior State Advocate Beverley Edwards was tasked with handling the case against the fugitive in the lower court.[3]

Krejcir's legal team, headed by Advocate Mannie Witz, argued that he was no longer a citizen of the Czech Republic, as he had given up his nationality when he became a citizen of the Seychelles. Witz argued that Krejcir was now protected by South Africa's Constitution.

Krejcir sat in the dock and smiled at foreign reporters who had travelled to South Africa to witness the case. He was 38 years old; he looked young and was smartly dressed despite having spent a month in jail awaiting trial.

The Czech Government told the court that Krejcir allegedly defrauded the country of about 9.5 billion crowns. The Czech authorities had four warrants of arrest for him.

Krejcir's lawyers claimed, however, that he was trying to enter South Africa to receive medical attention. He needed an MRI brain scan. One of his attorneys, Hugo van der Westhuizen, said Krejcir was experiencing stroke-like symptoms that involved intense headaches and memory loss. The symptoms were at their worst when he was under extreme stress, the attorney said.

At one of his court appearances, a special delegation of state and defence witnesses from the Czech Republic were ready to testify. Government ministers, diplomats, senior police officers, and Krejcir's mother and his son Denis, were in court to hear his fate. Then, in what was described as a shock twist, South Africa's most wanted international fugitive was released on a legal technicality. It was June 2007 – his lawyers argued that the 40 days the state had had to receive extradition papers from the Czech Republic had elapsed. The magistrate ordered Krejcir to be released from prison.

A shocked South African Police Service (SAPS) spokesperson for Interpol, Senior Superintendent Tummi Golding, said they planned to rearrest him. For days, the state had no idea where he was. All airports were alerted and the police began to search.

It turned out he was not plotting his escape, however. He was buying blankets to donate to old-age homes, and soccer balls for underprivileged children. His next charity crusade was to start soup kitchens. His lawyers made sure the media and courts knew every detail of his charity work during his stint of freedom. It had probably been a clever marketing ploy to show the authorities he cared about the country, and would be a citizen worth having on our shores. But, after eight days, he handed himself over to the police.

A Czech delegation comprising state attorneys Petra Pavlanova and Vladimir Tryzna, two Justice Ministry clerks and two policemen argued persuasively in the Kempton Park Magistrate's Court that Krejcir was wanted in his home country for fraud, tax evasion, counterfeiting, kidnapping and conspiracy to murder – all to no avail. Magistrate Stephen Holzen granted him R1 million bail on 6 July on condition that he report to the Lyttelton Police Station twice a week.

Holzen believed Krejcir's version of events and said it was clear he was running away from persecution rather than prosecution and he banned Interpol from arresting him. Considering it could take up to three years to finalise the extradition, it would not serve the interests of justice to keep Krejcir in detention, he said.

The state argued that Krejcir was a flight risk, that he had entered South Africa illegally, with a forged document under a false name, and that he had no emotional attachment or financial assets to keep him in South Africa.

Holzen said he found it strange that the charges against Krejcir were very old, some going back to 1994, while he was still living in the Czech Republic, and yet he had never been arrested there for the charges the Czech Government were now placing before his court. He said Krejcir had been legitimately issued a Seychellois passport, even if it were under a different name. Krejcir, he argued, had in the meantime bought properties and a business in South Africa. And he had told the court of his desire to bring his son and wife to the country permanently.

When he heard he was allowed to go free, Krejcir was all smiles. He told journalists he was impressed with the South African justice system: 'This is a country under constitutional law … and I am convinced that I have done the right thing. It's nice, very nice. Next step? Now I will pay bail and I have to take some rest,' Krejcir said.[4]

He said he was convinced more than ever that he would never go to a Czech prison.

As soon as he was out of custody, Krejcir applied for asylum in South

Africa, claiming he would be persecuted in his homeland and that the former government had ordered his father's murder.

The following year, Holzen would pass a judgment refusing to extradite Krejcir.

For two years, Krejcir appeared to lie low. There was not a peep from him in the press. He bought a magnificent home in Kloof Road, Bedfordview, commanding 180-degree views of Johannesburg. He bought up businesses, one being Moneypoint, a gold and jewellery exchange opposite the busy Eastgate Shopping Centre. Katerina joined him from the Seychelles and soon they would have their second son, Damian.

However, according to the testimony of many who became involved with him around this time, Krejcir was busy setting himself up in the South African underworld. He made friends with characters who knew how to make fast money, by every means possible, and he got cosy with members of the Crime Intelligence Division of the SAPS.

He befriended spies and, in doing so, infiltrated the hidden depths of South Africa's criminal world. His charming personality, wit and the lure of millions in his pocket drew people whom he needed to him. Krejcir never had a problem making new friends.

But the friend who was the key to opening all the doors for him was the man he met in the jail cells at the Kempton Park Magistrate's Court: George Louca (or Louka or Smith, depending on which ID book he decided to use at any given time).

Louca was a well-connected low-life who wheeled and dealed his way through the Bedfordview mafia. Louca's ID, under the surname Smith, was issued in January 2006 and it gave his place of birth as South Africa. But those who knew him said there was no doubt he was an immigrant from Cyprus. It emerged he had been a special-forces operative in the Cypriot military and had been identified as a professional hit man in the Gauteng underworld. Louca had also allegedly served seven years in a Swiss prison for drug trafficking. Staff at a Bedfordview cafe told *The Star*[5] that Louca was aggressive, but they put up with him because he was strip-club king

Lolly Jackson's friend. 'He was like an animal. He was a drug addict,' said the manager.

Their meeting in jail was one of the most fortuitous encounters of Krejcir's life and they developed a strong bond.

According to statements Louca later made to his attorney, Krejcir had just been arrested and brought to the cells of the Kempton Park Police Station (which shares the building with the magistrate's court) when they met. Louca had meanwhile been arrested on charges of theft. The two were both foreign born and this drew them to each other, along with the fact that Krejcir boasted about how rich he was. Louca had experience helping well-pocketed men – for a fee.[6]

It was Louca who introduced Krejcir to Bedfordview. He found him the R13 million mansion that Krejcir would call home for the next six years and he introduced him to the key players in Johannesburg's then fragmented underworld.

Krejcir soon identified a restaurant in Bedford Centre, the area's most upmarket shopping mall, where he could spend his days eating good Mediterranean food and meeting the suburb's cosmopolitan residents. It was the kind of place where wealthy immigrants from all over the world gathered and talked business. The Harbour restaurant was perfect. Situated five minutes from his newly acquired mansion, it had the type of food he enjoyed and a clientele that fitted in with his plans for expansion.

According to his own statements, it was also Louca who helped ensure that Krejcir would not be deported to the Czech Republic.

Louca saw a man he could make money from, and Krejcir saw someone who could help set him up in this strange new country he was determined to make his home. And, within a month of landing in South Africa, Krejcir's tentacles, with the help of Louca, had already infiltrated the criminal-justice system.[7]

The alleged bribery to secure bail sealed the deal. Louca carried out the payment and proved he could be trusted by Krejcir.

Louca said in his statement that in August 2007 he was waiting outside the courtroom for his case to be called when he was approached by a person involved in the bribery. Louca was told: 'Your friend has let me down; he hasn't made the other payment.'

A few days later, Krejcir asked Louca to go with him to meet the person in Pretoria to 'sort out the problem'. In his affidavit, Louca said:

> I accompanied him to a restaurant. I do not recall the name of the restaurant ... Krejcir asked me to remain at the front section of the restaurant and to keep an eye on him while he approached and spoke with the person, who I noted, was already present and seated at a table. I could see both clearly. They spoke together for some time, after which Krejcir rose from the table and left the restaurant accompanied by me.[8]

Louca said that Krejcir had told him, while driving from the restaurant, that they had agreed on a reduced payment of R500 000 from the original R3 million he had asked for.

Confident that he was now in South Africa to stay, Krejcir began to climb the social ladder. His first move: to make friends with the powerful and eliminate any enemies from his past who still posed a threat to his new life.

CHAPTER 4

ASSASSINATIONS PLANNED, ASSASSINATIONS THWARTED

They were heavies, two men who helped out in tense situations. And the foreign man in the company of George Louca looked like someone they could do work for, make some easy money from.

Louca explained to the two security guards that the man he was with, Radovan Krejcir, was a billionaire and that he was the ex-president of the Czech Republic.

This was great stuff, they thought, and they made sure they swopped telephone numbers before the evening was done.[1]

It was 4 November 2007 and it was Krejcir's birthday, the first birthday he was spending in his newly adopted country, and he was celebrating at The Grand, an upmarket strip club in Sandton. The two men were security guards at the club and they knew Louca well. That night Louca was causing trouble as usual. He had got into a fight with Mike Arsiotis, an employee of Krejcir, and they had to kick him out of the club. Later Louca apologised and the bouncers let him back in.

The next day, Krejcir invited the security guards to his house. He was looking for men like them who could help him out in difficult situations.

And it soon turned out he would need them. A few months later, in March or April 2008, the two men got a call from Louca asking them to meet him at Bedford Centre. He explained that Krejcir was having some trouble with a Russian man, Lazarov, and needed backup. They met at the Harbour, where Krejcir was known to spend most of his days.

Krejcir informed the two men that Lazarov had told him that he had been sent to South Africa under instructions to kill him. But the Russian man didn't want to kill Krejcir. Instead, he wanted his money. If Krejcir paid over hundreds of thousands of euros to him, then he wouldn't carry out the hit, Lazarov had told him.

Lazarov had asked to meet him, but Krejcir was worried that the meeting was a set-up, that Lazarov might come with someone else and carry out the hit while Krejcir was off guard.

The security guards and Louca were sitting at a nearby table, ready, in case there was any trouble. Then Lazarov arrived, alone. He was a short man, in his 30s with fair hair. He sat down next to Krejcir and they spoke for half an hour. Lazarov then got up and left.

Krejcir told the men afterwards that the Russian had repeated to him how he had been sent by someone in the Czech Republic to kill him and that he wanted money from him.[2] Krejcir asked them to follow Lazarov and find out where he was staying. The three men got into a white bakkie that was fitted with blue lights.

'George also had a police card as well, so everyone would think we were cops,' the guards later said in an affidavit.[3]

They drove to a hotel in Katherine Street in Sandton and spotted Lazarov outside.

'George then stopped the bakkie and jumped out and grabbed this guy and before the guy could do anything, George brought him to the bakkie and opened the back door and I helped to pull him in,' one of the guards said.[4] They then drove, with the blue lights flashing, to a house in Boksburg. Krejcir arrived shortly afterwards.

There are different versions of what happened next. The guards and Louca gave different accounts years after the kidnapping had happened. They all wrote sworn statements, which were signed by a commissioner of oaths. One thing they did all agree on, though, was that Lazarov was tortured.

According to Louca, the man who carried out the torture was Krejcir; according to the two guards, it was Louca, while Krejcir sat and watched. According to the guards' version of events, Louca started asking the Russian man questions. He was hit after each question.

'The guy fainted and when he opened his eyes I took water and woke him up. He said he wanted vodka and George was laughing. George took a beer from the fridge and gave it to him,' one guard said.[5]

Louca repeatedly asked Lazarov who had sent him. The guard held him down while George hit him.

'I may also have hit him, but I don't remember,' the man said. 'George wanted to stab Lazarov in the hand with a screwdriver and I stopped this from happening.'[6]

Krejcir also asked questions and every time the man answered, Krejcir accused him of lying, the men said.

'I was making some hot water and sugar to drink and the kettle was boiling. George then took the kettle of boiling water and poured it on him [Lazarov] … He poured it into his ears first and when the guy started crying, he poured it into his mouth. Krejcir was watching all of this.'[7]

The guard said he grabbed the kettle away, scalding himself in the process.

'George wanted to stab this guy with a screwdriver,' he said, but the other guard screamed at him to stop, because George now wanted to stab him in the eyes.[8]

Lazarov eventually started to talk. 'Lazarov told Krejcir that he had followed Krejcir to the Seychelles to kill him and that he brought a gun into the Seychelles hidden in a generator,' the guard said.[9] He said he had been paid about €500 000 by someone in the Czech Republic to kill Krejcir.

Louca said Lazarov had admitted to being a hit man and that they should 'take him to the bush and kill him and make his body vanish'.[10] But the two guards say they protested – they had been to his hotel and there were security cameras, so they would be the first suspects.

Instead they decided to take the Russian man to Bedfordview Police Station, where Krejcir would lay a complaint that he had come to try and kill him. Glad to be alive, Lazarov cooperated. He didn't breathe a word of what had been done to him.

The guards were paid R20 000 each for the part they played in the kidnapping.

That is the guards' account. Louca remembered things slightly differently, however. He said that, after the meeting at the Harbour, Krejcir had told him he did not feel safe with Lazarov, that he knew too much about his activities and he believed Lazarov posed a threat to his life.

He said that the Russian answered some of Krejcir's questions when he had been kidnapped, but refused or could not answer others.

'Krejcir began to torture him with a screwdriver which he pushed into Lazarov's neck below his ear,' Louca said.[11] He said that it was Krejcir who beat Lazarov up and tortured him with boiling water:

> He poured boiling water over Lazarov's ear and the side of his face, all the time asking Lazarov to tell him who had sent him here to kill him. This went on for approximately an hour, during which he continued to torture him alternatively beating him and pouring boiling water on the side of his face until the man told Krejcir that he had been hired by Pivoda.
>
> I should mention that Krejcir knew Pivoda. They had at one time been friends in the Czech Republic and shared a keen interest in riding and racing fast motorbikes, but had later fallen out with one another.
>
> Krejcir told me that he believed that Pivoda had learned of a planned attempt on his life, in Prague, which had been arranged by Krejcir earlier in the year and that it was for this reason that Pivoda had, in turn, hired an assassin to kill Krejcir.

He said Krejcir gave orders to the security guards to kill Lazarov and throw his body into the Loskop Dam.

Louca claimed that it was he who had said that Lazarov should not be killed, as he had been abducted outside of a hotel where they may have been captured on security cameras kidnapping him.

They called the police and Lazarov was arrested. After a few months in jail he was deported to Russia when Krejcir withdrew the charges against him.

It was not the first time Louca had been called to help Krejcir out in sticky situations. Except, according to Louca, it was Krejcir ordering the hits.

Going by the sworn statement of a Bedfordview resident who let his flat to a man called Tony, who was born in the Czech Republic and an employee of Krejcir, Louca was believed to be Krejcir's hit man. Krejcir was paying the rent for the flat that Tony lived in.

The owner of the property said that in 2009 he got a call from Tony asking to meet him at a restaurant called Medium Rare, in Van Buuren Road. Louca, who was someone he recognised from living in the area but did not know personally, was also there.[12]

'I noticed that there was some sort of atmosphere between Tony and George, as if they were challenging the pecking order below Radovan Krejcir,' the man said.[13]

In his sworn statement, the man said: 'George Smith came right out and said, "Radovan wants to employ you to do a job for him. He wants to send you overseas to do a hit on a guy and wants to know how much of a fee you will charge for doing this." I was completely taken aback by this, but did not want to immediately shut off the conversation, as I was curious as to what they were talking about.'

It was not made clear why Louca would approach this man to do a hit, and the landlord indicated in his statement that he, too, did not understand why he had been asked to do this. Louca's strange behaviour was remarked upon by many who had dealings with him. Perhaps it was his alleged drug use that led to this odd behaviour, or perhaps the nature of the criminal world he was surrounded by meant that talking about murdering someone didn't seem out of place to him.

Louca then told him they would send him to Germany to do a hit and a weapon would be provided there.

'The way he said this, it was clear he was bragging about their abilities to set up hits and arrange weapons and so on. He said they had been doing this for a while.'[14]

Tony told him Louca was Krejcir's hit man. But Louca claimed he was rather 'an agent, a fall guy' for Krejcir and he would arrange payment, trips, weapons and so forth.

The man said he later made it clear to Tony he would not help them and that he thought he was crazy getting mixed up with this kind of thing.

After he turned down the job, he said that Krejcir stopped paying the rent for his flat. The landlord said he decided to tell someone what had happened. He knew a man called Kevin Trytsman who he thought was an employee of the National Intelligence Agency, but who later turned out to be another employee of Krejcir. The landlord met with Trytsman and told him about the planned hit.

He said that because the rent wasn't paid things became tense between him and Krejcir. He was owed R15 000 and argued with Krejcir about the money over the phone.

'Krejcir said … something like, "Listen, everything will be taken care of, we will arrange the flights, the weapon will be handed to you and we will give you addresses, photographs, everything."'[15]

The man said he was not in that line of business and that he just wanted his rent paid. They swore at each other.

He said he later got a call from a powerful man, a security expert with political connections, a man called Cyril Beeka. Beeka told him he would sort the situation out and the man's rent money was paid into his account the next month.

Tony fell out with Krejcir too and left the country at some point.

Louca said that he visited the Czech Republic on two occasions for Krejcir.[16] The first time was to resolve some concerns over payment for a garage owned by Krejcir and he stayed with Krejcir's mother. That trip was uneventful, Louca said.

The second time, he flew to Prague with Tony. They were told they were going to make payments for Krejcir. They met up with a third man, called Tasso. Louca said that they arrived at a hotel and that night Krejcir called him and told him to go to their hired car in the hotel parking area and unlock the boot, then to leave the car for a while. He had to return later and remove a package, which he was told to give to Tasso.[17]

Louca did as he was told. He looked inside and said he found cash – €55 000 – and two pistols. He called Krejcir to ask about the weapons. Krejcir refused to tell him anything and told him to give the package to Tasso.

'It was obvious that Krejcir had a different agenda from that which he had disclosed to me in South Africa, prior to our departure. It appeared to me that an assassination had been planned,' Louca wrote.[18]

Tasso, he said, told him that he had orders from Krejcir to secure the services of an assassin who was to kill three men in the Czech Republic.

'I told Tasso that I was not prepared to place my hands in anyone's blood; nor would I take part in any plan to murder; and further that I did not care whether Krejcir became upset or ugly as a result of my refusal to cooperate.'[19]

He said he told Tasso there had been only €5 000 in the boot. The men packed up and left. When Louca arrived back in South Africa, he said he gave Krejcir the remaining €50 000 back.

The event was the start of a souring in their relationship, Louca said: 'I complained that he had not been open with me and should not expect me to participate in or be involved with murder. My position on this matter resulted in a falling out with Krejcir. He was angry with me and frustrated by my conduct.'[20]

CHAPTER 5

THE DEATH OF LOLLY JACKSON

Lolly Jackson, the 'king of teaze', looked down into his own grave.

He was in a tuxedo, a white rose in the lapel, and his head, cast downward, was set at the perfect angle to allow him a long look into the six-foot chasm that held his mahogany casket.

It was just a black-and-white portrait, *The Don*, as his family called it, but the knowing smile on his face and the angle of his tilted head gave the odd impression that Jackson knew what he was looking at.

His wife, Demi, dressed all in black and wearing stilettos, walked up to the image of her late husband, kissed it, stroked the surface with her bright-pink nails and whispered 'my big boy' before breaking down in tears.[1]

The sound of her distress was the only emotion on show at the strangely low-key event at South Park Cemetery on the outskirts of Boksburg on 10 May 2010. Jackson's grave was a few metres away from apartheid struggle hero Chris Hani.

Then a gust of wind blew *The Don* down. Shards of shattered glass went skidding across the dry brown grass and into the grave. Jackson's brother Costa chuckled, 'At least he went out with a bang.'[2]

It was a strange event. The family arrived in a Hummer limousine and, if you looked closely, the black suits of the businessmen were Gucci and other expensive labels.

Hanging at the back were women with pale skins, puffing on cigarettes – the Teazers girls, one had to assume. They said not a word, some were clutching supermarket flowers. They left on a bus that had been laid on for them.

Jackson's family threw dirt and yellow rose petals onto the casket. Following Greek Orthodox tradition, bottles of olive oil and red wine were poured into the open grave, followed by a Teazers shirt. The four corners of a Greek flag were held by Demi, Jackson's two sons, Manoli and Julian, and his daughter, Samantha, who placed the flag on the red mahogany coffin.

Vincent Marino, a friend of Jackson for 35 years, gave the eulogy. 'We all know that Lolly was a rough diamond. Rough on the edges in his mannerism, speech and action. But those who had the privilege of knowing him could see beyond the brash exterior, for within he was a man of true quality, committed to what he was responsible for'.[3]

He said Jackson was 'a renegade, the anti-hero who lived by his own rules'.[4] But, despite Marino's attempt to bring some humouristic reminiscences of Jackson's life to the event, the 200-plus crowd wasn't biting. They just stood and stared, waiting for the whole thing to end.

Perhaps it was the horror of what had happened to the man in the casket that made them shudder. The image of how he had been killed in a spray of bullets was too graphic to shake from their thoughts.

The funeral felt as far removed from the life of this man, who had always lived large, as it could be.

Lolly Jackson started out life on the rough streets of Germiston. He saw the business opportunity of strip clubs catering for men's fantasies, of classy girls dancing naked in front of them.

He opened his first Teazers club in Primrose, his childhood suburb, in the early 1990s. The franchise grew until there were six branches around the country. 'The teaze without the sleaze' was the company slogan.[5]

The stripping business made Jackson obscenely wealthy. He owned four properties in Bedfordview, including a huge mansion that eventually sold at auction for R9 million. Regarded as South Africa's own playboy villa, this five-storey, seven-bedroom, five-lounge house had been the scene of many parties featuring a jacuzzi filled with plenty of flesh.

Jackson was one of only three super-rich South Africans who could afford a R14 million Swedish-built Koenigsegg CCX, the world's fastest supercar at the time. His garage contained a fleet of the fastest, most colourful, most luxurious sports cars the world had to offer.

But his early years growing up on the mine-dumped East Rand suburbs never left him. Swinging between typical Mediterranean charm and a foul temper, he was constantly in trouble with the law. His most famous faux pas was in 2005 when he was caught travelling at 249 kilometres per hour in his Lamborghini, but claimed he was en route to church.

Jackson was not afraid of making enemies, from conservatives who balked at his risqué strip-club billboards, to competitors who accused him of sending death threats, and Ukrainian strippers arguing their contract terms with him.

Jackson once said of his competitor Andrew Phillips of The Grand: 'That man has been sleeping on his back for ten years now because he has such a hard-on for me. I know that with fame comes pain. I'm in a business where when I do something right, it is always wrong.'[6]

It was a comment made during a court case of an incident in which Jackson allegedly shot a former employee with a paintball gun containing rubber bullets.

Phillips, when he heard Jackson had died, wasted no time in telling *The Star* exactly how he felt about the strip king: 'I detested the man. He was trash – a bigot, racist, extortionist, megalomaniac. If there was a pie, he wanted the whole one. I won't pretend I'm shedding a tear … I think the world is better off. He was pollution, there was no other way to describe him. The air has been purified. He was a nasty guy.'

Phillips added, 'He lived rough and he's died rough.' [7]

But there were many who mourned the passing of a man they considered a legend. After his death his family, friends and business associates gathered at the Teazers in Rivonia. His wife and children had been inside the club from the early hours of the morning. The family's lawyer, Ian Jordaan, arrived to discuss family and business matters.

Jackson's public-relations manager, Sean Newman, described him as a mentor, an inspiration and a man he deeply respected: 'He was a truly genuine human being. You always knew where you stood with Lolly.'[8]

Lolly died in the same way that he had lived his life – dramatically. It was a late Monday afternoon, 3 May 2010. South Africa was in an energetic mood. The World Cup kick-off was a short time away and everyone was excited about the prospect of having thousands of tourists flocking to our cities.

It was a strange time for the murky secret of our criminal underworld to blast its way to the surface of our consciousness. But that's just what happened when Gauteng police intelligence head Major General Khanyisa 'Joey' Mabasa received a phone call the night Jackson was killed from a man he later claimed had been a police informer, but whom they had to turn loose because of his drug use. It was George Louca. He was crying, Mabasa said. 'I have done something very bad.' Louca told him he had killed Lolly, Mabasa told the *Mail & Guardian*.[9]

Leaked cellphone records later showed Jackson had made his last call, which lasted 27 seconds, to Louca. They also show Louca was in touch with Krejcir on the day of the killing. The call to Mabasa lasted 96 seconds, and a log of the cellphone tower that routed the call indicated Louca was not at the crime scene.

Police rushed to the house where Louca had been staying as a tenant in Kempton Park. They found it locked and had to fetch the owner to open up for them. They found Jackson's bullet-riddled body lying in the garage, a trail of blood indicating that he had been dragged there from the lounge.

News of the murder quickly leaked. In his book, *Lolly Jackson: When Fantasy Becomes Reality*,[10] Sean Newman describes arriving at the scene after he had been called by a journalist and told of Jackson's death. The house had been cordoned off by the police and all that could be seen from the street was a blood smear in the passage near the door.

Demi arrived, stumbled out of the car, screaming, and collapsed in the driveway. She was rushed off to the paramedics. Jackson's son Manoli insisted on going in and seeing his dad. He came out white-faced.

Newman was surprised when he heard that Louca had confessed to the crime. He knew of Louca, having briefly seen him with Jackson a few times.

Initial reports indicated that Jackson had been shot as many as 15 times, but the autopsy report, as described by Newman in his book, showed his body had in fact been hit by six bullets. He was shot three times on the left side of his chest, resulting in a fractured rib and perforated lung. The fourth bullet entered his stomach. Two shots were fired into his head.

'The sixth shot entered 3 cm in front of Lolly's left ear. This was executed at close range, resulting in tattooing of the skin from the gunpowder,' writes Newman.[11]

Ironically, the autopsy showed that if the bullets hadn't killed him, his heart would have.

Forensic pathologist Johannes Steenkamp noted that his heart was enlarged and showed signs of severe cardiac disease. The 53-year-old had been on the brink of heart failure.[12]

In the week following the murder, surprising details began to emerge, bringing the muddy underworld that Jackson had been involved in to light. Rumours that Louca had been a hit man for hire, working for Jackson and Krejcir, began to emerge in the public domain.

Police told journalists that when Louca had called Mabasa, the latter told him to meet him at the Harbour. Mabasa said he organised backup and went to the restaurant, but Louca, who had been there earlier, had already left. Krejcir said he and Beeka had been entertaining friends at the restaurant when Louca arrived. He said Louca had told them that he had killed Jackson, had bought two packets of cigarettes and then left.[13]

Louca was driving Jackson's Jeep Cherokee. The vehicle was found a few days later abandoned on King's Road, Bedfordview, around the corner from Kloof Road, the millionaires' row of the neighbourhood, where, at one point, the in-your-face strip-club king, the Czech fugitive and the hit man with different identities had all lived. Jackson was at number 40, Krejcir at 54a and Louca lived next door at number 54.

A man who openly admitted his animosity towards Jackson revealed a bit more. Pawnbroker businessman Michael Kalymnios had previously laid charges of attempted extortion, attempted kidnapping, intimidation and *crimen injuria* against Jackson, claiming that he had threatened him and his girlfriend, former Teazers stripper, Yuliyana Moshorovs'ka. Jackson demanded R50 000 from the couple after she left the club.

Kalymnios wasn't shocked by the murder. 'If you lived by the sword, you die by the sword. Lolly was a thug. God must forgive me, but I am so happy he is dead,' he said.[14]

He also described Louca as a thug. 'He did all Lolly's dirty jobs,' Kalymnios said. 'He was his right-hand man … He was running around with three passports with Jackson's help.'[15]

In a bizarre twist, Kalymnios said Jackson had hired Louca to kill him. 'I only learnt now that he had hired a hit man to kill me. I am supposed to be dead, not Lolly. He is a scumbag.'

Kalymnios revealed to *The Star* that he had always known Jackson wanted him dead. He had caused problems for Jackson by suing him for R5.2 million for threatening him, defaming him and for putting pictures of his girlfriend on the Internet: 'That's why he was trying to get rid of me. The wheels turned and he was killed – not me.'[16]

Kalymnios said he had met Louca at gambling houses in Joburg: 'He was a gambler and a drug addict, always high on cocaine. I won't be surprised if he was high when he killed Lolly.'[17]

It later emerged that Jackson had claimed Kalymnios was trying to kill him using Louca. The strip-club king had before his death given affidavits to the *Saturday Star*. Journalist Kashiefa Ajam revealed that a month before he was killed, Jackson claimed that Louca had been offered R100 000 to kill him.[18]

But there was more to Jackson's murder than an old feud over a stripper. In the days following the discovery of his bullet-riddled body, police raided numerous houses and premises across Gauteng looking for Louca, but their searches yielded nothing.

Krejcir's lawyer, Ian Small-Smith, told journalists that Krejcir had agreed to become a state witness and was not a suspect in the murder. In a two-hour meeting with police he told them everything he knew about Louca. In return, it had been agreed to let Krejcir off the hook with the extradition order he was fighting and to offer him immunity from prosecution in several other criminal investigations, including the trafficking of women from

Eastern Europe and Asia, and money laundering. All were cases nobody knew anything about. Journalists were told Krejcir was considered a vital cog in Jackson's murder case.

Interpol spokeswoman Golding said they were furious over this alleged deal. 'What happened does not make sense. Krejcir, who was one of Jackson's best friends, came to this country illegally on false documents and now he is being allowed to escape from the law,' she told journalist Graeme Hosken. 'The Czech Republic sent a team of specialists to South Africa with supporting documentation as to why he should be returned to stand trial. But now he is being allowed to stay. We need to know why because [this suggests] that it is all right to allow people who enter South Africa illegally to stay without any consequences.

We do not need his help ... We can solve this crime without his help. He only wants to save his own skin.'[19]

Golding was not the only law-enforcement official who was furious because of this move. Suddenly, the National Prosecuting Authority (NPA) remembered who Krejcir was and the embarrassment he had caused them when they lost his extradition case two years earlier.

They called for a review of the magistrate's decision not to send him back to the Czech Republic. In the Johannesburg High Court the state said Magistrate Stephen Holzen had shown bias during Krejcir's bail application. They quoted Holzen saying the state's case was 'questionable'.[20] The Director of Public Prosecution's legal representative, Laurence Hodes, suggested Holzen had been hostile towards the state.

After Krejcir was granted R1 million bail back in 2007, the state applied for Holzen to recuse himself, but he refused. He subsequently presided over the extradition case. Ruling on the extradition, Holzen said he 'could not help but feel there was an element of sour grapes on behalf of the (State)'. He accused the state of 'forum shopping', in other words trying to have a case heard before a court that would favour its position.[21]

But, this time, the state won and Krejcir's extradition case was reopened. Judges Philip Koppen and Piet Meyer ruled that Holzen should have recused himself when the state filed for his removal from the case.

Meanwhile, Krejcir had been smart. By applying for political asylum, the extradition case against him would be held up until the asylum bid had been completed. His application for asylum, which was refused in 2008, eventually reached the Refugee Appeal Board.

It later emerged that, one way or another, he had brought in – by his own estimate – about R60 million of the fortune he had amassed in Europe. He could now afford the best lawyers money could buy. The extradition requests went nowhere in a hurry – in part, reportedly, because he was helping police and intelligence officials in 'key matters of security'.

Krejcir was allegedly tipped off in 2010 about confidential plans by South Africa's priority crime investigation unit, the Hawks, to arrest him on charges of having fraudulently obtained his temporary permit as an asylum seeker. His attorney, Small-Smith, and immigration specialist Chris Watters rushed an application to the High Court to interdict the move. They obtained it, which prohibited the Department of Home Affairs and police from arresting or detaining Krejcir until his asylum application had been concluded.[22]

Krejcir told the court he had received an anonymous phone call in which he was warned of a plan to have him arrested and sent to the Czech Republic on the basis that his asylum permit was fraudulent. He argued that if he were deported to his home country, his life, and the lives of his family members, would be in peril.[23]

He was set to appear before the Refugee Appeal Board, when another delay was introduced. This time it was by the media, who had caught the Krejcir bug and had started to suspect the depth of his alleged shady dealings. Independent Newspapers, Media24 and the *Mail & Guardian* teamed up in a legal bid to try to gain access to the hearing, which was due to take place behind closed doors.

The media argued that Krejcir was an important public figure and that the public had a right to know about his asylum bid. He did not want the media there, he said, because he planned to call high-profile foreign politicians, police, lawyers and other professionals from the Czech Republic and the Seychelles to help him win refugee status, and it was important that the identities of those people were protected.[24]

The Refugee Appeal Board refused to grant the media access, maintaining that South African statutory and common law, and international norms and treaties, require the state to ensure asylum proceedings are confidential. Asylum seekers need the reassurance of absolute confidentiality to disclose fully and truthfully why they needed asylum, the board explained.[25]

The media took their fight to the Constitutional Court where the question was whether absolute confidentiality of refugees is a justifiable limitation of the right to freedom of expression. The highest court in the land ruled that Section 21(5) of the Refugees Act was unreasonable because it did not allow the Refugee Appeal Board the discretion to open its proceedings to the public in appropriate cases. The court gave the board the option to decide if the proceedings should be open or not.

The case was postponed numerous times over the years and all the affidavits were filed, but by the time the case was ready to be heard Krejcir was already facing numerous criminal cases. Knowing that, with criminal charges, he would never succeed at being declared a refugee, he dropped the appeal.

All the media attention had started to make life difficult for Krejcir. And he was not the only one under their scrutiny. Jackson's death had also shone the spotlight on the intelligence chief, Mabasa. Why was Mabasa the first person Louca called after the murder? What was his connection to the murderer and to Krejcir?

It turned out to be more than the fact he was a good spy with informers in the right places. For a start, Mabasa's wife, Dorcas, and Krejcir's wife had a business together. Krejcir claimed there was nothing sinister about this and that the two women planned to sell energy drinks.

Krejcir told journalist De Wet Potgieter that Small-Smith had introduced him to Mabasa at a time when he feared kidnapping or death at the hands of Czech secret agents. 'I needed a contact in the police to help me secure my safety in the country. Joey is a good policeman who was always prepared to help me if I felt my life was threatened,' he said.[26]

However, Juan Meyer, a former business associate of Krejcir, alleged after Jackson's murder that Mabasa was in Krejcir's pay. 'I saw half-a-million rand given in cash by Radovan to Joey Mabasa on two occasions,' Meyer said. [27]

Mabasa denied the allegation. Later, in September 2011, Mabasa was asked to leave the police force, along with the entire top brass of the Crime Intelligence Division, including national crime intelligence chief, Richard Mdluli, and the financial officer, Major General Solly Lazarus, on allegations of corruption, fraud, maladministration, nepotism and theft.

Police confirmed they were probing Mabasa's alleged interference with the Hawks' investigation into Krejcir. 'The probe is understood to focus on allegations that crime intelligence engaged in extensive phone tapping of Hawks members and others involved in the Krejcir investigation,' the *Mail & Guardian* reported.[28]

It was alleged that, in at least one case, intercepted conversations found their way to targets of the Hawks' investigation, which included not only Krejcir, but also a number of his associates.

'It was felt that it was in the interest of the SA Police Service for [Mabasa's] services to be discontinued. We felt we no longer needed him. The bad publicity around him in the media also contributed in some way,' then Hawks spokesman McIntosh Polela said.[29]

Mabasa, however, was never formally charged or arrested, and these allegations remain unproven.

Meanwhile, Krejcir's links to Lolly Jackson and his mysterious deals with the police had drawn more than just the media into his orbit. He had by now become the focus of a man who had a reputation for being a bulldog for justice.

About a year before Jackson was murdered, Irish-born independent forensic investigator Paul O'Sullivan began to look into the Czech fugitive who had quietly been making inroads into South Africa's criminal and intelligence communities. Krejcir didn't know it just yet, but the man who was to become his nemesis had entered his life.

By 2010 O'Sullivan's stern, piercing blue-eyed stare was well known. His face had been on the front pages of every newspaper in the country and on the television sets of every news channel. He had spent the last eight years relentlessly investigating former police chief and Interpol head, Jackie Selebi, successfully helping the state topple the highest police officer in the land when he was convicted for corruption. That was no small feat and there was no arguing O'Sullivan was a force to be reckoned with. His methods were often unorthodox, though, and he was loved and hated in equal measure.

But one thing was certain, when O'Sullivan set his sights on someone, they were in for a difficult time. And Krejcir was about to find this out.

During his investigations into Selebi, O'Sullivan had spread his net wide. He had sources and undercover operatives whom he used to infiltrate transnational organised-crime syndicates.

According to a written submission,[30] which O'Sullivan quietly placed on the chairs of everyone who attended Krejcir's refugee appeals tribunal, he had identified two men who he thought might be linked to Selebi: Lolly Jackson and Kevin Trytsman. He believed both men were involved in criminal activity. But, with Selebi as his main focus, O'Sullivan moved on to concentrate on bigger fish.

In 2009 when Trytsman, who claimed to work for the National Intelligence Agency (but, as was always the case with spies, nobody was really sure), interfered with an investigation O'Sullivan was working on, the Irish expat went back and took a closer look at the two men.

In the course of his investigation, Trytsman revealed to O'Sullivan that there was a man called Alekos Panayi, a banker, who could link Jackson, Krejcir and Louca to a large money-laundering scheme.

Who was this Krejcir? O'Sullivan was about to make it his life's work to find out.

Trytsman had been known in the underworld as 'Mr Fix-It' because he could make court actions and other legal headaches go away. He had received amnesty from the Truth and Reconciliation Commission after testifying that he'd had access to a secret arms cache as an uMkhonto we Sizwe cadre. He ran an information-peddling operation and Krejcir employed him to do undisclosed work, O'Sullivan revealed.[31]

'I investigated Trytsman, because he had interfered with certain state witnesses, and in so doing attempted to derail the investigations [into Selebi],' O'Sullivan said in a sworn statement.[32]

He said he found that Trytsman had been paid large sums of money by Krejcir. O'Sullivan met with Trytsman in October 2009 and told him he had enough information to have him arrested. Trytsman allegedly agreed to give him information if he left him alone. 'He alleged that I would find evidence of Lolly Jackson being involved in large-scale money laundering.'[33]

But before O'Sullivan could get the full details of what had been happening, Trytsman was murdered. In December 2009 he was allegedly shot by his lawyer, George Michaelides, in the attorney's offices in Bedford Centre.

'George Smith subsequently invited [Michaelides] to lunch with Krejcir, who wanted to show his "appreciation" for the killing of Trytsman,' O'Sullivan said.[34]

Before Michaelides could be held accountable for the shooting, he fled the country with millions of rands of trust money from his clients.

O'Sullivan then went to look for Panayi, the lead Trytsman had given him before his death. Panayi was of Greek Cypriot origin and had worked at the Laiki Bank, which was registered in Greece and Cyprus, with a representative bank in Johannesburg. The bank closed down in South Africa in 2008.

When O'Sullivan tracked Panayi down, he found a man terrified for his life. Panayi said he was being threatened by Jackson and did not know where to turn. He spilt the beans in a revelatory affidavit signed under Section 204 of the Criminal Procedures Act, absolving him from prosecution for giving evidence.[35]

In it Panayi said that when he worked for the bank, he had helped Jackson to transfer funds offshore: 'I would match him up with people that were in another country, that wanted to bring funds into South Africa without declaring the existence and Jackson would pay them cash, in rand, and the transfers would take place into off-shore accounts of Jackson, in either euros or US dollars.'[36]

He said he acted as the middleman in these transactions, keeping Jackson's money until the foreign currency was placed in Jackson's offshore account.

'The frequency of these transactions would be in the order of every three or four weeks. The amounts involved would range from R500 000 to R2 million per transaction,' the banker said.[37]

Panayi said his first contact with Jackson was in early 2007. Jackson already had money in his Greek account at the time: $900 000 and €300 000, and he asked Panayi to help him buy a luxury sports car, a Zonda, from an investment company in Singapore.

'I had to source Jackson some euros. He paid the person I found approximately R2.3 million in two tranches,' Panayi said.[38]

The banker said he earned a commission for the transactions he helped Jackson with. He said that things became difficult with the last transaction, a few weeks before the bank closed.

Krejcir was introduced to the bank by Louca. Krejcir's offshore company had an account with Laiki Bank in Cyprus. Krejcir said he was relocating to South Africa and that he needed to start bringing in funds, Panayi said. His main needs were to bring in money to purchase his house in Bedfordview.

'I did a transaction with Jackson to swap R1 million for euros. As the transaction was taking place, funds were being transferred from an account of George Smith, in Cyprus, as Krejcir could not hold an account in his own name in Cyprus. Smith was the name and front for the account, but Krejcir had signing powers on the account.'[39]

In January 2008 the bank refused to process the transfer, stating that it appeared to be money laundering, Panayi said. The sale of euros was put on hold until Krejcir made alternative arrangements to transfer the funds from an account in Poland held by Krejcir's mother.

'... [H]is off-shore company, Banara Trade Limited, also had an account with Laiki, which was frozen at the same time as the hold was put on the George Smith transfer. I was told by the office in Cyprus that the reason they were taking these steps was that they believed both Smith and Krejcir [were] involved in money laundering and that Krejcir was a fugitive from justice,' said Panayi.[40]

Panayi said that, with Jackson's approval, he gave Jackson's cash to Krejcir.

'Jackson wanted the transaction [made] before the bank closed, but it was out of my hands as it was the people in Cyprus that made these decisions,' the banker said.[41]

Around May 2008 Panayi said he received a call from Jackson accusing him of theft and threatening his life: 'He said that I had taken the money. He said I started a new life with the money. He said he would send someone to fuck me up, and fuck up my family and make my life a living hell. I was scared.'[42]

The first thing he did was set up a meeting between Jackson and Krejcir, as they had never met each other. Panayi said that, at the meeting, Krejcir admitted having not paid the funds, as he was unhappy with the rates on prior transactions.

'When I go to meet Krejcir I see ten or so armed guards hanging around. I think they are either ex or current cops,' the banker said.[43]

Krejcir allegedly agreed to pay €40 000 of the funds and insisted the figure was correct. This meant that Jackson would have been out of pocket to the tune of €60 000. Jackson blamed Panayi for what had happened. Terrified, he gave Jackson $12 000 from his own money in Cyprus, as well as a further R50 000. But the threats did not stop. 'He demanded I go to his offices in Rivonia,' Panayi said:

> He swore at me and threatened me ... Then he started assaulting me and slapping me around the face. He demanded I sign an acknowledgement of debt, saying that I owe him R650 000. I signed it because I was scared that he would cause harm to me or my family. However, I never owed him any money at all.[44]

Panayi's statement was dynamite. With it, O'Sullivan believed he had proof of money laundering. He contacted intelligence chief Mabasa to hand over the statement, so that the police could carry out an investigation.

'About one hour after my meeting with Mabasa, I got a call from one of my contacts. They told me to watch out and that Mabasa was at that exact moment in time at the Harbour Cafe meeting with Krejcir ... Shit, what had I done? I had no idea he was connected to Mabasa,' O'Sullivan said.[45]

He then looked deeper into the matter and discovered that Mabasa's wife was in business with Krejcir's. O'Sullivan said he then contacted Jackson and told him about Krejcir's past and what had happened in an attempt to get Jackson's cooperation on a case against Krejcir, who he now believed was a transnational criminal.

'Lolly had just agreed to turn state witness, when he was killed,' O'Sullivan said.[46]

CHAPTER 6

GERMAN CAR SPECIALIST UWE GEMBALLA LURED TO HIS DEATH

On 6 February 2010 Christiane and 16-year-old Marc said goodbye to Uwe Gemballa. The husband and father was leaving for Dubai and then South Africa. The goodbyes were brief: there was nothing unusual about his trip, as Uwe travelled for business all the time.

The 55-year-old German owned a company that did luxury-car conversions. He was renowned for his conversions of high-end cars, such as Porsches, Lamborghinis and Mercedes-Benzes. He had made millions through car sales to celebrities such as singer Michael Bolton and former Arsenal midfielder Freddie Ljungberg.

Gemballa was excited about his trip to South Africa. He had been in talks for a few months with Johannesburg businessman Jerome Safi, who was keen to open a Gemballa franchise in the country. Safi said his investors were willing to place R100 million on the table. It was a lot of money, especially since there was talk that Gemballa's business was in financial trouble. The millions made in previous years seemed to have dried up. The timing of the deal was perfect for him.

Three days later, at 10 pm, Christiane received a phone call from a number she did not recognise. It was a call that would change her family's life forever.[1]

It was Uwe. He was speaking in English, something he never did. He told her he needed a million euros. He told her to start preparing the money and he would call her again with the bank details of where she should make the deposit.

She asked him what was happening. Why did he suddenly need the money? Why did he sound so strange? Why was he speaking in English?

Uwe did not answer, but repeated the same sentence over and over again, asking her to prepare the deposit.

'I realised subsequently that he was being forced to speak English to me, as he had been kidnapped and was being held against his will,' she said.[2]

Christiane did not know it then, but it was the last time she would talk to her husband. She immediately called the police.

In the next few days her family were involved in an intensive investigation. She was put through days of questioning. She endured countless hours of waiting for some sign that her husband was still alive. It did not seem to come to an end. The call she was expecting from Uwe to tell her where to send the money never came.

'Our family experienced oppressive sorrow, worrying for the life of my husband and for the reasons for his hijacking, day and night. The anxiety and uncertainty imposed a psychological burden beyond belief [on] the whole family,' Christiane said.[3]

The German police contacted their South African counterparts explaining that a German national was missing and had seemingly been kidnapped. But all the police had to go on was emails between Safi and Gemballa planning their business venture. Gemballa had come to South Africa to meet the man who was set to become his new partner. Gemballa had written in an email shortly before his trip:

> Dear Jerome.
>
> It was a pleasure to talk to you today and a big nice surprise that you like so much our products and that you have decided to apply being our importer in South Africa. In general I would say we are open doing business with you and it is good that you have lots of passion and that you are not a standard car dealer.
>
> Regards from Germany and looking forward to start a successful business with you.[4]

Gemballa explained that he aimed to sell 12 converted cars in the first year,

15 in year two and 20 in year three. He wanted to make €350 000 turnover in year one.

Ludi Rolf Schnelle was a detective inspector with the SAPS organised-crime unit. He was tasked with investigating what had happened to Gemballa. At first there wasn't much to go on. The first thing Schnelle established was that Gemballa had arrived in South Africa on 8 February 2010.[5] He had entered the country on an Emirates flight around 9.30 pm from Dubai. He had a return flight booked two days later. The blond-haired man was travelling alone and it was unknown where he had been planning to stay.

Schnelle's colleague, Senior Superintendent Mbotho, arranged an interview with Safi to find out if he had met Gemballa and if he knew what had happened to him. Safi agreed to meet the police in the presence of his lawyer, at the offices of Botha, Du Plessis and Kruger in central Johannesburg.

Safi told the police that Gemballa was to travel to South Africa to meet him to discuss the business proposal with all the other role players, including Krejcir, who was to provide the financial backing. Safi also mentioned that Gemballa had business interests with an Angolan partner.[6]

In 2012, Safi told the police that he had sent his girlfriend, Tenielle Dippenaar, and his uncle, David Safi, to the airport to collect Gemballa.[7] Meanwhile, Safi waited with Krejcir at the Harbour. Later, Safi received a message from Tenielle saying that she had not seen Gemballa at the airport and had decided to return home.

Video footage at the airport, however, showed Gemballa walking into the immigration area at 21.26. The footage revealed an unidentified, slim man dressed in a white shirt, black jacket, black trousers, and white-brimmed hat with a black band, arriving at the airport an hour earlier. He drove a VW Golf GTI and parked in the customs and police parking area at the international arrivals section. He briefly met another unknown man outside the airport, out of view of the camera. They walked into a toilet together and parted ways when they came out.

The man wearing the hat stood at the international arrivals hall with a white board in his hands and waited. Police assumed Gemballa's name was written on the board.[8]

Gemballa came through with a baggage trolley at 21.47 and walked to the man holding the board. They left for the parking area together. The man with the hat pushed the trolley. Gemballa walked with this man freely, and did not seem distressed or forced in any way, Schnelle noted.

The policeman noticed Tenielle and Safi's uncle in the footage. They walked past the international arrivals area a few times for about an hour before leaving.

The next move was for the police to try to trace who had made the phone call to Gemballa's wife. The call was traced to the Dowerglen and Klopperpark area. The phone's SIM card was prepaid and had recently been purchased by a Zambian national. It had been used only to call Mrs Gemballa. Schnelle found that airtime for the phone had been bought from the Gardenview Shell garage in Smith Street, in Bedford Centre.[9]

Surveillance footage again provided the next clue. It showed a woman running into the shop and buying the airtime vouchers. She wore a uniform: black trousers, white shirt with a distinctive black collar and lapel, and a black apron. It was the uniform that staff at the Harbour wore.

A waitress from the restaurant identified herself in the footage. She said a customer at the restaurant had sent her to buy the vouchers. They asked who. 'She became very scared and informed us that she was in fear of her life if she revealed the identity of the person that sent her to buy the voucher.'[10]

She told the police she was far more scared of the people who had sent her than she was of being arrested.

'She refused to supply us with any information. Later on she offered co-operation, even though she was very frightened. She said there was a group of about six people at the restaurant that night.' They included Krejcir, Safi and Krejcir's treasurer, Michael Arsiotis. Arsiotis had asked the woman to buy the airtime.[11]

From then on, the investigation stalled and it took seven months before the police were able to make a real breakthrough. O'Sullivan by this time had become involved in the case. He had been hired by Christiane Gemballa to try to find out what had happened to her husband. He became a key player in discovering witnesses and helping police find the kidnappers.

Then, a key witness, gold refiner and former Krejcir business partner Juan Meyer came forward to O'Sullivan with an affidavit,[12] in which he linked Krejcir to Gemballa's disappearance. Meyer said that Gemballa and Krejcir had been connected through a money-laundering scheme.

Meyer had been regularly meeting Krejcir and security expert Cyril Beeka to start a gold-refining business. Meyer had the business know-how and the contacts, and Krejcir was supposed to supply the money. According to Meyer, when it came time to pay, Krejcir's cash never materialised. Meyer alleged that Krejcir, through Mabasa, had arranged to have him arrested to intimidate him. Meyer was angry and he went public with what he alleged had happened.[13]

It wasn't long after Lolly Jackson's death and Meyer's revelations drew speculation that Krejcir had become some sort of criminal boss in South Africa. He had now been linked to Jackson's murder and Gemballa's disappearance.

Meyer revealed in his statement that he had helped Jackson avoid paying tax. The strip-club owner had lots of cash that he needed to hide to avoid paying his dues to the South African Revenue Service (SARS).

At the same time as he was doing this work for Jackson, Meyer was planning the gold-refining venture with Krejcir. He revealed how Krejcir allegedly played two opponents off against each other to benefit from their downfall.

'At one stage Radovan told me he was going to buy Teazers from Lolly, but he did not want to pay a market-related price for it. He was also trying to buy Andrew Phillips's business, The Grand,' Meyer said in his affidavit. 'We discussed how Lolly would help Radovan to bring money into the country, so that they would get lots of cash and use it to apply pressure on the business of Andrew Phillips and that they would then try and buy him out.'[14]

Meyer said he was present at meetings where Krejcir told Phillips the same plan, and that they would try to buy Jackson out.

'I was not sure who was the real ally and who was the real target, but do recall being at a lunch meeting with Jackson one day, to talk about how we were going to bring in lots of cash to apply pressure against Phillips and the same night was at a meeting with Radovan, Beeka and Phillips to discuss how we would take down Jackson,' Meyer said in his statement.[15]

At one of their meetings, Meyer said Krejcir told him he had a few people and companies moving money for him into South Africa. The people involved were Jackson and Gemballa. He said Krejcir would buy Porsches from Gemballa. A vehicle would arrive in South Africa with dollars or euros stashed inside it. The money would be exchanged on the black market.

But, in September 2009, something had gone wrong. Krejcir had bought a Porsche from Gemballa, but when the car arrived, the money was missing. Meyer said he heard Krejcir arguing over the phone with Gemballa about the money while at the Harbour restaurant.

'Radovan had said that if Gemballa did not pay, he would get "trouble". Gemballa then told Radovan that if he threatened him, he would not see his money. Radovan then said something, I don't know what, then put the phone down. He was angry. Radovan then said it was Gemballa and he said he would organise a surprise for him.'[16]

While Meyer's revelations of what Gemballa had been up to shed some light on the possible motive for his disappearance, the information caused even more distress for his wife and son. Christiane wrote in her statement that their son keenly felt the loss of his beloved father, as they had been very close:

> Our son was traumatised and suffered from insomnia due to the daily coverage in the media, which would follow him into the classroom. The emotional distress was neither fully processed then nor is it fully processed today. Matters are made worse by media speculation that my husband died as a result of an illicit relationship he had with a criminal by the name of Radovan Krejcir. Other media speculation was that my husband had 'faked his own disappearance'.[17]

She said the speculation was so intense that it caused Gemballa's creditors to pull out. That, and the fact that the owner had disappeared, pushed the company into bankruptcy. Christiane said all her husband's wealth had been tied up in the business and when it went bust the family was left penniless: 'A continuation of the Gemballa business without the owner, founder, and representative was not possible any more and our entire existence was shattered. When my husband was alive and at the helm of the company, we lived a high-quality of life and [enjoyed] luxury holidays.'[18]

They went through months of not knowing what had happened to Gemballa. He seemed to have simply vanished. But behind the scenes the police had been busy, and in September 2010, they swooped. On 28 September the Gemballa family received the news they had been dreading, through the media.

It was one of the fastest arrests, charging and sentencing that had ever been witnessed. Investigators had linked the cellphone data to a 29-year-old, Thabiso Melvin Mpye. Within hours of his arrest, Mpye told police that he and three other men had murdered the car specialist. He also pointed out where they had buried his body. A bit of digging and there he was: in a shallow grave in an old cemetery in Lotus Gardens, Pretoria.

Within just 24 hours of his confession and revealing where Gemballa's body was buried, Mpye appeared in the Johannesburg High Court. He had made a plea bargain with the state and pleaded guilty to kidnapping and murder.[19]

In his indictment he said he had acted on the orders of other people and had been paid in two instalments: R25 000 and R10 000. Judge Frans Kgomo sentenced Mpye to 28 years – 20 for Gemballa's murder, five for kidnapping and three for theft.

Mpye said that he and the other three had kidnapped Gemballa from OR Tambo International Airport shortly after his arrival from Dubai. He told state prosecutor Riegel du Toit that they had taken Gemballa to a house in Edenvale and kept him there for several days.

They covered his head in duct tape, then forced all of the air out of his body by sitting on his chest. They wrapped his body in a black plastic sheet, which they tied with duct tape. Then they buried him. Mpye admitted stealing Gemballa's iPhone after the murder.

The autopsy report confirmed Gemballa had died of suffocation: 'The face and head have been tightly bound or wrapped repeatedly with grey duct tape. Beneath the tape is a black plastic bag, taped over the face (covering the mouth and eyes but not the nose). Both hands have been tied behind the body with grey duct tape. Both feet have been tied together with grey duct tape.'[20]

Another five months passed before the other three members of the gang were rounded up and charged. Thabo Mohapi, Garland Holworthy and Kagiso Joseph Linken, also known as Thabiso Lincoln Ledwaba, were arrested in March 2011.

Experienced criminals, these three were no strangers to the justice system. Holworthy and Linken were in prison for crimes they had committed later in 2010, after Gemballa's murder. Holworthy had been sent to Krugersdorp Prison for his involvement in a house robbery committed in June 2010. Linken was charged with robbery and murder for being part of a heist in Langlaagte. A policeman, Sergeant Gert du Toit, was killed during a high-speed chase and shoot-out with the cash-heist robbers in Protea, Soweto. Du Toit had chased the robbers from the N1 south into Soweto after the gang of 15, in five cars, had successfully pulled off the heist near the Maraisburg off-ramp. The gang was armed with AK-47s, and R4 and R1 rifles.

Mohapi's mother, Panki, told the *Saturday Star*[21] at their first appearance in the Johannesburg Magistrate's Court that it felt like she was living in a nightmare: 'It feels as if I am watching a movie. How did he get himself into this mess? Where does he know all these people from?' she asked.

She said it was not the first time Mohapi had been arrested. He had allegedly robbed a Pep store in Rustenburg shortly after he had been released having served four years in jail for another crime. She said she suspected her son's criminal behaviour had begun shortly after his father was found dead in a Soweto police station: 'He was 14 at the time. Ever since then he's always had a deep hatred for policemen. He is always angry. Even when he was in the army I had to be called in because of his anger issues.'[22]

With one member of the gang having confessed to the crime and revealing what had happened, the trial of the other three should have been swift. However, the wheels of justice turned slowly and it would take another five years, until 2016, before the courts concluded the case.

During all that time the spectre of Krejcir hung over the trial. Everyone now knew who had carried out the killing. But who had ordered the murder of Gemballa?

Two years after the murder, the man who had brought Gemballa to South Africa revealed another version of events. In 2012 Safi admitted in his statement that he had lied to police in 2010, that he had left out a lot of detail about why he had become involved with Gemballa:

> I was put under extreme mental pressure not to say anything that would incriminate Radovan Krejcir in the murder of Gemballa. This mental pressure consisted mainly of my feeling that Krejcir was extremely dangerous.
>
> Reflecting back, I can now see that I made the right decision not to be open and co-operative with the state. I believe that if I had co-operated, my life would have been at risk and I may even be dead today, at the hands of one of Krejcir's many criminal associates.[23]

Safi had previously worked for Jackson as a manager at the Teazers in Midrand. He first met Krejcir in October 2009 when George Louca introduced him to the Czech. Safi lived near the Harbour at the time and from then on he saw Krejcir regularly. In his 2012 statement, Safi said:

> Some evenings I would walk across and have a beer and a chat with [Krejcir]. He would tell me about where he was from and where he studied. But he never confided in me about any of his criminal activity. At the time he came across as a charming and intelligent guy and I was happy to be able to help him out here and there and make a few rand on the side. We took to each other and the relationship was mutually beneficial. I was able to help him out with odd jobs here and there and was happy with the arrangements.[24]

Safi remembers there being a jovial atmosphere at the restaurant, with a core group of men often chatting and setting up business deals while eating and drinking. He also recalls there were parties held on the deck overlooking the rear car park of the shopping mall. At one of Krejcir's birthday bashes there was a fireworks display. At the 2010/11 New Year's Eve party, Safi said he saw Krejcir take a gun from Beeka and fire shots in the air.

Safi said he met Jackson and Krejcir at the restaurant and they told him he could make a lot of money: 'Lolly pointed out Krejcir's car, a white Porsche 911 with a Gemballa conversion. The Porsche was parked in Krejcir's parking and we looked at the Gemballa conversion kit. The car looked great and I was impressed with it. ... Both Krejcir and Lolly were into their cars in a big way.'[25]

They asked Safi if he thought these car conversions would work if they were done in South Africa. Would they make money?

'I was surprised they were asking me,' he said, 'as they were the car experts, but I agreed that if they did this, there would be a good market for it.'[26]

Krejcir told Safi that a man called Uwe Gemballa did these conversions and they wanted to open one of his franchises in South Africa. Safi said they told him that if he put the deal together, they would give him a share of the business. Safi was excited because Krejcir had said he would invest R100 million in the business. Safi called Gemballa, who said he was interested in the business proposal.

'I felt this was going to be a big thing. Because of Radovan's behaviour and continuous boasting about cash, I thought that R100 million would be a drop in the ocean for him,' Safi said.[27]

Before making contact with Gemballa, Safi had been told not to mention who the investors in the business were. 'If Gemballa looks into me and sees my background and Lolly being involved in strip clubs, he might not want to do business with us. It would be better if he just comes here and we meet him and he sees who we are,' Safi said he was instructed by Krejcir.[28]

They made plans for Gemballa to come to South Africa.

Safi said that on the night Gemballa arrived in the country he was at the Harbour with a group of about ten men, including Krejcir. 'We were having a few drinks. There was a party atmosphere. As I have it, they were all going to The Grand in Rivonia that night, to continue partying and look at some girls. I was a bit reserved. I did not want to drink too much, in case I was going to meet Gemballa for business discussions. I felt it would have been rude and given the wrong impression to arrive for the first meeting smelling of liquor,' Safi said.[29]

He started to call Gemballa after his plane was scheduled to have landed. The first few times the phone just rang. He then asked his girlfriend and uncle to go to the airport and meet Gemballa because he could not get hold of him. They went to the airport, but did not see him. In his statement, Safi explained:

> Radovan was sitting nearby, and I was walking up and down trying to get hold of Gemballa. I then … told Radovan, 'The guy has supposedly landed and I can't get hold of him.' I then told him that I had sent Tenielle there to try and meet him. I did not mention my uncle. Radovan was put out that I had sent Tenielle there and told me that Gemballa was a big man and he would be able to look after himself. I was now confused. Radovan had been pushing me the whole week to get Gemballa here and now he did not want me to meet him.[30]

The other men went to The Grand until the early hours of the morning.

Safi said he had tried to call Gemballa the next morning, but his phone was still off. He then called Gemballa's office in Germany to ask if they could contact him, or if he had another number.

'Now I was worried. I met Lolly and Radovan at the Harbour and told them I could not get hold of Gemballa. Radovan said something like, "Maybe he's changed his mind and doesn't need someone in South Africa. If he doesn't want to speak to you don't chase him." I still tried to get a hold of him anyway … continuously.'[31]

About two days later, the police called Safi because Gemballa was missing. He told Krejcir that the police wanted to see him. Krejcir arranged for his lawyer, Ian Small-Smith, to go with him.

Safi said he was scared to tell the lawyer anything about Krejcir because he knew it would get back to the Czech. The police made Safi undergo a voice stress test. They kept him at the police station for about ten hours and showed him papers detailing Krejcir's overseas criminal activities. Said Safi:

I now realised that I had been 'played', but I also knew that if I mentioned the truth to them, I would probably be killed. I had seen all these files from the cops on kidnapping and stuff. I would be in grave danger. It was at this time that I gave a sworn statement, but I deliberately played down Radovan Krejcir and Lolly Jackson's involvement, as I knew that if I showed that they were instrumental in Gemballa coming to South Africa, I would have serious problems.[32]

Safi said after this he noticed a difference in how the group of men at the Harbour treated him. He felt like he was no longer part of their inner circle, but on the outside looking in.

When Gemballa's body was found, Safi said the atmosphere at the restaurant was tense, that 'the shit had really hit the fan'.

'I now realised that I had been duped into bringing Gemballa to South Africa and he had been murdered as a result,' he said.[33]

Years later, Louca would reveal what he knew about the Gemballa murder. In an affidavit never made public before, Louca told authorities that Krejcir had told him of his plans to bring Gemballa to South Africa.

Louca said that Krejcir had told him Gemballa was a wealthy businessman who operated a successful motor-vehicle business in Germany providing specialised conversion and modification services for Porsches.[34]

Louca said Krejcir's plan was for him to register a new company in Louca's name and to invite Gemballa to visit South Africa to consider establishing a South African agency for his European business.

Krejcir allegedly proposed that Louca should advise Gemballa of the fact that although there were many wealthy Porsche owners in South Africa, nobody provided a service of the kind Gemballa offered and that this presented an excellent business opportunity.

Louca said in his statement that Krejcir had told him that before his arrest in the Czech Republic, he had sent a Porsche GTS to Gemballa's workshop in Germany for modification.

'He told me that after work on the car was completed, Gemballa refused to release the Porsche to him because of a disagreement over certain costs which, as I understood it, had not been paid by Krejcir ... Krejcir said that he had insisted Gemballa return the vehicle, but Gemballa would not do so, and kept Krejcir's Porsche. For this reason Krejcir was angry with Gemballa and sought revenge.'[35]

Louca said Krejcir wanted to persuade Gemballa to visit South Africa, have him kidnapped and force him to transfer €2 million to a bank account identified by Krejcir. He said: 'Because of the dispute between them, Krejcir explained that the invitation could not come from him, nor should he be identified as being associated with the so-called "business opportunity". Gemballa would not have accepted an invitation to visit this country if received from Krejcir or from anyone who Gemballa knew was working in association with Krejcir.'[36]

The Cypriot said he refused to help Krejcir with his plans, believing it likely that Krejcir would have Gemballa killed after getting the money. He was not prepared to be part of such a scheme.

Krejcir persistently asked him to help. But when he finally realised Louca would not budge, he got very angry and told him to 'go to hell'.

'The incident damaged my relationship with Krejcir,' Louca said.[37]

These revelations have so far amounted to nothing, however. Krejcir, whose motive was seemingly just to seek revenge for losing money, has never been charged with arranging Gemballa's kidnapping or murder. He repeatedly denied involvement in the murder, telling the *Mail & Guardian*: 'I saw Gemballa once in my life for a couple of minutes at a car show in Prague in 1995. This is the first and last time I saw him, even talked to him. But maybe it is the reason why I want to kill him, because I saw him 15 years ago?'[38]

Krejcir claimed he had meant to set up the business with Gemballa, but he disappeared before he could meet him.

Halfway through 2013, two years after their arrest, the High Court was ready to put Mohapi, Holworthy and Linken, the men charged with kidnapping and murdering Gemballa, on trial.

The Palm Ridge High Court was packed with journalists waiting to hear what revelations the state's key witness, Mpye, the man who had confessed to the crime, would make. The atmosphere in the courtroom was expectant. Prosecutor Riegel du Toit was confident as he called Mpye to the stand. He had no idea Mpye was about to turn on him.

'I don't want to waste the court's time. These two statements were taken through torture,' Mpye told Judge George Maluleke.[39]

He claimed the three men in the dock were his friends, but had had no part in the murder. Three completely different people had been his accomplices.

The court was stunned. Du Toit called for a short adjournment to speak to his witness. It made no difference. Mpye refused to speak to the prosecutor.

Maluleke declared Mpye a hostile witness. He was transferred from Johannesburg Central, the prison he was sharing with the three co-accused, to serve his sentence at Leeuwkop Prison. Department of Correctional Services spokesman Ofentse Morwane said this was in the best interests of justice. But the move made no difference.

Sally Evans, writing in the *Mail & Guardian*, said Mpye appeared meek.[40] He wore reading glasses while sitting waiting to testify. On the stand, however, the glasses were gone and he came across as cocky and arrogant. At one point, Du Toit asked him a question that Mpye ignored. He was reading his book in the stand and refused to answer. Judge Maluleke added another year to his sentence for contempt of court.

His girlfriend testified that, after Mpye's arrest, she had received a call from Holworthy and Linken. They told her to tell Mpye not to say anything to the police or to anyone else.

Mohapi, Linken and Holworthy all had the same contrary attitude; they laughed during court breaks, as if the trial meant nothing to them.

Finally, in 2015, five years after Gemballa was murdered, the trial reached conclusion. Mohapi, Linken and Holworthy were found guilty of kidnapping, murder and theft. Cellphone information and CCTV footage linked the three men to the crime. Judge Maluleke said they stole a laptop, iPod, wallet and clothing from Gemballa.

'The established facts are that the accused all arrived at the airport. Accused number three (Holworthy) is the person who met the deceased and walked away with him, and after this the deceased was never seen alive again,' Maluleke said.[41]

'The cellphone data placed all of them at the graveyard where the deceased was buried – at very awkward hours, when people don't attend funerals. It was almost 11 o'clock at night. The inference is that the accused, together with Mpye, kidnapped Gemballa from the airport, took him to Edenvale, killed him or had him killed, and then buried him in a shallow grave.'[42]

Du Toit said in his closing arguments that there were more people involved, hinting at Krejcir's involvement: 'We would like to have everybody who was involved, but you need evidence. So we have to start somewhere.'[43]

Then, three days before sentencing, Linken escaped from court.

He was at the Palm Ridge Magistrate's Court for his murder and cash-heist case when, according to News24, he got hold of a firearm and pointed it at an officer in the holding cells below the court.

'I saw Ledwaba [Linken is also known by this name] pointing a gun at our colonel. He was still shackled. I saw the colonel handing his firearm to him because he was pointing a firearm at him and taking the keys from the table,' an officer told Judge Cassim Moosa.[44]

O'Sullivan described the escape as a 'tragic indictment of the criminal justice system, which now seems to be completely broken and in need of fixing'.[45]

A court orderly was arrested that week for helping Linken escape. The anti-corruption task team viewed CCTV footage of the escape that showed a police constable, an orderly at the court, placing a bag where Linken could find it. In the bag was a weapon, which he used to get out of court.

The footage shows the constable, in his police uniform, placing the bag between two cars in the staff parking lot of the court. He then took out his cellphone and made a call. When the truck carrying the prisoners arrived, Ledwaba waited for everybody to get out first, then waited at the back before retrieving the bag.

When questioned, the constable allegedly told the task team that the person he called was Linken, who had a cellphone despite being on his way to court in a police van.

O'Sullivan said Linken was known to be a dangerous criminal who did not think twice about killing someone. He said there was no doubt he would commit a crime again.[46]

Sentencing for the other two went ahead. Mohapi threatened the prosecutors, investigators and journalists covering the case. As he came into court, he said, 'I'm coming after all of you people because you made this personal.'[47]

Mohapi and Holworthy received lengthy jail sentences. Mohapi got 25 years for the kidnapping and murder. Ten of these years would run concurrently with his previous 34-year sentence for armed robbery. This meant he got an overall sentence of 9 years and would only be eligible for parole in 33 years, in 2048.

Holworthy was sentenced to 25 years for murder, five for kidnapping and two for theft, all running concurrently.

Judge Maluleke said there was no way of knowing what financial damage the murder had caused to South Africa's economy, having been committed shortly before the 2010 Soccer World Cup.

As they were led down to the cells below the court after sentencing, Mohapi shouted, 'The battle is not over.'[48]

For the Gemballas, Mohapi's words were certainly true. Christiane Gemballa had written to the court to ask for justice for her husband's murder. It still hurt them to know that Uwe would never return to her and her son. They would never be able to say goodbye to him. She wrote in a statement used during aggravation of sentencing:

> The manner of his death was particularly brutal and I shudder to think about his last moments on earth. The planned assassination of my husband and father of my son has most brutally ruined our lives. Until today I am suffering nightmares … Nobody can understand the extent of the damage this incomprehensible act of violence has done to me, my son, and our family.[49]

Although the conviction would not return him to them, it would at least allow them to know that justice had prevailed.

'I therefore ask that the courts show my husband's murderers no mercy ... unless of course, one of them would clearly set out, in detail, exactly why my husband had to die and who was ultimately behind his horrific murder,' she said.[50]

So far, they have not.

CHAPTER 7

BECOMING A CRIME BOSS: CYRIL BEEKA GUNNED DOWN

His nickname among gangsters was the Lieutenant. He was a man known to broker peace deals in turf wars among gangsters, whose links to the country's spies and high-placed political figures put him a step ahead in business – both legal and illegal – and whose black-belt karate skills left you in no doubt about who was in charge if you crossed him.

But, in the end, it didn't matter how powerful Cyril Beeka was, how well connected or how physically strong: he didn't stand a chance next to an armed, well-trained killer who attacked when he least expected it.

It was 5 pm on 21 March 2011. Beeka was in the passenger seat of his BMW 4x4. His driver, a man people only knew as Sasa, was behind the wheel. He was Beeka's bodyguard and he was armed.

They were travelling along Modderdam Road in Bellville, Cape Town, and Beeka made a quick call to arrange to meet his brother at the V&A Waterfront.

Five minutes later, a few hundred metres from the University of the Western Cape, on a busy road, they stopped at a red light. A motorcycle pulled up alongside them. There were two men on the bike. The passenger at the back was holding a firearm. The trained killer lifted the weapon and began to shoot.

The first shot penetrated Beeka's eye, and as his head swung from the velocity of the bullet, five more shots were pumped into his head. They were close to each other, the mark of an extremely good shooter.

Investigating officer Paul Hendrikse testified later that 17 shots had been fired. Beeka was also hit in the chest and arms. Sasa, the driver, was also shot in the arms.

Despite his injuries, though, Sasa sped after the motorbike and fired shots in its direction, but soon he lost control of the vehicle and crashed into a fence.

He later told the *Mail & Guardian* that he recalled hearing two loud bangs: 'I was hit in my right arm as well as my left one and I noticed that Cyril had been hit in the chest. It sounded like a shotgun went off. There was smoke and glass and I was confused. I then came to my senses and I noticed a motorbike on my right-hand side. Then more shots were fired in succession.'[1]

He told the paper he slammed the car into reverse, probably saving his own life because the bike could not easily reverse. He then gave chase, firing several shots at the bike. 'The next thing I recall was my motor vehicle lifting from the ground and I lost control.'[2]

Police received an anonymous call telling them there had been an accident and people were trapped inside a vehicle. When they arrived at the scene they found the crashed BMW with bullet holes in the side.

Sasa, who was in his 30s, was taken to Vincent Pallotti Hospital in a critical condition. There was no hope for Beeka.

As the sun set that day, relatives and friends comforted each other at the cordoned-off crime scene next to the Cape Flats Nature Reserve, where Beeka's mangled vehicle lay.

Security experts could immediately tell the killer was a professional hit man. Some of the shots had been fired when both the car and motorbike were moving, and yet the bullets were in a tight cluster.

Beeka, 49, had been living in Pretoria, but was from Kuils River. He frequently visited his relatives in Cape Town and often went there for business dealings, his brother David Beeka told journalists at the scene.

David said his brother had spoken to him minutes before the shooting. Relatives had been planning to meet Beeka later that evening at the

Waterfront. He stared in disbelief at the wreckage of the silver BMW and his brother's body, which was covered by a blue blanket.

'It's a shock. It's a huge shock for all of us. He was well loved by everyone. He had a heart of gold,' David said.[3] They were a close family, he said, with six brothers and two sisters.

Beeka's wife, Sonia, was on her way. He had three daughters and a son. He was set to celebrate his eldest daughter, Megan's, 21st birthday the following weekend.

Another relative said: 'A lot of unsavoury things were said about Cyril, but to us he was a beautiful person.'[4]

His relatives may not have admitted it at the scene of his death, but Beeka had lived a gangster's life. For years he had been a prominent underworld figure. Drug trafficking, extortion, money laundering, assault and forgery were all charges he had managed to evade over the years. There were also unproved allegations of murder.

Despite the long list of criminal allegations against him, Beeka never spent a day in jail. He was a former Umkhonto we Sizwe (MK) informant and no stranger to ANC top circles. In December 2007, at the ANC's elective conference in Polokwane, the then national intelligence boss and associate of President Jacob Zuma, Moe Shaik, created a stir by bringing along Beeka as his bodyguard. After the murder, Shaik told Independent Newspapers: 'I'm saddened by Mr Beeka's death. My prayers and thoughts go out to his family.'[5]

After MK was disbanded, Beeka returned to his home turf in Cape Town, where he quickly fitted into the world of protection rackets involving Moroccans and Russians, and the anti-drug vigilante group Pagad (People Against Gangsterism and Drugs).

He was known to many powerful men in the city. Beeka knew Hard Livings gang boss Rashied Staggie. He kept the company many years ago of Vito Palazzolo, who was convicted *in absentia* of Mafia-related offences in Italy.

Beeka also associated with former apartheid intelligence operatives Gert Nel and Dirk Coetzee, the latter the one-time Vlakplaas commander.

He was respected for his karate skills, having represented Western Province in the 1989 national championships. His reputation and short-fused temper terrified many.

Beeka owned Pro Access Security and, together with his brother Edward, who owned Red Security, was allegedly a key figure in Cape Town's night-club security scene. Beeka commanded respect in the underworld and was hailed for a truce he brokered among the gangs in Cape Town.

In 1994 he was involved in a fist fight outside of court with one of two men accused of murdering two of his employees. In 1998 Presidential Investigation Task Unit head Andre Lincoln laid intimidation charges against Beeka and Palazzolo.

In 1999 Beeka and a German man were charged for assaulting a woman from an escort agency. In 2000 Beeka's security company co-director Jacques Cronje and others were charged with murdering a Chinese sailor in a brawl at the Saigon Karaoke club, in Cape Town. Police told the court that Beeka and his brother Edward, through Red Security and Pro Security, controlled 90% of the city's nightclub scene, an industry from which they solicited protection money. They were linked to 427 alleged offences, including ten of attempted murder, 262 of assault and 73 of serious assault.

In 2002 the Scorpions investigated Beeka for charges of drug trafficking, corruption and contraventions of various customs, excise and tax regulations, as well as illegal interception and monitoring using phone tapping.

But the investigations always fizzled away. The rumours swirled around him like a low-hanging cloud, but he always cleared the air of any real threat of prosecution. There were never any convictions.

The *Weekend Argus* reported that the tense turf war for club scenes saw Beeka trade in his leather jacket and jeans for a corporate suit in the early 2000s.[6] He left Cape Town and headed for the offices of a courier company in Johannesburg, where he became the national security adviser for courier service RAM. Graeme Lazarus, the joint managing director of RAM, said he was in shock after Beeka's murder.

The speculation that Beeka worked for military and national intelligence would not die after his death. Eventually the State Security Agency told the *Saturday Star* that 'the domestic branch of the State Security Agency had no dealings whatsoever with Beeka'.[7]

Just before his death, Beeka allegedly became involved in bringing Eastern European girls into the country as strippers and exotic dancers. He had a profitable sideline arranging for girls to be supplied with residence papers and work permits under the corporate permit system designed to allow the movement of migrant workers from neighbouring countries to South Africa's mines. This allowed hundreds of workers to enter the country legally. The girls were 'sold' to strip clubs and, in some cases, to brothels. According to Juan Meyer, Beeka, along with Krejcir, was allegedly looking to move into the sleaze industry in Gauteng.[8]

Of course, none of this was spoken about at his memorial service or funeral. Independent Newspapers reported that Beeka's family broke down at the memorial they held at the scene of his death about a week after the murder. Beeka's parents, siblings, some of his children, and nephews and nieces gathered at the scene to lay wreaths and pay their respects.

'We lost a brother, son, father and uncle. He impacted the lives of so many people from different walks of life,' his brother Edward said. 'As a family all we want is to embrace the good memories of him, that's how we will remember him.'[9]

Relatives placed a wooden cross, a picture of Beeka and flowers against the fence the car had crashed into.

'This is overwhelming and unreal,' his wife said. 'When I got the call to say he had been shot, I just cried and cried. I don't want to believe that he's gone. I am just feeling anger, frustration and a lot of sadness.' They had been married for 16 years and her late husband was 'everything' to her, she said.[10]

In the same week, his daughter Megan turned 21 and Laura 16. Megan's mother, Debbie, from an earlier marriage, said that her daughter was devastated and did not want to be at the memorial. She was close to her father and was feeling very angry.

Beeka was buried in Plumstead Cemetery. Hundreds of people attended the ceremony at the Good Hope Christian Centre in the southern suburb of Ottery. No reference was made to his shady past. The funeral opened with

Frank Sinatra's 'My Way'. Photographs of Beeka's life were displayed on large screens around the centre. He was buried with an ANC flag draped over his coffin. It looked out of place at the funeral of a gangster, but to those closest to him it was a sign of respect shown for the days when he had been an MK fighter.

Security at the funeral was tight. Guards with hand-held metal detectors scanned all who entered. Burly ushers in dark suits, each with a radio receiver in their ears, patrolled the aisles. They were members of one of Beeka's security companies.

With such a public, violent death of a prominent, although shady, personality, police had to be seen to be moving quickly. Western Cape police deployed several high-profile squads in their hunt for the assassins.

Their sights first moved back to 2007 when Beeka's then business partner Yuri 'the Russian' Ulianitski had died in almost exactly the same circumstances as Beeka's – shot dead in an ambush while in his car. Yuri's four-year-old daughter, who was in the car with him, became an innocent victim of her father's murky life.

Both men owned a security company. Ulianitski also owned the Castle Adult Entertainment Club, a strip joint in Castle Street, Cape Town.

The modus operandi for the two hits was also the same. Unknown gunmen driving alongside Ulianitski opened fire while he was on his way home. He died in a hail of 20 bullets.

Asked for comment at the time of Ulianitski's death, Beeka said of his associate: 'It is terrible for anyone to be killed like that.'[11]

According to the underworld gossip mill, Beeka was behind Ulianitski's killing. But, as always, nothing stuck and the Russian's death went unsolved.

Now organised-crime detectives reopened the investigation into Yuri's murder to determine whether the killers were the same. They also looked at the man Beeka had been in a meeting with before he was shot. He had visited the alleged former Sexy Boys gang leader, Jerome 'Donkie' Booysen. At the time of the murder, police believed Beeka was trying to broker a peace deal with Booysen to avoid a nightclub security turf war.

'The meeting was to say "let's all stick to our own areas",' a source told *The Star*.[12]

Booysen confirmed that he and Beeka had met for a brief business meeting: 'Both of us buy properties. It was a formal meeting but it did not last long. I was very busy and he had some place he needed to be at too. We have a 12-year friendship, you know,' said Booysen.[13]

The investigating officer, Hendrikse, confirmed the meeting during his testimony in court, and said Booysen was a suspect in the murder. 'It's very suspicious because they'd just left his place and coincidentally he was the first person on the scene,' he said.[14]

The policeman never spoke about the supposed peace deal between the two, however. He maintained the meeting had been about Sasa, Beeka's bodyguard. Sasa had been planning to open a second-hand shop, had wanted to renovate the premises and had submitted plans to the city council. But there had been a hitch on the approval for the renovations. Beeka got in touch with Booysen, who had worked for the City of Cape Town for many years, to get someone from the city council to help Sasa.

Booysen later said he did not know why Hendrikse had said that he was a suspect in Beeka's murder. 'What could possibly be my motive?' he asked.[15]

There was no doubt the tentacles of his underworld life had caught up with Beeka, but was it his past in Cape Town that led to his death? While the police kept their eyes on suspects from the seaside city, it wasn't long before they also set their sights further north – to the glittering lights of the country's business hub, Johannesburg.

In particular, they zoned in on a certain Czech fugitive who in the past few months had been seen almost constantly in Beeka's company.

Beeka's name had come up in affidavits and the testimonies of witnesses, such as Jerome Safi and George Louca, claiming he had been with Krejcir both before and after Lolly Jackson and Uwe Gemballa's murders. Beeka arrived with Krejcir at the house in Kempton Park where Jackson had been found dead in May 2010.

It emerged, however, that in the weeks before the bullets flew, the relationship between the two men had deteriorated. 'They had a big argument, and business dealing started going sour, and things haven't been the same since,' a security expert said.[16]

This was the world of Cyril Beeka – a world that was constantly shifting. You never knew who to trust. Your best friend one minute could become your murderer the next.

After his death, those who had been involved with Beeka were on edge. Their boss had just been murdered and deals had been interrupted. They were scrambling to determine the new underworld pecking order. It appeared things had been tense for a while and Beeka's business dealings in Joburg became rocky a few months before the shooting.

According to the media, Beeka had fled Cape Town eight years before after a serious argument with another security company guarding nightclubs in Cape Town, but he visited the city once a month to see his children.

A police source said: 'He was never very comfortable here [in Cape Town]. Even this time, he had a bodyguard who was armed, so that says enough.'[17]

The relationship between Beeka and Krejcir soured a month before his murder, when the two got into an altercation involving a stripper. Krejcir was allegedly embarrassed when Beeka attacked him in full view of patrons at the Casa Blanca, a nightclub in Green Point, Cape Town.

'Cyril hit him right through the chairs and tables, and Krejcir had to go to hospital to get stitches,' one source told the *Weekend Argus*.[18] Krejcir denied it, however, saying it was a bar fight involving about 20 men.

The paper reported that Beeka learnt that Krejcir had allegedly put a hit out on him. But Beeka was fond of Krejcir and would not believe it. He met Krejcir twice in Cape Town after learning of the hit. 'They discussed the issue over lunch. Cyril asked him whether it was true he had a hit out on him, and Krejcir in turn told Cyril he thought Cyril had a hit out on him. Both denied it to each other,' a source said.[19]

Police soon revealed that they thought the assassins were trained Eastern European killers. Three of them had been brought into the country to do the job: one Serbian and two Albanians.

The Hawks decided to take action. It was supposed to be a public-relations success story: they would storm Krejcir's Joburg mansion in the middle of the night, with journalists and investigator Paul O'Sullivan in tow, and arrest the man who had by now become the South African public's version of Dr Evil.

After attempts to arrest Krejcir had been scuppered by strange deals with crime intelligence after Lolly Jackson's murder, the Hawks decided the best move was to act quickly and bring Krejcir in before his connections or legal team could put a stop to the arrest: 'police win, criminal goes down' was the idea.

They wasted no time. One day after Beeka's death, on 22 March 2011, the Hawks swooped into Bedfordview's millionaires' row. They used an armoured vehicle to batter down the gate as task-force members scaled the walls. Helicopters hovered overhead and police wearing balaclavas broke open doors and windows to get into the Kloof Road mansion.

It was an impressive show of force. Except it was the wrong house.

Simon Guidetti told *The Star*'s Shain Germaner that he had received a call at midnight from his domestic worker telling him that his house was being ransacked. He rushed home and found a platoon of police cars outside his home.[20]

His rammed, twisted metal gate was completely off the rail, the ceramic pot next to it lying shattered from the storming of his home. His side-entrance door and front door had been smashed. His possessions lay strewn across the floor, every cupboard ransacked and each of his indoor security gates removed from their frames.

He just happened to live next door to Krejcir.

Police finally realised they were in the wrong property and told Guidetti they were on top of it and would sort it out. They eventually left to raid the house next door.

Hawks spokesman McIntosh Polela tried to talk their way out of the mess: 'We are dealing with an international fugitive whose house looks like a fortress. We had to use the Nyala [an ambush-protected military vehicle] because we were dealing with a scumbag. We had to gain access to the house,' Polela said.[21]

The Hawks spokesman said they did not need an arrest warrant but admitted they went to the wrong house.

In the right home this time, they found Krejcir was not there.

According to the police, however, the operation was not the total waste of time and money the public thought it was. They held Krejcir's teenage son, Denis, and two of his employees, Michael Arsiotis and Miloslav Potiska, the latter a Serbian national who was allegedly acting as a bodyguard for Krejcir. They were all made to lie on the floor and had their hands cuffed behind their backs. (Denis later complained about the treatment, saying police had manhandled and threatened him. The Hawks denied the claim.)

The police speculated that Potiska had come to South Africa a few weeks before to help organise hits for Krejcir. They said he had helped fly hit men into the country.

Polela said that inside Krejcir's safe they found a hit list written in Czech. At the top of the list was Beeka's name.

Also named on the list were Paul O'Sullivan, Dr Marian Tupy, a doctor who had just been charged for forging a medical certificate for Krejcir in an insurance-fraud case, and advocate Riegel du Toit, the prosecutor in the Gemballa case.

Tupy had entered a plea bargain deal the week before to receive a suspended sentence in exchange for giving evidence against Krejcir.

'The others on the list, including myself, are there because we pose a threat to his freedom. He is trying to build himself up into a powerful organised mob boss and he will let nothing stop him. He has people, including senior police officials, who he will use to ensure any threats to him are eliminated,' O'Sullivan said.[22]

Polela said they invited the media to observe the raid because police wanted Krejcir to know they were looking for him and they wanted the murders to stop.

The taxman also used the opportunity to pounce. SARS investigators confiscated a Lamborghini and a Ferrari during the Bedfordview raid, whose combined value was between R5 million and R6 million.

'Oooh!' a crowd outside the house winced as millions of rands' worth of luxury cars were towed away the next morning, grating along the driveway – their suspension profile was a little too low for the winding drive.[23]

Police revealed they were investigating 15 people in connection with an international financial fraud network that involved cash, gold and expensive cars. They believed Krejcir had links to human trafficking, prostitution, corruption, money laundering, drug, gold and diamond smuggling, and murders.

But the raid had failed to catch the big fish. He was still swimming in open water.

Instead of lying low, Krejcir's lawyer, Piet du Plessis, came out blazing. He said they had asked police for search and seizure warrants but had not received any. He said that if police wanted to see their client all they had to do was ask and they would meet them at their earliest convenience.

Three days later, Krejcir's lawyers said he would hand himself in either at the Pretoria or Joburg Central Police Station. While police were waiting, they received word that Krejcir was at the Rosebank Clinic. By the time they arrived there he had left. 'We were told that he had been at the clinic for medical advice for supposed cancer. He has been playing cat and mouse games with us today,' Polela said.[24]

He said someone within the Hawks may have tipped off Krejcir about the impending raid on his house. Polela said Krejcir's wealth had helped him make numerous connections in the police and he had escaped because he had a bottomless pit of cash and was being informed by snitches, some of whom were corrupt officers.

'He has counterintelligence and, unfortunately, some of them are in our employ,' Polela said.[25]

Then, after three days of playing games with police, Krejcir handed himself in to the Hawks at midnight on 24 March 2011. He was questioned for Beeka's murder, and arrested and charged for the cancer fraud case involving Tupy.

Polela said Krejcir had run out of options: 'He had no passport. He was an international fugitive. He did not have the option of presenting himself to another country because Interpol would have picked him up. We had to put pressure on him and his lawyers. He knew it was just a matter of time.'[26]

De Wet Potgieter reported that the enormous distrust between the Hawks and members of the Crime Intelligence Division led to Hawks chief, Anwa Dramat, insisting that all cellphones be switched off and their batteries removed before, during and after Krejcir's handover. Dramat allegedly told them their phones were being tapped and information was being leaked to people not connected to the investigation.

The next day, the *Saturday Star* ran a picture of O'Sullivan on its front pages. He was sitting at Krejcir's favourite table at the Harbour, behind the bulletproof glass Krejcir had had installed to stop assassination attempts. He was seated in Krejcir's chair and had parked in Krejcir's parking bay. He drank a Guinness, called a source in the Czech Republic and told him of Krejcir's arrest. He said he liked rubbing salt in wounds: 'I feel good. It is Czech mate for Krejcir. He will never sit here again enjoying himself. In fact, he will never eat anywhere else in South Africa again.'[27]

Raising his glass, he said, 'Cheers, Radovan!'

It was too soon to gloat, however. Even when it appeared he was backed into a corner and had no way out, Krejcir was planning how to get out of trouble. O'Sullivan had over the past year amassed a mountain of evidence against Krejcir, but he and the Hawks did not yet know quite the extent of his influence and corruption over the police.

Krejcir's lawyers accused the Hawks of a 'high-handed, jack-booted display of force in the execution of an ill-conceived raid on his house'.

Polela said Krejcir's lawyers were involved in a media war. 'If he was so willing to give himself up, why was he on the run for two days?' he asked.[28]

While Krejcir and his legal team planned their next move, the police looked more closely at the scene of Beeka's murder.

Beeka's driver and bodyguard, Sasa Kovacevic, was discharged from hospital a week after the shooting. He had taken the first bullet, Beeka's wife told the *Cape Argus*.[29] She wanted to meet Sasa to get answers about her husband's death. She said a friend had gone to see him, but he did not want to talk.

A search on Google showed Sasa worked as a software designer and developer at Siemens. He listed interests in security, design and security for clubbing venues. Polela said he was being treated as a witness and if he felt he was in danger he needed to tell them so they could protect him.[30]

In a surprise move, Kovacevic was arrested in December 2011. Police told the press they believed the Serbian national was a hit man and that they were looking into the possibility that one of the five bullets that hit Beeka was fired from within the car because the exit and entry wounds left by one of the bullets were not consistent with having been fired from outside the car, a source told the *Cape Argus*.[31]

Journalist Henriette Geldenhuys said authorities had admitted they did not know who Sasa really was. South African and Serbian authorities were working together to try to figure out his identity. Although he had been identified as Sasa Kovacevic, they believed he might be Dobrosav Gavric, a member of the Serbian mafia.

A Serbian television and radio network, B92, reported that Serbian Interior Minister Ivica Dacic had said the man was arrested in Johannesburg, but could not confirm if he was Gavric. Gavric had been found guilty in Serbia of murdering Zeljko 'Arkan' Raznatovic, the hit-squad commander for former Serbian president Slobodan Milosevic.[32]

Gavric fled Serbia in 2006, shortly after being sentenced to over 30 years in jail for the killing. Arkan was Serbia's most infamous wartime paramilitary leader and mafia boss. Gavric, who killed two other people during the attack on Arkan, was wounded by a bodyguard.

Police first turned their attention on Kovacevic/Gavric because they found 5 grams of cocaine in his bag in Beeka's car. It didn't take long for the South African authorities to determine that one of Serbia's most wanted hit men had been living right under their noses: Kovacevic was in fact Gavric.

He appeared in court for a bail hearing for his possible extradition. It was during this that the investigating officer, Hendrikse, opened up about what police knew of Beeka's killing. In the Cape Town Magistrate's Court he laid bare the links between prominent businessmen and an organised-criminal network operating in Cape Town and internationally. Gavric, 38, faced a 35-year jail sentence in Serbia for murdering two people, including Arkan, 12 years earlier.

Hendrikse testified that at the time of Beeka's killing, the police's organised-crime unit in Gauteng had been investigating Beeka for murder, drug trafficking and dealing in illegal diamonds. About a week before his murder, Beeka and Gavric had attended a rugby match at Newlands where they occupied a private hospitality box owned by controversial businessman Mark Lifman. 'He [Lifman] is also being investigated by organised crime,' Hendrikse said.[33]

All of these powerful men seemed to be connected. Lifman was linked to Jerome 'Donkie' Booysen as well as Krejcir; Gavric played cards with Krejcir and Lifman. Beeka, Krejcir and Gavric were business associates involved in trading in gold, and in other ventures, Hendrikse said. After Beeka's murder, Gavric flew to Johannesburg regularly to spend time with Krejcir, Hendrikse told the Cape Town court.

It was also revealed in court that Gavric had arrived in South Africa in 2007 under the alias Sasa Kovacevic and befriended Beeka a year later. Hendrikse read from Gavric's affidavit: 'I heard he [Beeka] was connected to the police and if ever there was a threat to me, my family would be warned.'[34]

After being convicted of Arkan's killing, Gavric had fled Serbia and travelled to Bosnia where he picked up the passport bearing the name Sasa Kovacevic, Hendrikse said. '… I'm not saying [Gavric] is involved in drug trafficking, but these areas are drug capitals,' the policeman said.[35]

Before arriving in South Africa, Gavric had travelled to Ecuador, Peru and Cuba. He managed to obtain a driver's, firearm and business licence in South Africa using his false passport. Police confiscated the illegally obtained pistol he had used during Beeka's assassination, a 9-millimetre Glock.

Gavric asked later if the gun could be returned to him for self-protection. He handed himself to the Hawks after his identity was confirmed and Serbian authorities requested his extradition.

The revelation of who Sasa really was opened up a Pandora's box of Serbian gangsters who had made their way to South African shores. O'Sullivan said that Krejcir had surrounded himself with Serbian bodyguards: 'They get into SA on fake papers saying they're tourists. They seem to be immune from deportation and are being employed to kill people, rob people and run cocaine. The central and eastern European mafia see SA as a safe haven. It's the new Brazil, and they now prefer SA.'[36]

A Serbian journalist told the paper that a prominent Serbian organised-crime syndicate may have set up operations in South Africa.

An accomplice in the Arkan murder, Milan Djuricic, had also fled to South Africa. Police were on the hunt for him and for one of Serbia's most powerful drug traffickers, Darko Saric, who they believed was hiding in the country after he fled from Serbia to Montenegro in 2010.

Saric was accused of smuggling several tons of cocaine, Serbian papers reported. Police believed he now lived in Johannesburg. Both Krejcir and Gavric denied knowing Saric.

Saric was charged *in absentia* in Serbia with smuggling more than 2.5 tons of cocaine from South America into Europe. Serbian police said he led a drug syndicate that laundered its drug money by investing in property.

Gavric, meanwhile, applied for refugee status, so he could stay in South Africa. By 2016 he was still being detained awaiting a decision to be made.

When news leaked that there were delays in Beeka's estate being wound up because of claims made on it by Krejcir, his dealings in Beeka's life became even more suspicious. Could Krejcir have killed Beeka for money, people wondered?

Beeka owed Krejcir R1.2 million, it emerged. Beeka's family was trying to settle the debt 'to get Krejcir off their backs', reported Geldenhuys.[37]

A few months before his death, Beeka and Krejcir had bought a house, a posh property in Plattekloof, Cape Town, for R1.9 million at an auction Beeka attended with Booysen in November 2010. The house was then put on the market for R3.9 million, but it was unclear who would benefit from the sale.

Some said Beeka's wife, Sonia, and their three children should get the assets. Other friends of the family said they should go to Beeka's love child, a 22-month-old boy, the son of Natalia Mordvinova, with whom Beeka had an affair. Mordvinova owned an agency that recruited strippers, mostly from Russia, to work in South Africa, Geldenhuys reported.

The house was in the name of Beeka's brother Edward. The *Weekend Argus* reported that Edward had paid Krejcir R250 000 against the sum on the deposit that Krejcir paid for the house.[38]

Krejcir, it seemed, had no shame in demanding money from Beeka's children either. A black BMW 3 Series that Beeka had given his daughter for her 21st birthday had been forfeited to Krejcir as part of the repayment arrangement.

Krejcir also wanted nearly R500 000 from Beeka's family for a consignment of firearms that were due to be sent to Mozambique. Krejcir claimed he was owed the money for a controlling stake he had bought in one of Beeka's companies. Confidential Deterrent Systems (CDS) was started by Beeka and former *Big Brother* contestant 'Bad' Brad Wood. The weapons, mostly Glocks and Heckler & Kochs, were to be used in anti-piracy operations in Mozambique.

Krejcir claimed that R480 000 was later used to buy up Wood's half of the company. The weapons were in the possession of a security company in Johannesburg. The *Cape Argus* reported that Krejcir was putting immense pressure on the Beeka family to get the money back.[39]

Krejcir confirmed to the paper that he and Beeka had invested in the anti-piracy company, which was preparing to operate along the African coastline up to the Red Sea. 'We wanted to provide protection from pirates for ships moving along the coast. We were in the process of acquiring boats,' Krejcir said, confirming they had bought 50 weapons.

Chad Thomas, a forensic investigator at IRS Forensic Investigations, corroborated this. Thomas knew Beeka well and confirmed that he was getting involved in anti-piracy maritime security. Thomas said Beeka was talking about it constantly just before he died. He said that anti-piracy was the new buzzword in the security communities at the time because piracy incidents were at an all-time high. Everyone wanted to get involved in it, Thomas said. He said Beeka created an anti-piracy network group for people who could use it to recruit staff and access information on what was happening.

'[Beeka] thought it would get him away from all the clandestine work he had been doing in intelligence and all the underworld activity,' Thomas said.[40]

When they heard that Krejcir wanted to get hold of the weapons, Thomas said the police were determined not to let it happen.

Cape Town detective Lieutenant Colonel Mike Barkhuizen led the Hawks operation to seize the arms cache. A total of 43 out of the 50 weapons, including semi-automatic rifles, were seized from Zonkizizwe Security Services in Randburg. Seven were missing.

Beeka's company SMG agreed it would pay Krejcir's wife and her companies Groep Twee Beleggings and Cross Point Trading, in an attempt to settle the debt Krejcir said was owed to him from the estate. The deal guaranteed Krejcir would drop his claim against the anti-piracy maritime company, CDS, in favour of Edward Beeka taking full control.

Krejcir's claims didn't end there though. There were allegedly further demands for krugerrands worth R500 000, a Ferrari, two Toyota Corollas and a Mercedes-Benz, which delayed the winding up of Beeka's estate.

Weeks later, Krejcir denied any involvement in Beeka's murder or that he had written a hit list. He told eNews that he had been close to Beeka and that his arrest had stopped him from going to the funeral.

'I have never been involved in this Beeka murder. Beeka was my friend, very good friend of mine. I felt very uncomfortable because I couldn't go to his funeral,' he said.[41]

For now, he was a detained man, however, and his plans in the next few weeks would centre on how he could get out of jail.

CHAPTER 8

THE CHAMELEON WITNESS: MARIAN TUPY

When Chris Couremetis was gunned down after the wedding of his best friend at the upmarket Cradle Nature Restaurant, police originally believed the young businessman was the victim of an increase in crime in the area.

They thought he was the target of the infamous Rolex Gang, who had been on a recent spree of murders and robberies in the northern suburbs of Johannesburg. The gang analysed their wealthy victims, knew their movements and always struck when they were sure to get away with a swanky watch. Had the gang now killed the best man at this wedding? Was he the target of their bullets because of the shiny R400 000 bauble on his wrist?

It seemed obvious. The gang had been busy lately. Just a week before the wedding, another man had been shot and killed for his Rolex watch in Joburg. He had been returning from a shopping centre when his car was forced off the road by the robbers.

It didn't take long before police changed their minds about the motive for the wedding killing, however.

Very few people at that Sunday-night tragedy in October 2010 knew about the 35-year-old's secret life and identity. A bit of digging by the police, however, revealed that Couremetis was known as 'Mr Big' to his connections in South America and 'Mr Cocaine' to those who knew of his other life in South Africa.

Months after his death, a picture of what Couremetis had been up to slowly started to come together. It appeared he was a drug trafficker with deep intercontinental connections in the dangerous world of narcotics, where he earned himself the nicknames and a luxury lifestyle, with properties across the globe that not even his nearest and dearest knew about.

But, just like Beeka, it didn't matter how illustrious Couremetis's underworld reputation was, or how deep his connections or his overflowing wealth – a bullet cannot be stopped.

The fancy wedding had been a success and Couremetis, together with a woman and a British couple, made their way out of the venue at 7.30 that warm Sunday evening. The two women were already in the back seat of the car. Couremetis was walking around to the front of the vehicle with a friend when the two gunmen started firing shots.

Twelve bullets from an AK-47 and a 9-millimetre pistol were fired, all of them at Couremetis.

Warrant officer Odette van Staden told Solly Maphumulo from *The Star* that two bullets hit Couremetis in the chest and hand.[1] The rest of the bullets left his luxurious car, a Cayenne worth more than R1 million, riddled with holes.

Van Staden said a bullet penetrated Couremetis's heart: 'I think this must be the shot that killed him. The bullet wound in the hand was not serious. When the paramedics arrived at the scene, he was certified dead.'[2]

When he dropped to the ground, his attackers took his watch and a moonbag containing R10 000 wrapped around his waist.

The guests inside the restaurant scattered in panic, some hiding under tables. The two women who had been in the back seat were later rushed to hospital where they were sedated and treated for shock.

Something didn't feel right, wedding guests speculated afterwards. Nobody else was targeted. Everything about the shooting pointed to it being a hit. Immediately, the police picked up one thing that was suspicious: the other three people who were with Couremetis also had valuables, but they had not been targeted at all. All the bullets had been aimed at Couremetis.

'Once they got their target, they fled the scene. This makes us believe he was targeted either for his Rolex or it was a hit. The modus operandi makes us suspicious,' said Van Staden.[3]

A mysterious phone call to Talk Radio 702 explaining that there was a recent crime wave in the Cradle of Humankind was immediately dispelled by the authorities. It was untrue and they could not understand where the information had come from.[4] And the general manager of the wedding venue, Chandre Buys, said he had worked at the special-functions venue, situated on a 3 000-hectare nature reserve, for ten years, and in that time he had not experienced any major crime there.

All guests have to sign in at the main gate, giving their vehicle registration and ID number before driving about 3 kilometres along a dirt road to the parking lot where Couremetis was killed. The killers, it seemed, had got into the venue posing as wedding guests, even dressed the part in suits, and had waited six hours to pounce on Couremetis.

Police established that three men, two of them in a light-blue Volvo, a stolen vehicle, had entered the premises during lunchtime posing as wedding guests. A third suspect later arrived on a large motorcycle. He said he was delivering a wedding gift and he had something tucked away under his jacket.

Nobody was sure if the killers had attended the wedding ceremony, but no one had seen anyone who wasn't supposed to be there. Said executive head chef Adrian Cook, 'Many guests were walking around with expensive jewellery and watches. There were many Rolexes. This was a rich, high-profile wedding.'[5]

The wedding couple, who were due to honeymoon in Mauritius, cancelled their plans so that they could bury their friend of 17 years. Couremetis's family and friends were devastated.

The day after Couremetis's murder, convicted drug trafficker Glenn Agliotti, who had played a pivotal role in the assisted suicide of mining mogul Brett Kebble, Tweeted that he had 'lost a dear friend in a shooting … yesterday at a wedding. Say a prayer for Chris. Grazie.'[6]

Couremetis was his neighbour and had helped Agliotti when robbers broke into his upmarket Sandton townhouse.

The connection between the two was an immediate red flag: Agliotti was also known to be a friend of Krejcir. After Agliotti was acquitted in 2010 for masterminding Kebble's assisted suicide, one of the first people he spoke about was Krejcir. It seemed the Czech was a friend who had stuck with him during his darkest days. 'I have met with Mr Radovan. He's got a gold refinery in South Africa so it's one of the things we looked into. He has not been convicted in the country so you can't say he's a criminal and that people should not do business with him,' Agliotti told *The Star*.[7]

Later Agliotti admitted to taking a R400 000 loan from a company owned by Krejcir's wife, which he had paid off with interest.

For several months the suspicions around the shooting began to settle. Then, in April 2011, when alleged Cuban drug lord Nelson Pablo Yester-Garrido was arrested, a major international drug cartel was unravelled and the role that Couremetis had played in that world suddenly came to light.

Police spokesman Colonel Vishnu Naidoo said the Cuban's arrest came after an eight-month joint operation between the Organised Crime Unit of SAPS, crime intelligence and the Brazilian Federal Police in São Paulo.[8] The arrest happened after the Hawks had seized more than 160 kilograms of pure cocaine concealed in a container filled with used canola cooking oil in Port Elizabeth. Calculated to have a street value of more than R140 million, the cocaine was in trans-shipment from Paraguay to Bulawayo in Zimbabwe.

Yester-Garrido was in possession of a pistol, a Smith & Wesson Desert Eagle revolver, registered in the name of Couremetis, who police now knew was a cocaine trafficker.

They had also discovered that a bag of illicit diamonds had been stolen from his car when he was killed.

Couremetis was planning to go to Yester-Garrido's house in Morningside when he died. The last text message on his phone was sent to the Cuban, saying he was on his way. Yester-Garrido and his Italian girlfriend were hosting a party that day to celebrate the birth of their first child.

The *Saturday Star* reported that in the months following the Port Elizabeth drug bust, Couremetis had been keeping a low profile, living a clandestine existence in Spain, fearing for his safety in South Africa.[9] He wanted to attend the wedding of his friend, though, so he had flown to South Africa. Because of the risk to his life, Couremetis had told very few people he was coming. But as soon as he landed, he was contacted by Djordje Mihaljevic, owner of the Sandton Gold and Diamond Exchange, and a business partner of Krejcir. Couremetis collected his Porsche and met Mihaljevic on the highway before they both headed to the wedding.

The paper said the murder took place while a massive deal in illegal diamonds was being concluded. As much as 10 000 carats of illicit stones were said to be at stake. The deal was allegedly sealed during the wedding reception. Police revealed that as Couremetis lay dying, one of the attackers leapt onto the car shouting, 'Where is the bag, where is the bag?' The British tourist, who was in the back seat, threw her handbag at the attacker, who then left. The handbag was later found discarded in the car park.

It turned out, according to the *Sunday Times*, that Couremetis was in fact known in underworld drug circles.[10] He owned a five-star villa called Samui Palace on Thong Krut Island in Thailand, a nightclub in Brazil and numerous local mansions. Mihaljevic admitted that Couremetis lived life to the fullest. 'The saying goes that everyone dies, but not everyone lives. Chris lived life. He only wanted the best, and everything he had was the best you could get,' Mihaljevic told the paper.[11]

Couremetis also owned a multimillion-rand collection of cars, including a Ferrari and a Porsche Cayenne, a collection of watches, including six Rolexes, valued at more than R2 million, a home in the exclusive Icon complex in Hyde Park and another in Fresnaye, Cape Town, and a R7 million home in the Savoy Estate, Bryanston, where his neighbour was Agliotti. His grieving parents, Costas and Judy, were trying to unravel the complex details of his assets. Couremetis's wealth was largely unexplained.

Intelligence sources told the *Mail & Guardian* that underworld sources suspected Couremetis had orchestrated the police bust on the cocaine in Port Elizabeth, with a view to secretly recovering some of the cocaine.[12] Some say the bust involved 250 kilograms, but only 166 kilograms of the drug was booked in as evidence. There had also been a break-in at the police laboratory in Port Elizabeth, which appeared to be targeted at the cocaine haul.

It wasn't long before Couremetis was added to a growing list of the dead who had in some way been connected to the Czech fugitive. By the beginning of 2011 there were five names: Trytsman, Jackson, Gemballa, Beeka and Couremetis. Krejcir's name filtered through all the stories of Mr Big's death because of his connection to Agliotti and Mihaljevic. It was rumoured Krejcir had somehow been involved in the drug run gone bad.

Would a Slovakian-born doctor with an alleged addiction to Valium soon be added to the list?

Marian Tupy was one of the four names written on the hit list found in Krejcir's home during the Hawks' March 2011 raid. The 59-year-old urologist had turned on Krejcir in the Alexandra Regional Court one week before Beeka's death by identifying the Czech fugitive as the alleged mastermind of a multimillion-rand insurance-fraud case involving Liberty Life.

Tupy admitted to falsifying documents, saying Krejcir had cancer so he could avoid being extradited to his homeland. Krejcir also used the claim to get a R4.5 million payout on a life-insurance policy. Tupy was convicted of fraud and sentenced to seven years, suspended for five in exchange for testifying against Krejcir.

Tupy entered into a plea bargain agreement with the NPA and agreed to testify that his diagnosis was fraudulent and that he had swapped the samples of a person who he knew had cancer, with samples of Krejcir, indicating that Krejcir was sick.

News24 had affidavits written by Tupy that revealed the money was paid out to Krejcir by Liberty Life after a pathologist's report confirmed the presence of secondary stage cancerous cells in a bladder biopsy.[13] Discovery Healthcare also suffered R250 000 in losses as a result of the alleged scam.

O'Sullivan, the third name on Krejcir's hit list, had found out about the alleged fraud and brought Tupy to the authorities. It seemed that the net was finally closing in on Krejcir: with a doctor admitting he had falsified a medical report so that Krejcir could make a life-insurance claim, the case appeared watertight.

In statements given to the state, Tupy claimed that Krejcir had first broached the 'possibility of making false diagnosis' in April 2008.[14] The two had met in early 2008 at a house in Gallo Manor. Krejcir told Tupy he was having some medical problems and asked to see him in his consulting rooms at the Flora Clinic in Roodepoort. Tupy said in his statement that Krejcir complained about having blood in his urine and he said he had had an MRI done in the Seychelles, as he had a problem with his memory.

Tupy said blood in the urine can be related to lifestyle issues, but cancer should be eliminated as the cause of the problem. The problem could also be caused by high blood pressure. Tupy then carried out tests. The initial tests did not reveal any serious health problems, but as Krejcir kept complaining, Tupy did more invasive tests. Then the possibility of making a false diagnosis came up. Krejcir said this would help him with his extradition case, as he would be less likely to be sent back to the Czech Republic if he was terminally ill, Tupy said in a statement.[15]

The doctor said it was at this point that he decided to make enquiries into who Krejcir was. 'I ascertained that he was alleged to be either the first or second in command of a mafia-type organisation that was based in Eastern Europe, with its headquarters in Prague,' Tupy said.[16]

Tupy said he told Krejcir he would comply, but he intended to drag it out as long as he could, hoping that Krejcir would move on to another country. Instead, however, Krejcir started treating him as a personal physician, calling him constantly and at all hours. Tupy asked to be put on a retainer and started complying with Krejcir's demands: 'I swapped the samples of a person that was known by me to have cancer, with samples of Krejcir, thereby indicating that Krejcir was sick.'[17]

Tupy said that Krejcir often bragged that he could buy anyone he wanted: 'Indeed there were rumours that he had senior cops in his pocket. There were many people that mentioned about the high-level politicians, cops and prosecutors ... that he had paid large bribes to ... I wanted to get rid of him and his problems. However, I also feared that if I just dropped him, he might do something unexpected.'[18]

Tupy said he decided to speak to O'Sullivan, as he had started to get fearful of Krejcir because of things he had heard while in his company. The first was a conversation he allegedly had with Krejcir's mother, at OR Tambo airport in June 2009, where he claimed she had half-joked about killing Krejcir's wife. 'This sent goose-bumps down my body and made me very scared,' said Tupy.[19]

When he was later asked about this, Krejcir described Tupy as 'crazy' and 'sick', and said his mother and his wife were close and the best of friends.

'Then, in or about January or February of 2009, Krejcir told me that he was having a problem with George Smith, and he would have him extradited. This made me realise that Krejcir was able to buy anyone to do anything,' Tupy said.[20]

On one of Krejcir's visits to his consulting rooms, Tupy said he asked Krejcir why the media was linking him to some German guy who had gone missing, Uwe Gemballa. 'He smiled. I then asked what had happened to Gemballa and he put his hand to his throat and drew his hand across his throat, making a cutting sound with his mouth and then he pointed to his own chest and said, "It was me." I realised that he is a very dangerous man indeed,' Tupy said in the statement.[21]

After Jackson's murder, Tupy said that Krejcir was calling him every day asking for the false medical file. The doctor called O'Sullivan again and handed him the file to be photocopied before making his statement to the NPA.

Tupy described how he was then called to meet Krejcir. At the meeting a number of Krejcir's associates stood and watched as Krejcir handed Tupy the statement he had made to O'Sullivan. The investigator had given the statement to the police and the fact that it landed in Krejcir's hands revealed just how many corrupt police officers he had in his pay. 'My heart stopped beating ... Pictures of me being forced into the boot of a car ran through my mind. I really believed that I was going to be murdered that day,' Tupy said.[22]

He denied having made the statement and Krejcir allegedly said to him that if he found out that Tupy had made the statement he would kill him. Krejcir demanded his medical file and Tupy said he gave it to him.

According to journalist De Wet Potgieter, Krejcir then convened a crisis meeting with his closest confidants after receiving the statement.[23] He allegedly told the group of men a hit squad had been brought into the country and they discussed a list of targets.

Meanwhile, national Hawks head, Dramat, the Gauteng Hawks head, Major General Shadrack Sibiya, National Director of the NPA, Menzi Simelane, and state prosecutor, Riegel du Toit, met in Pretoria to strategise how they would arrest Krejcir following their breakthrough with Tupy's statement.

There was talk of a Krejcir hit list but Potgieter said that the police did not take it seriously. Then, Beeka was gunned down. Said Potgieter: 'All hell broke loose, personal security was tightened around all the high-risk individuals and the plan to raid Krejcir's home had been brought forward.'[24]

Krejcir said he offered to assist the police from the start, but that the Hawks rebuffed all his attempts to help them with their investigations.

Krejcir's lawyers also sent a letter to Du Toit explaining that he was willing to cooperate in the medical-insurance fraud investigation. The letter was written two days after Tupy entered into the plea bargain with the state and four days before Beeka was killed.[25] In it the lawyers asked the police not to arrest him until he had given a full statement.

'In the event you do eventually decide to prosecute him you will give our offices notice of your intention and we will facilitate his surrender,' said the lawyer's letter. BDK Attorneys said they had sent several letters to the Hawks offering assistance. 'Disquietingly, however, all of these letters have gone without the courtesy of a reply. All of Mr Krejcir's tenders of co-operation and even surrender were rebuffed by the authorities, seemingly contemplating a public display of clumsily executed military intervention,' the lawyers said.[26]

Krejcir was held at Johannesburg Central Police Station in a cell for high-risk prisoners when he was finally arrested.

The deaths of Jackson, Gemballa and then Beeka had feaured so prominently in the news that everyone thought Krejcir would be charged with their murders, but it turned out the only charge he faced was the R4.5 million medical-fraud case.

But perhaps it was the small case that would catch the big fish? This was a strategy police used often to bring in high-profile criminals, who were so busy concentrating on protecting themselves from being caught for the big crimes that they slipped up and revealed evidence on the smaller ones, which carried lesser sentences.

But a jail cell was still a jail cell in the end, and once the big enchilada was behind those steel doors, the authorities had more space to investigate his criminal network, which had so plagued society. The mere fact that the boss man was behind bars often scared his minions enough into making them talk just that little bit more during interrogations.

Had Krejcir been netted by one of the oldest crime tools in the book? Perhaps, but, as time would teach us, there were very few tricks Krejcir fell for. He seemed too smart, or perhaps it was the fact he was loaded – both with cash and a reputation. The lure of making easy money was too tempting for his accomplices, who loved material possessions so much. Perhaps the yellow dust of the gold mines of Johannesburg had seeped too far under the skin of some of its residents. The glint of riches too tempting, no matter what road it took to get their grubby, greedy hands on them.

Right now, Krejcir used his riches to secure good lawyers. And immediately they turned the public's thoughts from the more serious crimes and made everyone start wondering if the mafia-style crime boss was infallible enough to actually have cancer? Krejcir's health was a concern, said his lawyer, Du Plessis, hinting at the cancer Krejcir said he had in order to make the insurance claim.

'The man handed himself over to the police and we must remember he is only being charged with fraud. How many people appear in court on fraud charges every day in this country? I think the Hawks will make a show of it. Let them have their fun. What matters is what will be said in court,' Du Plessis said.[27]

On 28 March 2011, in his first court appearance, Krejcir would face one of the men on his hit list: Riegel du Toit. Journalists were warned in advance that security at the Johannesburg Magistrate's Court would be heightened and that a security contingent would arrive with the prosecutor. Du Toit turned up at court with four police officers flanking him, all armed with R5 riles. Their sirens could be heard as far away as downtown Johannesburg.

Katerina arrived in a creaseless, tailored business suit and stilettos. She climbed out of a black Mercedes after one of her two bodyguards opened the door for her. She was accompanied by their son Denis. They ignored the media.

The first appearance was a mere formality. It was over in ten minutes. Krejcir stared at Du Toit the whole time, *The Star* reported.[28] The prosecutor seemingly paid no attention to Krejcir, but beads of sweat could be seen on his forehead.

At the next appearance, a few days later, in the old, statuesque court building, the question of bail arose.

Du Toit argued that Krejcir should be kept in prison at least for another week, *The Star* reported.[29] He said that Krejcir knew several of the state witnesses and where they lived. Reading from the affidavit of investigating officer Dumisani Patrick Mbotho, Du Toit said it was alleged that Krejcir had brought three Serbian assassins into South Africa on 18 and 19 March to kill some of the four people named on the list found in his home.

Krejcir was considered a flight risk because he had family and funds overseas. The prosecutor said police had also been informed of two other people whom Krejcir wanted killed: businessman Jerome Safi and gold refiner Juan Meyer.

The defence team, led by Mike Hellens SC, said Krejcir was a man who was literally trapped in South Africa, and would not attempt to flee the country if he got bail. 'I have nowhere to go in the world,' said Krejcir in a statement, adding that if he was extradited to the Czech Republic he would be killed. His statement also revealed that his mother had deposited about R40 million into a local bank and was allegedly planning to move to South Africa.[30]

Krejcir added that he had brought R60 million into the country over the last few years. Using the wealth he had brought into the country was a strategy his lawyers used often. It suggested he would not easily flee a place where his money was stashed and it highlighted, in their minds, what an important, responsible person he was to the court.

The court was told that Tupy said the original purpose of the medical fraud was to keep Krejcir from being extradited, as he would serve two jail sentences in the Czech Republic. The money was just an added extra.

But Krejcir's legal team insisted he was a very sick man, deliberately creating confusion to poke holes in the state's case. They said he had bladder pain and Tupy had operated on him eight times. Krejcir said he had gone for tests in February when possibly cancerous lesions were found in his bladder. He said that if granted bail, he would go for further tests.

According to the defence, O'Sullivan had persuaded Tupy to lie about the insurance fraud claim and he was the 'architect' of the case. Hellens called O'Sullivan a 'self-proclaimed white knight' in South Africa, who perceived himself to be above the law.

In the end Magistrate Philip Venter freed the Czech on bail of R500 000. He said the state had not provided enough concrete evidence to prove that Krejcir would intimidate or harm witnesses. He said it was ironic that it would be joyous news if Krejcir had to find out he did in fact have cancer. He also denounced O'Sullivan and Tupy as unreliable witnesses because Tupy had already been convicted for the fraudulent claim and O'Sullivan consistently expressed his dislike for Krejcir in the media.

Turning to the journalists with a smile, Krejcir said, 'I always believed in the justice system of South Africa.'[31] He said he would be going home to enjoy his mother's Czech cooking and to play with his 17-month-old son.

He was not worried about all the accusations surrounding him. 'Accusing me of these and other crimes is like accusing me of the killing of Marilyn Monroe, Michael Jackson, Elvis Presley and President John F Kennedy. It is ridiculous,' Krejcir told journalist Graeme Hosken.[32]

After his release, Krejcir went straight to the Harbour, took his usual seat at the restaurant, where O'Sullivan had raised his glass two weeks earlier, lifted his favourite Czech beer and said, 'Salut, Paul O'Sullivan. Here I am, back again. I first have to sanitise my seat for the cockroaches before I can take back what belonged to me.'[33]

But, while he may have won the sympathy of the courts, the public at large was not so convinced of Krejcir's claims of innocence. By now people believed Krejcir was a criminal, and watching him being set free by the courts was not doing the criminal-justice system any favours.

Krejcir claimed that some of his possessions had been stolen during the police raid – expensive watches and pens, and several pairs of Louis Vuitton shoes. He said he believed bugs may have been planted to eavesdrop on him and he would search his house.

O'Sullivan was angry, blaming Krejcir's release on his legal team. Du

Plessis sent an email to the South African Press Association saying that O'Sullivan had attacked them.[34] He said O'Sullivan's attack was without merit and in bad taste. The lawyers approached the High Court to have O'Sullivan interdicted from making threats against them in the media. 'We were never and will never be deterred in our duty by any threats of violence or any other underhand tactics by people dissatisfied with the dedication we approach our profession with.'[35]

Du Plessis claimed that O'Sullivan had threatened his life and that of his family in an email.

O'Sullivan said the allegation was all lies. The two publicly showed there was no love lost between them.

Du Plessis said he was going to lay intimidation charges against O'Sullivan and attempt to get a restraining order against him. The investigator responded by sending the law firm a scathing email demanding that they stop lying about him in the media and to stop opening false dockets against him.

Stacey Swanepoel, the wife of Arsiotis, who was arrested on the night of the raid, and Denis Krejcir also laid charges of assault against O'Sullivan. Denis claimed he was hit by police and threatened with rape. The law firm claimed O'Sullivan had led the raid.

'That you have chosen to lie to the media against me, and persuade your gangster friends to open false dockets against me, makes you move very quickly onto my radar screen,' O'Sullivan said in an email titled 'you have crossed the line'. It began with the words 'Hello scum' and said it was a 24-hour-warning notice.[36]

O'Sullivan said he would leave no stone unturned in bringing their business down. Sending threatening emails was a strategy the Irish-born investigator had used before – when he brought down Selebi. His tactic was to work up the people he was investigating, making them angry and never letting them forget that he was there watching them. Some believed his actions were pure madness; others thought he was brilliant. Sometimes it worked by forcing people into a corner; other times it backfired and O'Sullivan got caught in the hot seat.

His relentless bulldog approach seemed to work a lot of the time. Others would give up and move on. But O'Sullivan kept on their scent. There was no question that his methods were unorthodox, however, and his brash, in-your-face personality irritated many. But, when it came to Krejcir, many of the witnesses who had come forward and signed sworn affidavits did so through O'Sullivan. He was making inroads into this case like no one else.

It was no wonder he was on Krejcir's alleged hit list and had become the focus of his lawyers. O'Sullivan made no secret of the fact he hated defence lawyers almost as much as the alleged criminal he was focusing on. He believed they too were criminals for defending what he believed was the indefensible. O'Sullivan said they bogged investigators down with lawsuits that took up their time and money in an attempt to distract them from looking too deeply into their clients. The lawyers argued they were just doing their jobs.

Du Plessis said they would not allow O'Sullivan to 'drag them into a mud-slinging match of low morality'. The legal team then obtained a restraining order against O'Sullivan, who said he had no intention of breaking the law but would continue his criminal investigation into them. 'Frankly, I expected nothing less from the lawyers of gangsters who have demonstrated that they are strangers to the truth.'[37]

In an answering affidavit before the High Court, O'Sullivan revealed that he had been threatened by Krejcir.[38] The investigator said he had been called by someone he believed was Krejcir after he had been to the Czech Republic to speak to authorities there about Krejcir's criminal history: 'Hello clown, you want to fuck with me? I will show you who is Radovan. When you will come to South Africa, I will make you suck my cock, then I will kill you, to show you, you fucking with the wrong guy.'

Another call said: 'It's Radovan, you fucking *poes*. You fucking finished, I'm gonna kill you very soon, you fucking *poes*.'[39]

Du Plessis said O'Sullivan had taken a 'self-appointed biblical role' as a dispenser of justice. 'Persons such as Mr O'Sullivan could quite evidently be dangerous in society if left unchecked,' said the lawyer.

Eventually, after months of catty comments, threatening emails and verbal attacks, a white flag was raised, reported *The Star*'s Germaner.[40] Both sides agreed to pay their own legal costs. The side-show litigation came to an end.

In between the legal wrangling, the law firm applied to the court to get Krejcir's bail reduced from R500 00 to R250 000. Krejcir claimed he needed the money to carry out medical tests. His lawyers claimed that Krejcir had allegedly had two bladder operations in the meantime.[41] Magistrate Venter was not impressed, however, and turned down the application. He pointed out that during bail proceedings Krejcir made it clear he had a huge number of assets: a R20 million Bedfordview home, a R7 million house in the Vaal and numerous cars worth more than R1 million each. His mother had also brought R40 million into the country and invested it in the South African Reserve Bank. There was no argument against that.

In the middle of the legal bickering, another Krejcir made an appearance. Nadezda Krejcirova arrived in the country. SARS, intelligence sources and journalists were all watching and waiting for her grand entrance. She was questioned by officials minutes after landing, in what was described as a 'routine questioning of potentially high-risk people'.[42]

The then SARS spokesman, Adrian Lackay, said that no irregularities were found and she was released. Intelligence sources told the *Pretoria News* that while all eyes were trained on the blonde woman, they believed someone else slipped through with bags of her money.[43]

Listed by the *Prague Post* as the Czech Republic's tenth richest woman, Krejcirova walked into the arrivals hall in Johannesburg smiling for the cameras before rushing off into a waiting car, cellphone at her ear.

Things went quiet on the Krejcir front for about a year. Then, in a surprise move, in February 2012, this time with no journalists in tow, or armoured vehicles to bulldoze neighbours' gates, Krejcir was arrested again.

He was hauled in this time for allegedly having been part of an armed robbery in Pretoria. Krejcir was having a nap at his home when police came in.

Du Plessis lashed out at the police for the 'cowboy-style tactics' of the arrest of Krejcir and his two accomplices Veselin Laganin and Jason Domingues. The armed robbery had taken place in October 2011 at an electronics store in Pretoria West, Ali's Electronics, where R200 000 was taken.

The store was owned by Pakistani nationals. Du Plessis said they had dealings with one of Krejcir's friends. Krejcir's lawyer argued they were set up because they were trying to collect a R900 000 debt. Police said a gang of six held up the owner and a shoot-out ensued in which Domingues was allegedly shot in the hand.

Attorney Eddie Claasen said there had been no robbery: 'This is simply a botched charge brought by some Pakistani individual who my clients allege to be involved in illegal trafficking of money.'[44] Claasen said the alleged victim owed Laganin about R900 000 and had lured him to the premises on the understanding that he would be paid.

He said Krejcir was in no way connected, but confirmed he had been at the scene. Both parties laid charges of robbery. Domingues was arrested shortly afterwards but the case had originally been struck off the role because of insufficient evidence.

After appearing in the Pretoria Magistrate's Court, Krejcir received bail of R30 000 and his two co-accused were given bail of R10 000 each.

The case went nowhere fast and fizzled out when the NPA withdrew all charges. There was never any clear explanation about what really happened in the electrical shop that day.

Krejcir soon went from being a fugitive on the run, who was so wanted by the state that his house had been publicly stormed by the police, to having zero charges against him. In a move that sent shock waves through the criminal-justice system, the medical-fraud charges were withdrawn. The state's main witness, Tupy, announced that he could not testify after all.

It turned out that Tupy was not happy with the fact that he too had been charged with fraud when he had signed a plea agreement with the state. He wanted his conviction overturned. His application stalled Krejcir's case and all charges were provisionally withdrawn.

Tupy had turned to the High Court. His fraud conviction meant he could lose his medical licence, and if he was not practising he could not make a living. Having the conviction removed would allow him to carry on practising. He also faced an internal investigation by the clinic in Roodepoort where he had practised before his conviction.

His reasoning sounded simple at first: he needed to convince the Health Professions Council of South Africa that he did not have a conviction against his name. But, in his application to the court, a whole new version of events was suddenly presented to court.

In an astonishing move, Tupy turned on O'Sullivan.[45] He claimed he had signed the plea and sentence agreement under duress, that he had been unduly influenced by O'Sullivan and the Hawks. He claimed that O'Sullivan knew of the insurance claim before he signed a letter saying Krejcir had cancer, and that the investigator gave him the go-ahead to sign the false insurance claim form, saying he was a friend of the state. If he was working with the state, he should never have been charged with fraud, Tupy claimed.

O'Sullivan, however, said that Tupy had gone before a judge, had his own lawyer and thrashed out a plea bargain over many weeks – a process O'Sullivan had played no role in. 'I didn't tell him to sign anything. He is being economical with the truth. I went to the ends of the earth to help this man. I had no knowledge that he had signed those documents. I only found out in February this year and I took it straight to the Hawks and they took over,' O'Sullivan told investigative journalism body amaBhungane.[46]

Tupy, he said, had told him the false diagnosis was for Krejcir's extradition case. He knew nothing of the Liberty Life insurance claim.

O'Sullivan said he did not believe Tupy was of sound mind. 'I wish to indicate that given the vast amounts of liquor I saw him consuming at our various meetings, he might think that he told me about his Liberty Life claim. The applicant also admitted to taking vast amounts of Valium to keep himself calm,' O'Sullivan said.[47]

Tupy's allegations against O'Sullivan escalated. In his review application to have his guilty plea for fraud overthrown, he now claimed that O'Sullivan had stolen Krejcir's medical file from his offices, that he forged evidence, stole a biopsy, got Tupy so drunk that he didn't know he was signing affidavits, and set him up to sign a guilty plea when he thought he was getting indemnity from the state. He also said that Krejcir did in fact have bladder cancer.

O'Sullivan described the allegations as lies. The investigator said Tupy was back on Krejcir's payroll to ensure the state's medical fraud case against him disappeared. He also believed the doctor was being threatened to change his story and implicate O'Sullivan. (This version would be corroborated years later by Krejcir's employee Potiska, who wrote in the book *The Godfather African* that Tupy's family in Slovakia had been threatened and that the doctor had no choice but to change his version of events.[48])

Tupy's papers were filed against O'Sullivan, the NPA, the Director of Public Prosecutions and Hawks officer Mbotho.

Tupy said that O'Sullivan approached him and claimed he had proof that Krejcir wanted to kill him and his family. He said he would protect him, but only if he helped in the criminal case against Krejcir. O'Sullivan said it was the other way around – that Tupy had approached *him* asking for help with his Krejcir problem, one in which he had become so embroiled that he feared for his life.

Tupy said his offices at the clinic had been broken into and patient files went missing. Later at a meeting he claimed that O'Sullivan had pulled out Krejcir's file. He also claimed that O'Sullivan collected the biopsy samples from the pathologist. He laid a charge of intimidation against O'Sullivan. The investigator hit back at Tupy for claiming he had bullied him and plied him with alcohol. O'Sullivan said Tupy had handed him the medical file. O'Sullivan photocopied it and returned the file to the doctor, who then allegedly passed it on to Krejcir.[49]

In his responding papers, O'Sullivan denied all of Tupy's claims and attached a transcript of a conversation the two men had during which they discussed the statement Tupy had signed on Krejcir. O'Sullivan said he had all the recordings of their conversations proving that Tupy had falsified the medical diagnosis at Krejcir's behest.

O'Sullivan also sent a complaint to the Health Professions Council because Tupy had allegedly made reference to needing Valium. 'You will observe from the transcript that he has to be high on Valium before he can operate. Not sure that's in the best interest of his patients though,' O'Sullivan wrote to the council. 'Look at me. Look at my face. I'm on fucking constant Valium, man. Constant. Because otherwise I can't operate, I can't concentrate. Fuck, I'm a surgeon, man,' Tupy allegedly told O'Sullivan.[50]

According to O'Sullivan's version of events, he met Tupy in 2009 at the Krugersdorp Airfield.[51] He said Tupy had explained to the investigator that he had got himself into a situation with a very dangerous man and he needed some help to get himself out of it. The man was Krejcir. O'Sullivan said he subsequently met with Tupy in his consulting rooms and he showed him the files on Krejcir. Tupy allegedly told him he had agreed to create a false file for Krejcir, indicating that he was dying of cancer and the file would be used to persuade the Czech Government that Krejcir was not fit to return there to stand trial for various offences.

O'Sullivan said it was clear to him that Tupy was scared for his life and did not know what to do, so he advised Tupy to play along with Krejcir, but at no point should he supply the documents as requested, because if he did so Krejcir would no longer have any use for him and he could be killed. He told him to keep the file in a safe place and not let anyone know where it was.

After Jackson was murdered, O'Sullivan said he received a call to say that Tupy was scared because Krejcir had been paying him a lot of attention. He indicated he was under pressure to provide Krejcir with a letter indicating he had cancer and that the prognosis was not good.

O'Sullivan said he took a statement and sent it to the NPA. Tupy then handed the whole file to him for safe keeping, which he photocopied.

During this time, Krejcir had told Tupy that O'Sullivan was working with the Czech Government as a secret agent, and was going to help the authorities extradite Krejcir from South Africa. He was worried about having the investigator killed, as that would point too many fingers at him. Instead, he wanted to discredit him by claiming he was a foreign spy and crazy.

Du Toit, the prosecutor, also dismissed Tupy's latest version of events as a fabrication. He indicated that if Krejcir really had cancer, as Tupy now claimed, why would subsequent results and reports from a laboratory and specialists show otherwise? 'It seems incredible that the Applicant has been a victim since 2008. A victim of Krejcir, a victim of O'Sullivan, a victim of the SAPS, a victim of the NPA, etc. It is humbly suggested that the applicant was a victim of his own greed and bad judgment,' Du Toit said.[52]

Whatever the real story, there was no way Tupy would ever be called on now as a witness. 'He had recanted and varied his evidence on numerous occasions, thus dispelling any degree of credibility,' O'Sullivan said.[53]

And so, cancer or no cancer, Krejcir remained a free man. And he had R4.57 million safely stowed away in his pocket.

CHAPTER 9

THE GRUESOME DEATH OF AN INNOCENT MAN

His burnt body lay on the undercarriage of his overturned car, the only part still recognisable as human was his smooth skull, but even that was damaged. A scan later revealed that Ian Jordaan's teeth had been smashed out.

For the police, attorneys and businessmen who have been in some way involved with Krejcir, it is this image that haunts them – the body of an innocent man lying on the car – because everyone who had died so far had lived and died by the gun. Each one had in some way been a part of the murky underworld of international crime: Kevin Trytsman, a wheeler and dealer who claimed to be involved with intelligence, Lolly Jackson, a strip-club king who was laundering money, Cyril Beeka, a mafia boss who straddled the underworlds of Cape Town and Joburg, and Chris Couremetis, a drug dealer. Even Uwe Gemballa had a cloud hanging over him, with rumours that he had been involved in money laundering for Krejcir.

But Ian Jordaan?

Jordaan was a lawyer who had been representing Jackson for years. He had been in charge of winding up Jackson's complicated multimillion-rand estate. All he was ever tainted with was doing his job. An innocent man, he died a gruesome death.

On 20 September 2011 at 12.44 pm, Ian Jordaan sent a fax from his office at Jordaan & Wolberg, on Louis Botha Avenue in Norwood. It was sent to Karla Strydom Attorneys and concerned a claim on the estate of Emmanuel (Lolly) Jackson: 'Your client is hereby notified that the claim as lodged against the estate is rejected … Based on the documentation and information presently at our client's disposal, I can find no proof of the alleged loans as referred to in your client's claim.'[1]

Jordaan's client was Jackson's widow, Demi, and the person whose claim he had just rejected was Krejcir, through his wife's company Groep Twee Beleggings (Pty) Ltd.

The fax was a final rejection of claims of several millions of rands that Krejcir had made on Jackson's estate.

Trying to wind up Jackson's estate was proving to be an incredibly complicated task for the lawyer who had been by Jackson's side through numerous court battles in all the sleaze king's various run-ins with the law. Everyone had expected Jackson to leave so much money behind that his family would be swimming in it. But the colourful character had one fatal dislike: paying taxes. And this came back to bite his family while they were still trying to get over the shock of his brutal death.

According to the will filed in the Gauteng Master's office, Jackson left an estate estimated to be worth about R200 million, not counting the Teazers businesses or the fleet of luxury cars he had been so famous for.[2] The money was to be split between Demi and Jackson's three children, Samantha, Manoli and Julian. The will listed four properties, together valued at R33.4 million, furniture and household effects worth R300 000, intellectual property for the Teazers group valued at R80 million, letting enterprises of R70 million and various policies worth R41 million. The smallest amount named was a judgment order in a court case worth R1.25 million. Jackson was said to have a fleet of 14 cars estimated to be worth more than R42 million.

But in the file was a letter from SARS indicating their interest in the contents of the will, and they weren't looking at taking a million or two. It appeared that Jackson owed the taxman a significant amount of money.

After the man who ran the Teazers in Durban, Shaun Russouw, sued Demi Jackson for millions saying he owned half the Teazers logo and brand, Demi said people kept on coming forward trying to claim a piece of the estate: 'People think there are millions and millions out there, but they don't seem to understand that those millions are going to the taxman. I sold the Kloof

Road property to give money to the taxman and I had to give a R10 million life policy to the taxman.'³

SARS eventually won an application to have two curators appointed to take control of Jackson's assets. The tax bill was said to be as much as R100 million.

Krejcir was one of the people also wanting a share of Jackson's stash to come his way. On 30 May 2011 a claim was submitted to Jordaan's firm by Strydom on behalf of Katerina Krejcirova's company.⁴ Everyone knew that her name was there in name only: Krejcir was the real owner behind the business.

The claim was for various debts Krejcir claimed had been allegedly incurred by Jackson. Later the creditors included Groep Twee Beleggings, Krejcir's mother, and Czech company DKR Investments Praha (the acronym referring to Denis, Katerina and Radovan).

Krejcir's lawyers had sent through acknowledgments of debt that Jackson had purportedly signed before he died indicating he owed Krejcir money. Jordaan had been trying to get Krejcir's lawyer to send further proof of these claims, but none had been forthcoming. It appeared the loans to Jackson had been transacted through overseas accounts and there were no bank statements showing the money had swapped hands. So Jordaan rejected the claim by fax.

Six hours later he was dead.

Jordaan was known to be trustworthy and supportive of the family. He would always do his best for his client and had been trying to keep Krejcir away from Demi, who was being harassed to pay the debts. He told Krejcir's manager, Ivan Savov, to stay away from Jackson's widow and to deal only with him.

He put himself in the firing line, as lawyers often do, when he hit the 'send' button on the fax. One hour later, at 2 pm, he left his office. He was going to meet a potential new client, he told his colleagues. They had no idea who the new client was. Later he called his secretary and told her a man would be coming to the office to collect his laptop and that it was in order for her to give the computer to the man, who, he said, would be wearing a pink shirt.

Jordaan's fiancée, Joanne Rizzotto, worked for the same firm. She became concerned hours later because the motorbike Jordaan had travelled to work on was missing and he had not returned from his meeting with the client. He had taken his bakkie to the meeting, so she could not understand how the bike was gone. The couple were meant to travel together to their home in Kyalami together at the end of the day. Rizzotto filed a missing person's report at Norwood Police Station.

At 9 pm an overturned silver bakkie was found under a bridge on the Broederstroom Road, near Hekpoort in the West Rand – almost 80 kilometres away. The number plates revealed it was Jordaan's car. On top lay his body. Lieutenant Colonel Lungelo Dlamini of the Gauteng Police said that it was burnt beyond recognition.

City Press reported that a scan of the body revealed the man's teeth had been smashed out – probably in an attempt to stop the body from being identified through dental records.[5] But, police wondered why, then, was the bakkie's number plate still left on? It was a mystery they never solved.

'There was considerable damage to the mouth. He was probably dead when the body was set alight,' the paper reported.[6]

Forensic expert Dr David Klatzow said it was very difficult to smash out a full set of teeth. If there were no teeth left in the skull, it probably meant they had been pulled out.

Only DNA could positively identify that the man was the 55-year-old lawyer.

Jordaan's laptop had been used to facilitate the transfer of the money. In the hours after his death, R1.8 million was transferred from his trust account. It was money Jackson had placed in Jordaan's trust pending the outcome of a civil dispute between Jackson and his former protégé, Mark Andrews, over the ownership of the Teazers Cresta branch.

A judge had ordered Jackson to place the money in a trust after a court case in which Andrews had sued Jackson over the renovations and ownership of the Cresta Teazers. Jackson was instructed by the court to put the money aside until the case was finalised.

The Johannesburg High Court initially allowed Jackson to evict Andrews and his staff, but two months later the same court allowed Andrews to sue Jackson, but the case was never finalised.

The court decided R1.8 million should be set aside as a payout if the attempt by Andrews to sue him was successful. After Jackson's death Jordaan had allegedly been told by Demi to keep the money until the Jackson estate had been settled, possibly to use as legal fees. This money had been transferred from Jordaan's trust account into an overseas account on Jordaan's death, which the police traced to Andrews. They quickly intercepted the transfer and stopped it.

The news of Jordaan's death swept terror into those who had been close to Jackson. They began to fear for their lives. Sean Newman, Teazers former spokesman, said that if the hit was a murder, 'then it is the most disgusting thing ever. He is just an innocent individual who was caught in the middle.'[7]

The police had one clear suspect in mind: they needed to find Mark Andrews. The year before, Andrews had relocated to Thailand but had returned to South Africa to finalise his claim against Jackson's estate.

The conclusion of the Teazers Cresta case was impossible to identify, as all the court documents relating to it had been removed from the Johannesburg High Court. *The Star* reported that there was just one file with three pages inside that said Jackson was deceased and 'executors substitute themselves as defendants in the above action'.[8]

Andrews was Jackson's former partner in the Cresta branch of the Teazers strip club. In 2008 Andrews had been managing the branch at Jackson's behest but a personal fallout had divided the partners.

Jackson described in an affidavit he had placed before the court how the two had travelled to Europe together recruiting strippers. Jackson trusted Andrews to the extent that he loaned him cars from his legendary collection, allowing him full access to his garage when he was out of town.

But then Jackson discovered Andrews was romantically involved with a stripper called Micaela, which was strictly against company policy. Jackson said he had earlier fired Micaela from a Cape Town branch after she had a relationship with a business partner and then his brother.

The relationship between Andrews and Jackson deteriorated beyond any hope of repair after Andrews locked Jackson out of the branch's bank accounts and Jackson stopped receiving financial reports. Andrews took full control and renamed the club Decadence, spawning the court battle because the Cresta club was registered under a company owned exclusively by Andrews, giving him full control of the finances.

In the Johannesburg High Court in October 2009 Jackson was granted full control of the club, and Andrews and his staff were ordered to vacate the premises. But, first, Andrews trashed the place, ripping out light fittings and smashing mirrors. Andrews was then given permission to sue Jackson for R2.3 million.

So, now, he was the police's number one suspect. Andrews knew he was being looked for.

It had been seven days since Jordaan's murder and the burly 36-year-old spoke to his lawyer. He planned to hand himself over to the police.

Writer Julian Rademeyer from Media24 reported that Andrews was in deep financial trouble.[9] He had accumulated credit-card and other debts of close to R1 million in the five months since he had returned to South Africa.

He told his parents that he was being set up for the murder of Jordaan and he feared for his life. He visited his girlfriend, Candice Greef, at her workplace at around 11 am on 27 September. He borrowed her credit card to withdraw R200 and then left the card at the security desk at her office.

That was the last time he was seen by anyone close to him.

He was wearing white takkies and light-coloured pants – clothing that was easily picked up in the headlights of a police vehicle on the R59 in the early hours of the following morning. The two patrolling police officers found him alongside the deserted road at about 3 am on 28 September 2011.

Andrews's body was lying on the side of the highway between the Kliprivier off-ramp and Vereeniging. He had been shot execution-style. His hands were secured behind his body with cable ties. He was slumped forward after being shot in the back of the head, hitting his face hard against the ground. The only wound was an 8-millimetre bullet hole in the back of his head. There was no exit wound. Police believed he had been shot with a low-calibre bullet.

The Times reported that the murder was extremely professional with no trace of evidence left on the scene.[10] There were no footprints or car tracks. None of his personal belongings, including his cellphone, were stolen.

Andrews's distraught mother and sister arrived at the Germiston mortuary to identify his body. 'They did not handle it easily. There was a breakdown,' said one officer, who had been with them when they identified the body.[11]

Andrews's murder happened exactly eight days after the murder of Jordaan. Police now believed Andrews was only the middleman in the transaction of the R1.8 million and that he would have been given a small share of the money for the use of his account. But the deal came undone when Andrews, knowing the police were hot on his heels, decided to hand himself over. Their theory was that the masterminds then kidnapped Andrews and shot him to avoid his identifying them.

The fear factor in Jackson's circle escalated – 'I am terrified, but don't quote me in case it gives anyone ideas,' a relative told *The Star*.[12]

'Body number seven,' said a former employee of Jackson. 'I am really frightened today. This is scary.'[13]

After the week of bloody murders, the trail appeared to go as cold as the bodies of the men who had now been buried. There were no arrests or revelations about what had happened those two fateful nights in September 2011.

Even the claims on Jackson's estate died down, for a while. But soon the pressure was back on Demi and her fear had not gone away. The fearful widow hired Paul O'Sullivan to help her. She asked him to find out who had killed her husband.

The two of them went to the High Court to ask cellular service provider Vodacom to reveal if they had supplied a third party with their cellphone itemised billing data. O'Sullivan revealed in affidavits that he was used to threats because of the kind of work he did.[14] The investigator said that he had been called by a friend who had witnessed Krejcir asking Colonel

Sambo, the station commander at Bedfordview Police Station, why there had been so many phone calls between him and O'Sullivan on one particular day. When asked how Krejcir knew about these calls, 'he boldly bragged that he had my telephone records,' O'Sullivan said.[15]

The investigator said he immediately contacted Vodacom telling the operator that he believed his communication had been breached. Vodacom revealed that his cellular records had been requested by the police in March, April and June 2011. Again, proof was emerging that police officers were in Krejcir's pay, and they were handing information to him.

In the police's request for O'Sullivan's cellphone records, they indicated that there were dockets opened in Primrose and Tokoza of kidnapping, assault, theft, armed robbery and murder, which named O'Sullivan as a suspect. They were cases that O'Sullivan had no knowledge of. He believed that police had used these dockets to illegally listen in on his calls. O'Sullivan's ex-wife had also received disturbing phone calls telling her O'Sullivan would be arrested and that she would receive R1.5 million if she provided the caller with information that could be used to publicly discredit him.[16]

Demi also believed her phone records had been accessed. Another affidavit, this time filed in 2012 in the South Gauteng High Court by O'Sullivan's colleague, forensic investigator Kim Marriott, revealed that Demi had been getting threatening SMSes demanding she pay back a 'patient' Krejcir his money.[17]

Marriott shed light on the relationship between Krejcir and Jackson and the joint money-laundering operation they had conducted. She told the court that Jackson's alleged acknowledgements of debt to Krejcir had been forged.

Her affidavits, which included statements by Demi Jackson, alleged that Jackson used the forged documentation to cover up questionable financial transactions, a cover story prepared in case SARS or the Reserve Bank came to ask questions.

Marriott said that in the last few years of Jackson's life, he and Krejcir had been engaged in various transactions 'conducted in furtherance of an overall scheme to launder money':

> I believe that the (acknowledgments) were created as part of a sham transaction to be utilised in the event that the South African Reserve Bank became apprised of the cash dealings between Krejcir and Jackson.
>
> This is consistent with the modus operandi of both Krejcir and Jackson. I further believe that upon the murder of Jackson, Krejcir saw an opportunity to utilise the fictitious acknowledgments in order to obtain a pecuniary advantage in a claim against Jackson's estate by virtue of the fact that Jackson would not be alive to verify that the acknowledgments were fictitious.[18]

Marriott revealed there had been four separate attempts by Krejcir to claim from Jackson's estate since his death in May 2010, each one escalating in value.

The first attempt was made when Krejcir purported to be the buyer of Teazers. Krejcir claimed an amount of only R1.1 million. The full debt was said to be R6.6 million but Krejcir said R5.5 million had already been paid by Jackson.

Lawyers' letters showed the attempted takeover, in 2010, of Jackson's strip-club empire where the alleged debts would be written off as part payment of a R90 million price tag, allegedly agreed as a buy-out price between Krejcir and Jackson for the clubs.

Then two acknowledgements of debt were submitted with Jackson's signature. The second claim was for a sum of R8.1 million. The third claim came through an email sent by Krejcir's employee Ivan Savov, claiming R9.12 million and the third had escalated the value to R10.7 million.[19]

Jordaan was murdered at the time the second and the third claims were made. Savov had been contacting Demi, demanding the money be paid.

'I was tasked to try and sort out repayment on these loans … Radovan is being patient, but Lolly signed an agreement with Radovan and has also verbally agreed to sort out repayment by end of July 2010,' Savov said to Jordaan.[20]

The lawyer wrote back asking for more information on the debts that Jackson had allegedly had with Krejcir, explaining he had no proof of their validity: 'Without any answers to the questions asked, our clients are not in a position to accept and admit your client's claims.'

Then Jordaan and Andrews were murdered.

The affidavits revealed that the same day that Andrews was murdered, three people in the employ of Krejcir attended the Rivonia branch of Teazers. Marriott said they were very menacing and they made it clear they were there to collect the money owing to Krejcir: 'Radovan wants his money and he's getting impatient,' they said.[21]

After that things went quiet for a while. Then a fourth claim was sent, this time for R10.7 million. It was an application filed by Nadezda Krejcirova and Czech company DKR Investments Praha. The acknowledgement of debt had allegedly been signed by Jackson five days before he was shot.

DKR claimed that Jackson had borrowed money and had signed an acknowledgement of debt in April 2010, promising to pay $1 million within two years. The document said Jackson would pay back the money in five instalments of $200 000 each plus 8% interest per annum.

In response, Marriott filed an application before the court. She showed that, with every claim against the estate, the documents changed and the witnesses whose signatures were on the acknowledgement of debts denied they had ever signed them. The claims came with three acknowledgements of debt signed by Jackson but, according to a wealth advisor at Standard Bank, who was said to have certified the documents as true copies, neither the signature nor the stamps used to certify the copies were his.[22]

Marriott asked that Krejcir and Savov be prosecuted for charges of fraud, forgery and uttering a forged document. But, once again, despite overwhelming proof, nothing stuck to Krejcir.

The forgery case, just like the murders of Jordaan and Andrews, were filed in newspaper archives and gathered dust.

They were just another set of unsolved crimes.

CHAPTER 10

GEORGE LOUCA: DEATHBED CONFESSION

George Louca died an innocent man.

Despite being a top dog in one of South Africa's biggest international crime syndicates, despite having called the head of Gauteng crime intelligence and confessing to killing the country's strip-club king, despite fleeing the country when every police officer was looking for him and despite the state spending millions of rands to have him extradited back to South Africa, George Louca died an innocent man.

He was never to be found guilty, in any court of law in the country, of any crime.

His dying wish: to have his story told, so that his four children did not remember him as a murderer. Those were the words of a man riddled with cancer tumours in his windpipe, gasping between intakes of oxygen. His words were hard to make out – you had to lean in close to the frail body in the wheelchair to understand what he was saying.

They were the words of a man filled with remorse for the life he had lived on the edge. He was a man who his lawyer, Owen Blumberg, later said was a changed person, a change so great that it had inspired Blumberg to tell Louca's story. He was a client he could never forget. Blumberg had wanted to write a book on Louca, but he never had a chance: a heart attack suddenly struck, killing the kind-hearted lawyer.

The image of the remorseful, dying Louca was the man the public saw in 2015. But, five years earlier, back in 2010, when we left him last, he was the wild-haired, smug George Smith seen in the ID photo that the police circulated to the media. Then, he was the man who lived on the edge: arrogant, untouchable. A thug.

In the months following Lolly Jackson's death, the rumours around Louca would not die. Jackson's death had caused a storm, a whirlwind that kept on feeding itself. The public wanted, they demanded, to know what was going on in South Africa. What was this underworld that had suddenly been exposed to the light of day? After the death of Brett Kebble and the shaming of police chief Jackie Selebi, everyone thought this element of our society had been smothered. Now they had found out, in the bloodiest way, it had in fact become more entrenched.

And George Louca, with the big belly, double chin and multiple identities, who went grocery shopping on tabs that were never paid, was the key to opening the doors of our understanding. He knew what was really going on.

Police announced that they did not believe Louca had been alone the night Jackson was shot. The Hawks were said to have identified a different set of DNA and blood samples at the scene of the murder, indicating there was either an accomplice or possible witness to the crime.

But they had no way of finding out more. The key witness, the man who had confessed to being there that terrible night in May 2010, had simply vanished. It took two months after Jackson's death to establish that George Louca was in exactly the last place you would expect a fugitive from justice to be: at home with his wife and children.

Louca was in Cyprus. And he wasn't hiding the fact either. Members of the Greek community said it was no secret that George had been living in the seaside town of Limassol, where his wife and four children had been living for many years.

The police had formally asked Interpol to help locate him. 'All the airports and ports had been red-flagged after the shooting,' said police spokesman Lieutenant Colonel Eugene Opperman. A check by *The Star* revealed, however, that Louca's details and photographs did not appear on the SAPS or Interpol websites.[1]

There was talk of Louca sunning himself on the beach, telling everyone who asked that he knew the truth behind Jackson's murder. People speculated that he was living off Jackson's laundered money, which, they said, had been kept in a bank account in Louca's name in Cyprus. They said he and Krejcir were in regular contact over the phone.

To prove just how easily accessible Louca was, a source gave me his telephone number. I picked up the phone in 2011 and called him.[2] A man with a heavy Greek accent answered and admitted that he was Louca. He told me he had left the country through OR Tambo International Airport nearly a month after the murder and he spoke to his friends in South Africa nearly every day.

He told me he was 'not innocent [of] what happened that day', but said there was an explanation. Speaking in riddles, he called Jackson's death 'the accident', and said he was not responsible: 'I would never invite someone to my house and then kill them there,' he said.[3]

He said that if he told the truth about what had happened, a lot of people would be arrested in South Africa. He said he did not fear for his life after Jackson, Uwe Gemballa and Cyril Beeka's deaths. 'They die who deserved to die. I'm not scared. I don't deserve to die,' he told me. Louca said that he had saved Jackson 'millions and millions' and that 'he got killed for being greedy'.[4]

Louca added that the media reports about him were rubbish. 'I don't know why these rubbish articles are being written,' he said. 'Last year they said all sorts of things in them, accusing me of being things like a drug dealer. I don't know why they write them. Maybe they just love me so much,' he said.[5]

The story of my phone interview sparked renewed interest in Jackson's murder. Here was the dead man's professed killer, not in hiding like everyone thought, but living in plain sight, arrogantly speaking to the media.

Other journalists tried to call him. But, that first phone call had been a surprise. It had caught him unawares. He was more prepared the next time around. He started demanding R20 000 for an interview. He would not talk until the money had been paid. As a general rule, respected media organisations in South Africa do not pay for stories. Doing so could lead to anyone who wanted a quick buck making up a story. The rule is there as a safety measure, to ensure that the stories you read and hear are authentic and that a monetary incentive has not been behind their release. Paying a self-confessed murderer would be as ethically questionable as it gets. So Louca never got his money.

The *Sunday Times* decided to try their luck and sent a team to Cyprus to interview him anyway. It was a smart move and they had an exclusive, the kind of story every journalist longs to get. They found him easily enough and Louca the braggart gladly gave an interview to journalist Sashni Pather, sharing a pack of cigarettes and an authentic Greek meal with her.

Louca told the *Sunday Times* that he wanted to tell the truth about what happened, but he did not believe he would receive a fair trial in South Africa. 'If I go under, I will not go down alone, a lot of important people will go down with me. I will pay the consequences, but they will as well,' he said.[6]

He told Pather that he had arrived in South Africa in 1987 and had set up a supermarket in Polokwane. Home Affairs officials gave him the surname Smith.

He would not speak about the night Jackson died. 'Don't ask me that. I am alive because I am not a betrayer.'[7]

He told the paper that Greek banker Alekos Panayi, Jackson and he had laundered money, but Jackson found out Panayi was allegedly taking the money.

Louca told the *Sunday Times* that Panayi was eventually fired from his bank and this made Jackson 'furious':

> [Lolly] paid his henchmen R10 000 to beat Alekos again. Lolly was aggressive. Alekos agreed to pay Lolly R25 000 a week.
>
> That's when the problems slowly started with Lolly. He was meant to pay me R3.7-million for getting back his money, but he was doing it in dribs and drabs. I said, 'No, Lolly, this isn't our agreement.'
>
> There was no trust and, after six months, he didn't pay me. He owed me nearly R4-million – and I didn't have money.[8]

In typical Louca fashion, he even claimed he had made time to pay his domestic worker R12 000 before leaving the country on a flight out of OR Tambo International Airport. However, according to his own affidavits,[9] which he later signed, it was all nonsense. Within 48 hours of Jackson's death, Louca was out of the country, and not through the main airport either.

Others followed the *Sunday Times* lead. Police and private investigators got on planes and headed to Cyprus. In one recorded interview that later emerged, Louca confessed to seeing Jackson being murdered. He said he knew who the killers were and that if he ever came back to South Africa, his life would be in danger because of everything he knew.[10]

But, in every interview Louca spoke in riddles. He would say just enough to keep the interest in him alive, but not enough for everyone to know what actually happened the night Lolly Jackson was killed.

The police were embarrassed. The press was showing just how easy it was to trace Louca: Why were they not doing anything to solve Jackson's murder?

They had to act.

The wheels of justice moved slowly, but eventually it happened.

It was not so easy because South Africa did not have a direct extradition treaty with Cyprus.

Through Interpol, the NPA then put in an extradition request through the European Union. Eventually, it was two years after Jackson's murder before police, in an arrangement with Interpol and Cypriot police, pounced and arrested Louca in Cyprus.

He was arrested not only for Jackson's murder, but for one other case where he had been charged for fraud, theft and possession of stolen property – a case that he would have appeared in court for before he fled the country in 2010. This was the case that had landed him in the Kempton Park police cells that fateful winter in 2007 when he had first met Krejcir.

The NPA announced that Louca was believed to be a vital cog in revealing the details of South Africa's underworld. It was believed that he knew not just how Jackson had been murdered, but also how Eastern European and Asian women were being trafficked into South Africa for strip clubs and brothels, and about the money laundering through imported fast cars, the murders and the corruption of top police officers. The authorities believed he knew a lot more about the workings of leading criminal syndicates than any other person. But, the question was, would he open up and reveal all he knew? Or would we hear more riddles?

Sitting in a cell beneath the Limassol District Court, Louca told *The Star*'s Shain Germaner that even if he were extradited, he would never open his mouth and talk. He said he was not the man who had fired the bullets into Jackson, but that he was nothing more than a fall guy, a decoy to direct attention away from the real heads of the Joburg underworld.[11]

He made it clear from the start he would do everything legally possible to try to stop his extradition. His lawyer, Loukis Loucaides, asked for bail, arguing that Louca was an upstanding citizen, a father of three teenage daughters and a young son, who would not flee the country. Judge Elena Ephraim said the accusations against him were too great to be ignored.[12]

Louca said that if he was compelled to return to South Africa he would be killed. Louca's lawyer argued that his client would be assassinated because of the information he held, and that eight other people linked to Jackson and Krejcir had already been killed. Being extradited would be an infringement on the alleged hit man's right to live.

But his arguments came to naught: the courts ruled that Louca would return to South Africa to face the crimes he was alleged to have committed. Loucaides tried to appeal through the European Court of Human Rights, but they rejected Louca's bid to overturn the extradition order.

Two years after his arrest in Cyprus and four years after Jackson's murder, Louca would be coming back to South Africa. The news was met with joy by Jackson's family – although no doubt his accomplices were less than ecstatic at the news.

Paul O'Sullivan said he believed Louca's testimony would be key. He said both Jackson and Beeka had been murdered because they knew who murdered Gemballa:

> Lolly Jackson was murdered for one reason and one reason only – he knew the intimate details of who ordered the murder of Uwe Gemballa.

Cyril Beeka was murdered because he knew who ordered the murders of Gemballa and Jackson. George Louca knows what happened to all three.

It will be interesting to have him on the stand, but my worry is his credibility as a witness. He's a crack cocaine user, but that's not insurmountable, I've got other witnesses – he'd just be the icing on the cake. He'll come back to South Africa, he'll name names and we'll see the unravelling of the dirty underbelly of the crime underworld in this country and its links to dirty cops who have been corrupted as a result.[13]

In February 2014 South Africa's most wanted criminal was coming back to South Africa, courtesy of South Africa's Interpol extradition team. When Louca landed he was immediately handed over to the Hawks.

Demi Jackson said the family was relieved that Louca was back. 'We need closure. We need to know what happened that night,' she said.[14]

The fears that Louca would be killed before he could talk were real. He was kept under tight security and nobody knew where he was being detained. Every time he appeared in the Kempton Park Magistrate's Court a bomb sweep was done, and everyone who entered the court was body-searched and watched by tactical-response police members throughout proceedings.

Blumberg complained that he could not get private access to consult with his client. 'Correctional Services have precluded me from seeing the accused privately. [It has to be] in the presence of a prison official,' Blumberg told the court.[15]

In July 2014 an assassination attempt was revealed. Louca did not appear in court owing to a series of threats he had received. Sources told Germaner that Louca's security had been compromised and police had received intelligence of a plot to kill the Cypriot.[16]

At a previous court appearance, Louca was transferred in a civilian vehicle, instead of an armoured vehicle, further compromising his safety. Blumberg also argued that his client was no longer safe in his current place of detention. 'There is a very real possibility that my client will have to be placed in new detention facilities,' Blumberg told the court.[17] He had to be kept from the broader prison population. Blumberg came to an agreement with the court whereby Louca would appear on camera because of concerns over his safety while being transported to court. From then on, his appearances in court were through a Skype video feed.

It did not take long for the state to reveal what their case against Louca would be in its charge sheet – one that even an ordinary member of the public could see was full of holes.

They believed that Jackson had been lured to Louca's house. Louca and Jackson had had numerous phone conversations throughout the day, culminating in the meeting. The prosecutors believed a scuffle then broke out between the two of them in the lounge area. The brawl turned deadly when Louca allegedly took out his gun and fired several shots at Jackson. He then pulled Jackson's body into the garage before fleeing the scene.

Germaner pointed out in *The Star* that the state's version of events failed to explain the following:[18]

– Who drove the two vehicles? Louca's Peugeot Boxer was found next to Modderfontein Road and Jackson's Jeep was found abandoned in Bedfordview.

– Why was the firearm used to kill Jackson found in the garage only a week after the murder occurred?

– Why Krejcir was a state witness in the case.

– Why Mabasa was not on the witness list, even though Louca allegedly called him and confessed to the killing.

Blumberg told journalists that Louca had not committed the murder. He would be pleading not guilty. 'This is now about absolute honesty,' Blumberg said. 'He's got to be direct and forthright on every level and he intends to do so.'[19]

Did this mean Louca would talk? Would we finally know what had really been happening in Bedfordview, in those restaurants where groups of well-heeled men sat gossiping and making deals all day long?

Blumberg revealed that Louca had written five affidavits, admitting everything he knew about Krejcir and the criminal network he had been a part of, in his bid to get leniency from the state. Although journalists wrote about the existence of these written statements, only one saw the light of day: the one that described what really happened on that now-long-ago night in May

2010 when South Africa's flamboyant, bad-mouthed king of strip clubs was shot dead.

The journalists who had been working on this story from the start had waited five years for this. The frustrated phone calls where he spoke in riddles and the flights to Cyprus had all culminated in nothing. This secretive man had not revealed much. We all wanted to know more. We were rubbing our hands in anticipation at the revelations that were about to come.

That's when things took an unexpected turn. Life intruded, or, as so often has been the case in this story, death.

In February 2015 Louca was suddenly rushed to hospital. Blumberg told Germaner that Louca's health had deteriorated and that he had to be taken urgently to Chris Hani Baragwanath Hospital in Soweto.[20] The hospital was not appropriate for Louca, however, who required high levels of police guards after the series of alleged threats against his life. Even while he was sick, the security around him was the priority. He was then taken to another, unnamed, government facility where he remained for the weekend.

It seemed he had a severe chest infection and there was heavy fluid on his lungs. Blumberg said tests were needed to determine if his client was suffering from TB or another serious ailment. He said his client was on the road to recovery after his lungs were drained and that he was in good spirits. 'He's just happy he survived. He mustn't slip into a stage where it could be life-threatening.'[21]

He said his client remained in solitary confinement for up to 22 hours a day, which would be physically taxing for even those of the staunchest of constitutions. 'What sustains him is the determination to clear his name,' said Blumberg.[22]

However, a month later, in March 2015, Louca was still not better. He had to get a CT scan and have other tests conducted to find out what was wrong. It wasn't good news: Louca had extensive stage-4 lung cancer. It was terminal.

After the enormous effort and time it had taken the state to get him extradited from Cyprus to answer for what had happened to Jackson, it seemed Louca would not live long enough to testify – or clear his name.

In April Blumberg threatened legal action: either his client should be released from prison or transferred to a facility that could give him better medical treatment. Taking him to a hospital for medical interventions every time his health took a bad turn was not working out, especially since his security needed to be guaranteed every time he was moved. The lawyer said Louca had been denied access to the Steve Biko Academic Hospital following an incident where he struggled to breathe. He said Louca needed to be placed in a facility that could help in such emergencies: 'It is imperative that my client receive the best palliative care and support possible, given his terminal condition and advanced stage of the disease.'[23]

On 21 April 2015 a Section 49E application was brought before the court, whereby early release from prison may be granted if a facility can't provide adequate healthcare for a prisoner awaiting trial. Blumberg said all the necessary arrangements had been made to ensure Louca returned to Cyprus for medical care. If the application was successful, plane tickets had already been bought and Louca would immediately fly home to Cyprus. He badly wanted to be with his family in his last days.

It was a shock to see him in the courtroom on 21 April 2015. He had lost more than 35 kilograms and was barely able to speak because of the cancer slowly expanding in his windpipe. He was in a wheelchair and had to inhale oxygen every few seconds, clearly struggling just to breathe.

A letter produced in court from a leading oncologist at the Donald Gordon Medical Centre said Louca had between one and three months left to live. Sitting in his wheelchair at the stand, Louca told the court that all he wanted was for the truth about Jackson's killing to be revealed and for his four children to know he was not a murderer. 'I am just glad to have my story told,' he said.[24]

He told the court that as long as his family and the public knew his version of events, he could die without regret. 'What I'm asking you is to allow me to be next to my family if it happens that I pass away. Please. Please.'[25]

By means of an interpreter, given Louca's deteriorating voice, he told the court why he had fled the country after Jackson's death. He entered his whole version of Jackson's murder into the court record, so that if he did not survive, Krejcir and Mabasa could be tried. He said he had feared he would be killed if he ever told the truth of what had happened that night.

Now that fear was meaningless, as his death had come knocking regardless.

Louca said Krejcir and Mabasa had 'big business' dealings and he fought his extradition from Cyprus because of this corruption, not believing his safety would be guaranteed because of 'dirty' officials.

His legal team argued that his human rights were at stake, that he deserved the best palliative care and that he be allowed to die among his family.

During a break in court proceedings, Louca wept as he spoke to his brother in Cyprus on a cellphone.

Despite Louca's frail condition, Judge Geraldine Borchers ruled that he should remain in prison. Borchers said that although she felt compassion for Louca, she could not allow him to be released. She based this on his past behaviour, saying it was unlikely he would return to South Africa even if fit enough for trial.[26] She said Louca had not abided by the law when it suited him in the past and he had conceded that he had committed other crimes. She said that if she allowed his release, it would be tantamount to dropping the charges against him.

Krejcir's lawyer, Piet du Plessis, denied Louca's version that he had not murdered Jackson. 'What Louca is saying is total nonsense. There is no truth in it,' he said. He told the *Sunday Times*: 'This is absolute rubbish. My client is a state witness on the matter. George is trying to exonerate himself and trying to get off the case. As far as I am aware, he is the one accused of the murder of Lolly Jackson and not my client.'[27]

Mabasa told the *Sunday Times* that Louca was being economical with the truth: 'If George is innocent, as he claims now, then he must tell us why did he run away and not Krejcir, and even exhausted all the legal avenues in avoiding to come to South Africa, if he really wanted to clear his name?'[28]

Krejcir told Eyewitness News that he had two statements written by Louca in which he denied that Krejcir had anything to do with Jackson's murder. Krejcir said Louca had made one of these confessions to him while he was still in Cyprus. 'I have his confession over the phone,' Krejcir said. 'In a 20-minute call he told me exactly what happened here when he ran away from South Africa; I even offered my DNA to the police so they could go to the scene.'[29]

By 9 May, Louca was throwing up violently. He was meant to appear in court for the case about his possession of stolen property, but could not make it.

Three days later he was dead. He died at 7.30 pm in the Kgosi Mampuru II Correctional Centre in Pretoria.

Alone, with no family, 'he died like a dog', said a weeping Dimitri Panayiotou, Louca's brother. Panayiotou told *The Star*: 'We are very angry, hurt and disappointed, and we are speaking to our lawyers to see what action we can take … What about human rights? … the government wanted him to die in South Africa. They kept promising to release him, but never did.'[30]

The family was having his body repatriated to Greece for his burial. His brother said that Louca had been confident he would be released. He kept telling his brother he was coming home to die. 'But the past three days, he was unable to speak to me. I could hear he was getting weaker,' Panayiotou said. 'He died surrounded by strangers – it's just not right. They used him to get all the information they could about the Lolly Jackson murder case, then threw him away,' he said.[31]

Blumberg alleged that the NPA dragged out Louca's trial so that he could die of his terminal illness before Jackson's murder trial could take place. Blumberg said this would save them face after spending vast amounts of money and time extraditing Louca from Cyprus. It would have been seen as an enormous waste of resources if he turned out not to be the murderer after all.

But Louca beat death in one regard. He did not allow the Grim Reaper to have the final say, by ensuring his own version of events was the last thing everyone would remember.

In the courtroom, that day in April 2015, almost exactly five years after the fact, his voice failing, Louca revealed what had really happened to Lolly Jackson. His affidavit, which he had signed earlier, went into even more detail.

'Louca died an innocent man. In that regard, he won,' Blumberg later said.[32]

Louca wrote in the affidavit that it was a shared love of fast cars that had brought Krejcir and Jackson together. Krejcir was also interested in buying Teazers.[33]

Louca also revealed that Krejcir knew that Jackson 'was exporting millions in funds which had not been declared, through the service of Alekos Panayi who ran the Laiki Bank of Cyprus ... Panayi would arrange what was called a cash swap for residents of South Africa who wanted to send money offshore. Panayi transferred millions of rands for Jackson.'

Louca said that Panayi stole funds from Jackson: 'Jackson approached me with the request that I recover the amount stolen by Panayi. I was able to do so and as a result Jackson began to rely upon me to assist him in a number of ways.'[34]

He also arranged a Greek passport for Jackson, cementing the two men's working relationship. He said that Jackson confided in him that he was planning to leave South Africa as pressure was mounting over allegations of money laundering. That is why he needed Greek citizenship.

Louca said Panayi lost his job at the bank after it was discovered that he had been involved in money-laundering activities.

'In 2009 Krejcir approached Jackson and advised that he and his associate Cyril Beeka were in a position to make funds available offshore using a similar arrangement to the 'money swap' scheme operated by Panayi, allegedly using certain eastern European contacts of Cyril Beeka who had set up businesses in the Cape.'[35]

Jackson told Louca that he had agreed to use their services and that two or possibly three transactions involving 'small' sums of money, between R80 000 and R120 000, had been successfully concluded.

Louca's affidavit continues: 'In April 2010 Jackson contacted me urgently and told me that he and Krejcir assisted by Beeka had arranged a "transfer" of approximately R740 000 which amount he had given to Krejcir; but that an equivalent amount of funds had not been transferred to [Jackson's] account despite receipt by him of a document in the form of a "swift-transfer" which he explained to me, had, upon enquiry, proved to be fake.'[36]

Louca said that Jackson was angered by this development and in April 2010 he asked Louca to set up a meeting with Jackson and Krejcir:

I arranged a meeting but neither Krejcir nor Beeka, despite their commitment to attend, arrived for the meeting. I called Beeka and told him that in my opinion, this was not the behaviour expected from a grown man.

Krejcir called me to meet him at Harbour Cafe. Upon my arrival I spoke with Krejcir, and during the conversation Beeka came toward me, unseen, and punched me on the side of my head. I fell to the floor and was kicked several times by Beeka on my head and face. Krejcir didn't interfere in the assault in any way.

I was hospitalised, and once released attempted once again to set up a meeting between Jackson and Krejcir.[37]

Louca said that Krejcir refused to have a meeting at Jackson's home or office, insisting that the meeting take place at Louca's house in Kempton Park. 'It was agreed,' wrote Louca, 'that a meeting would be scheduled for the afternoon of the 3rd of May 2010.'[38]

He said that he and Jackson agreed to meet on Modderfontein Road in front of the Greenstone Shopping Centre. Jackson, driving his Jeep, arrived late afternoon, following Louca who was in a Peugeot van. Louca said his car broke down and they drove the rest of the way in Jackson's Jeep.

Louca said that, once at the house, he invited Jackson into the living room and went behind the bar to offer him a beer. Krejcir arrived some five or six minutes later and was also offered a drink. Louca said in his affidavit that, within moments, Jackson had begun shouting at Krejcir and was waving the copy of the swift transfer at him, which he said was fake:

Jackson swore at Krejcir, asking him 'who the fuck' he thought he was to steal Jackson's money. Krejcir lunged forward to grab the swift transfer from Jackson, who held it out of reach.

At this point Krejcir pulled out a firearm and shot Jackson once, Jackson fell onto the back of the sofa positioned directly behind him. Jackson looked shocked, and began to plead and beg for his life. Krejcir crossed the floor toward him standing over him and kicked him in the side of the chest saying: 'You want to know who I am, I will show you who I am you fucking cockroach.'

Krejcir then fired many shots into Jackson. Jackson appeared to be dead, and lay in a pool of blood.[39]

Louca stood there, horrified and frightened, he explained in his affidavit.

'Krejcir ordered me to pick Jackson up and take him down the corridor toward the garage. He wanted me to put the body into Jackson's car. I attempted to do as he said but Jackson was quite heavy. My shirt was quickly covered in Jackson's blood. I said to Krejcir, "I can't do that, I can't pick him up."'[40]

He said that Krejcir told him to get a blanket to carry the body. Louca's affidavit recounts the events that happened next:

I ran to my bedroom, removed the bloody shirt and put on a clean one taking a duvet off my bed and returned to the lounge where I succeeded in placing Jackson's body onto the duvet and dragging the body down the passage towards the door that leads into the garage.

I left Jackson's body in the passage just inside the door and stepped into the garage. I opened the automatic door on the left and noticed Cyril Beeka seated in a car just outside the garage on my right together with someone who I could not see clearly save to say that he had short light-coloured hair.

I reversed the Jeep into the garage right up to the doorway leading from the passage. When I stepped out of the Jeep in order to open the back of the car I found that I had parked it too close to the door to open up the boot.

At that moment I was in a state of shock and felt afraid for my life; I had just witnessed Lolly Jackson shot dead by Krejcir and wanted to get away as quickly as possible.

I got back into the car and drove away. I then called General Mabasa from my phone telling him that I had just witnessed Krejcir killing Jackson. He asked me who was present at the time of Jackson's murder and I told him that Krejcir and Cyril were there.

He asked me where I was. I told him that I was driving Jackson's Jeep. He suggested that I meet him at Bedford Centre, and that I should speak to Krejcir as soon as possible.

Mabasa knew of the problems between Krejcir and Jackson, having already been approached by Jackson to intervene and assist in facilitating a meeting with Krejcir. I too had spoken with Mabasa about the need for a meeting to be arranged between Krejcir and Jackson to resolve their problem. I didn't drive immediately to Bedford Centre but drove around for a while.

Radovan was calling me on the phone. I didn't take his calls at first. Later I called him, as advised by Mabasa.

He asked me to meet with him at Jannis Louca's Engen garage near to Linksfield. We met there.

He got there before me and I met him behind the garage. He wanted me to calm down, but I was extremely angry with him for what he had just done and didn't want to listen to his stories. He asked me why I had driven off and left the house. He said that I was supposed to have helped him to put the body in the car and then dumped it.

I drove off and then headed for the Harbour Cafe in order to meet with Mabasa. Upon my arrival I saw several people including Cyril Beeka, who was sitting with Hein Metrovich in the smoking area. I asked him whether Mabasa was there.

He answered that he had not seen Mabasa. I realised that I was alone and that Mabasa was not going to show up.

Krejcir then arrived at the Harbour Cafe and before speaking with me approached Metrovich, who handed him two cellphones.

He then turned to me and said we need to talk. We got to the parking lot and he told me that I should give him my cellphone and speak to no one. He said I should drive to the Nicol Hotel in Bedfordview.[41]

Louca said he went to room 26, as instructed by Krejcir, where he found a friend of Krejcir's from the Czech Republic, Martin. Louca said Krejcir arrived at 10 pm and told him that he had no choice but to leave the country:

As he put it: Lolly was murdered in your house. You were there when it happened. You are fucked and there is nothing you can do about it.

He reminded me further that I was due to appear in court the following day (on charges of theft) and that Mabasa had told him that I would get between ten and fifteen years on the charges.

He said I should leave as soon as possible for Cyprus, which he said had no extradition treaty with South Africa. He said he would send me money in Cyprus.[42]

Louca said he called his friend Yannis [Jannis] Louca, who came to meet him. They drove in Yannis's car across the border to Mozambique, from where he flew via Lisbon to Cyprus.

CHAPTER 11

KREJCIR THE TARGET:
AN AUTOMATIC WEAPON TAKES AIM

A dozen remote-controlled gun barrels emerged from behind the number plate of a car. Bullets flew towards where Krejcir stood. Then the car exploded into flames.

At first, Krejcir thought that someone had let off some fireworks, before realising that he was in fact the target of an attack.

A movie screenwriter couldn't have produced a better-scripted action scene. It was too fantastic to be true. And yet, when police, emergency services and journalists arrived at the scene, the fantasy was reality: there, for everyone to see, stood the burnt-out car, the gun barrels, which had been hidden behind a number plate, still smoking hot, and the bullet holes in the wall and in Krejcir's car.

It was a clear winter's day in Johannesburg, 25 July 2013, when Radovan Krejcir became the target of an assassination attempt. It was around 11 am, and he had just driven his R1.7 million bullet-proof, matte-black Mercedes-Benz AMG into the parking lot of Moneypoint, his gold and diamond pawn shop.

He had a parking bay right in front of the business, his usual spot. Krejcir hadn't noticed the red VW Polo Cross parked behind him, assuming it was a customer either visiting his shop or the estate agency next door, Remax One.

The boot of the Polo was positioned opposite the space where Krejcir always parked. He got out of his car, on a phone call. He was distracted, he said. According to his version of events, bullets flew towards him, fired out of several gun barrels. He had taken three steps towards the entrance of his shop when he heard a loud 'popping' noise, he told *The Star*.[1] At first, he thought it was fireworks and he carried on with his call but then he saw the bullet dents in his car and realised he was under attack. His colleague ran out to help get him inside the building as the car in the parking lot exploded into flames.

Later, police were able to piece together that, as Krejcir got out of his car, somebody, who was nearby, set off the secret weapon attached behind the number plate of the Polo by means of a remote control.

The back number plate blew off, revealing a dozen home-made gun barrels. At least 24 holes were found in windows and walls near the parking spot, but the projectiles were unable to pierce Krejcir's modified car, which merely had dents on the driver and passenger windows. Flames had melted the back of the Polo, probably from the intense heat generated by the firearms.[2]

Krejcir not only managed to survive the assassination attempt, but he did so without even sustaining a scratch.

'It was like something from a movie,' he said, shaking his head in disbelief. 'It's definitely a professional job.' He described the attack to Graeme Hosken from *The Times*: 'It was bang. Bang, bang, bang. Over and over again very quickly. There was no time to think. It was incredibly scary.'[3]

The police said the weapon was a battery-operated, remote-controlled device. They believed that once the assassin realised the job had been bungled, he probably fled the scene.

Real-estate agents at Remax One said they had noticed the vehicle over the past three to four days. Both adjacent businesses assumed the car was visiting the other. However, the car had not been there earlier that morning, and must have re-entered the premises between 9 am and 10.30. 'We ran out when we heard a bang and more popping sounds and saw the car on fire,' said estate agent Jarrid Rahme.[4]

Flanked by two associates, Krejcir told Lerato Mbangeni, a journalist from *The Star*: 'I don't know who did it, but if I did I wouldn't tell you.' Mbangeni said Krejcir looked nonchalant and described him as cheerful, puffing on a cigarette, as he joked that he would have to start going to church. 'It was a surprise for me, but I am not gonna get some bodyguards or anything like that,' he told her.[5]

Krejcir told Alex Eliseev, writing in the *Daily Maverick*, that he believed he was a lucky man. Eliseev said the swarm of detectives who were all over the scene, were, for once, not there to raid Krejcir's house or take him for a ride downtown. 'All my life is like James Bond stuff,' he told Eliseev. 'So it's usual stuff for me ... It's how I live my life.'[6]

Police confirmed the Polo had been stolen in April in Brixton and the number plates were cloned. The woman identified as owning the vehicle registered to the licence plates still had her vehicle. Those responsible had attached the cloned plates to a car that was exactly the same make, model and colour. The police opened a case of attempted murder.

Underworld sources told *The Star* that it was believed the weapon was linked to the Cape Town movie industry and that the hit may have had something to do with Krejcir's dealings with Cape Town gangsters over territory.[7]

Krejcir, however, denied claims that before the attempted hit he had met alleged underworld figures from Cape Town, and that this was somehow linked to the incident. 'No, no. I believe that's bullshit. People are talking a lot of nonsense,' he said.[8]

It emerged that three weeks before the bizarre attempt on his life, Moneypoint had been broken into and R3 million worth of jewellery stolen. 'The suspects gained entrance through the roof. Once inside the premises, the safe was cut open,' police spokesperson Lieutenant Colonel Lungelo Dlamini told *The Star*.[9]

The robbery had taken place at night, and it was discovered only the following morning that something was amiss.

Police believed the two incidents may have been connected. Besides the gold and diamond exchange, the business also gave instant cash loans without any credit checks. A source said that Krejcir knew who was behind the break-in.

A source told the *Saturday Star* that the attempted hit must have been done by a top gangster, and by someone, or persons, with a number of skills – from explosives handling to panel beating. 'There are only two or three [such gangsters] in this country,' the source said.[10]

A police source with knowledge of investigations into Krejcir said the attempted hit was designed to be a clear warning to the Czech national: 'This was a message. Steps will be taken to silence people. Especially those who are about to talk.' A team of detectives, including members of the police counter-terrorism unit, were involved in the case, he said.[11]

A military-arms expert said the weapon system used was intriguing:

> The way it was fired, the way ammunition was fed into the barrels and the fire afterwards indicate the designer knew exactly what he was doing. This device was built with a knowledge not everyone has. It takes years of design and practice. It was fired using a specialised electronic system possibly run through a radio frequency. It will keep our forensics teams busy, especially as the fire is likely to have destroyed whatever evidence was left behind.[12]

But, while the police were kept busy trying to figure out who was behind the attempted hit, those close to Krejcir started to get suspicious.

A Czech employee of Krejcir's, Miloslav Potiska, who lived in a room on the second floor of Krejcir's mansion, later revealed in a tell-all book that Krejcir acted afterwards like nothing had happened. He showed no signs of being worried and he did not increase his personal security in any way.[13]

Potiska said that behind the scenes Krejcir was broke and was coming up with all sorts of ideas to make some money. One of these was to cook high-quality crystal meth (also known in South Africa as tik), which was unavailable in the country, using European 'cooks', whom he brought into South Africa.

According to Potiska, Krejcir and an underworld character, Lebanese drug dealer Sam Issa, were working on exporting a big batch of meth to Australia.

Those close to Krejcir believed that while this deal was going down, he wanted to distract the police. Potiska said he thought that Krejcir was behind his own assassination attempt: there was no better way to create a diversion than by becoming the target of an assassination attempt.[14]

The police, however, had a different theory about what had happened – a theory that confirmed Krejcir had been the target. They believed somebody desperately wanted him dead. He had stepped on too many toes to get to the top of the underworld and someone out there thought it was time for payback.

But who it was, and why they wanted Krejcir six feet under, would emerge only a few murders and one bomb blast later.

CHAPTER 12

A CLOSE ASSOCIATE SPILLS THE BEANS

Miloslav Potiska arrived in South Africa in September 2010. He was in trouble with the law and he needed some distance from the Czech Republic. He had met Krejcir years before and heard from a friend that the fugitive wanted people he could rely on to help him out in South Africa.

Without hesitation, Potiska got on a plane and headed south. Krejcir put him up in a hotel and covered his expenses, glad to have a fellow Czech to work with, Potiska revealed in a book written by journalist Jaroslav Kmenta. Originally published in Czech with the title *Padrino Krejcir*, his book was translated as *The Godfather African*.[1]

Potiska was arrested along with Denis Krejcir when the Hawks raided Krejcir's mansion shortly after Beeka's murder. Police at the time believed Potiska had been brought into the country to organise three assassins who would fly into South Africa and take out the four people on the hit list that they had found in Krejcir's safe.

In the book Potiska describes himself as a man who just needed some work and who did not realise what he was getting into when he arrived in South Africa.

For two years Potiska was close to Krejcir. He stayed in his house for a while. He described Krejcir as a volatile man who drank, sniffed cocaine and pretended he had more money than he actually had. In Potiska's version of events, Krejcir was coming up with increasingly dangerous schemes to keep up the fast-paced, expensive lifestyle he had become used to.

He also revealed some details about Krejcir's private life, saying that he and his wife lived in separate homes. Katerina spent some of the time in a house in Pretoria because Krejcir made no secret of the fact he was dating a mistress, *Playboy* South Africa cover-girl Marissa Christopher. Potiska describes parties where Krejcir would start fights if any man looked at Christopher and there were frequent bloody punch-ups.

Potiska fell in love with a South African woman, Shimo Shield. He said that Krejcir wanted to use Shield to get close to a wealthy man whom he allegedly wanted to con. He said that Krejcir repeatedly rubbished Shield to him, claiming she was HIV-positive and had numerous sexual partners. But it was all lies, Potiska said. Potiska also maintains that Krejcir viewed women as less important than men and that even though he looked after his wife and respected his mother, men always came first for him.

When his plans did not work out, Potiska says he feared for both his and Shield's lives, convinced they would be taken out, like so many of Krejcir's other associates. In February 2012 the couple eventually fled South Africa. They now live in Prague.

Later, after publishing the book, Potiska spoke to eNCA's investigative current-affairs programme, *Checkpoint*.[2] During the documentary, which aired in December 2014, he told journalists that he had not come to South Africa to kill people. He said he had proof of everything he had revealed in the book, including some of the murders that had taken place. He had papers and messages, which he would hand to police. He said he would testify and collaborate with police if the conditions were right.

As soon as he heard that a close associate of Krejcir was spilling the beans, forensic investigator Paul O'Sullivan boarded a flight to the Czech Republic and went to get statements from Potiska. Later he was joined by a dedicated police officer who had become a part of a specialised Krejcir investigating team, Colonel Bongani Gininda, as well as tough, no-nonsense prosecutor Advocate Lawrence Gcaba. The state was bringing out the big guns and they were collecting as much information as they could to incriminate the Czech fugitive.

Through an interpreter, Potiska signed six sworn affidavits. Like Louca before him, it seemed Potiska really did have unique insight into Krejcir's world. He said in an affidavit:[3]

> I left South Africa because I could see that Krejcir was getting involved in so much criminal activity that, sooner or later, I would be dragged into it and even possibly murdered, like so many of his other 'associates'.
>
> I had been in South Africa only a few months, and had realised who this Krejcir person was ... I knew him from the Czech Republic, but he wasn't such a big shot there, not like the big psychopath he became in South Africa. I soon realised he was a dangerous man and would kill everyone who crossed him.
>
> Krejcir would make many deals with people but would not give them their money back and would threaten to kill them or even have them killed. There are many people who he wanted to kill in South Africa, he told me who they were. Some of them are already dead.

Potiska's statements implicated Krejcir in the murder of Beeka; he also said there was a conspiracy to have O'Sullivan murdered.[4] According to O'Sullivan, these statements 'also corroborated what George Louca said in his sworn statement about Krejcir having fiddled Lolly Jackson out of cash, using fake transfer documents, which they argued about before Krejcir shot him'.[5]

Both the book and Potiska's statements show just how intensely Krejcir hated O'Sullivan, who kept on getting in the way of his carefully orchestrated criminal plans. According to Potiska, Krejcir repeatedly referred to O'Sullivan as 'that muck'. Potiska revealed in a statement that, at one point, Krejcir got hold of O'Sullivan's telephone records for three months in 2011 from an employee at Vodacom.[6] In a case before court Vodacom had previously revealed that these cellphone records had been obtained by the police. Potiska said he had been asked by Krejcir to analyse whom O'Sullivan had been speaking to before and after the police raid on Krejcir's house.

In a separate statement, Potiska said Krejcir asked him at least three times if he could arrange for people from the Czech Republic to kill O'Sullivan.

Said Potiska, 'I told him "no", as I didn't want any part in anyone being killed. I also didn't want any attention as Lolly Jackson had recently been killed at that time.' He said Krejcir was very insistent and would not leave the matter: 'Krejcir said that he would give me a big gun and I could get a sniper to kill O'Sullivan.'[7]

Potiska said that Krejcir told him that O'Sullivan had an office near Melrose Arch and that he wanted Potiska to arrange people from the Eastern Bloc to attach a bomb to O'Sullivan's car while it was in the office car park. He told him that if he could not carry this out, then he was to follow O'Sullivan from work on a motorbike and bomb his car when it stopped at a robot, or shoot him.

'Krejcir had many ideas on how to kill O'Sullivan. He even asked me if I knew anything about remote controlled helicopters or drones,' Potiska said. He said Krejcir wanted him to land such a device, loaded with a bomb, near O'Sullivan and then with a cellphone detonate the bomb. Potiska said that Krejcir wanted camera footage of this attack. 'I think he may have been watching too much TV at the time when he came up with these ideas,' Potiska said.[8]

He also revealed that Krejcir was allegedly bribing police officers, in particular the then head of crime intelligence in Gauteng, Joey Mabasa. Potiska said that he believed Krejcir had a secret number for Mabasa. He claimed Mabasa would be picked up at a Shell garage near Eastgate and brought to Krejcir's home. The Czech explained how Mabasa would be hidden in the car and brought secretly into Krejcir's house, where they would have meetings. Potiska said he witnessed Mabasa being given cash on two occasions – between R5 000 and R10 000. But the money dried up when Mabasa was suspended from the police and Krejcir decided he was of no more use to him.[9]

Potiska said that Krejcir paid many police officers. He said they would meet at a Chinese restaurant at Bruma Market. Each time, Krejcir would have cash – R5 000 for each cop. 'These guys from the police started helping Krejcir smuggle cigarettes from Zimbabwe into South Africa. Krejcir used them for drug trafficking too,' Potiska said in the affidavits.[10] 'The SAP [South African police] guys from Narcotics would arrange a car and a truck at the Zimbabwe to South Africa border. Then they would follow this truck with the cigarettes in their car, and if they were stopped by the customs or other police, they would tell the police they were Narcotics police and had a reason for following the truck.'

But while he was handing out cash bundles to cops, Potiska said that Krejcir was conning others out of money. He said he would create fake bank swift transfers on Krejcir's instruction in the name of a bank account of one of his companies in Prague. 'Krejcir would show the person this document and they would believe that he [had] transferred the money into their bank account,' Potiska said in the affidavits.[11]

He said that Krejcir told him he did this all the time and that he had done something like this with Lolly Jackson. 'He said the important thing was that it should look real, the people ... would not know if it was real or not, and that the bank would never be able to give information to verify.'[12]

Potiska said Krejcir asked him to create fake bank statements for two Eastern European women to prove to South Africa's Department of Home Affairs that they had money because they were applying for work permits so that they could work in nightclubs.

Krejcir told him he was going to take all the clubs from Demi Jackson because he had an acknowledgement of debts from Lolly Jackson and that he would bring a woman who knew how to make work permits for about 200 women from the Eastern Bloc to use as prostitutes in these nightclubs.

'The acknowledgments of debt,' said Potiska 'were only for protection, whilst money was being exchanged between Jackson and Krejcir, and Krejcir knew [these acknowledgements] had no value, but said he would try anyway.'[13]

Potiska also spoke about Beeka's murder. He said that Krejcir first introduced him to Beeka as a friend with whom he was going into business. He saw Beeka a few times in Bedfordview and at The Grand, in Rivonia.

He said that on one occasion Beeka had told Krejcir that he could buy krugerrands for him. Beeka and Arsiotis then left to go and buy the coins with money Krejcir had given them. 'I was ... with Krejcir when Arsiotis returned. He said there was a problem and that he and Beeka had been tricked and did not get the Kruger Rands, but had handed over the money.

Krejcir was angry because of this and knew that Beeka was behind the "trick". Krejcir said that he would have to "sort it out" with him, which I knew meant to kill him.'[14]

Potiska said Krejcir said he would wait a while though because he had other business to finish with Beeka first – some gold business in the DRC and securing ships against piracy in the Horn of Africa.

He also said that Beeka, Krejcir and Arsiotis had flown to Cape Town for Beeka's birthday party. There had been a fight and Beeka beat Krejcir up. 'Krejcir's ego would have been very badly bruised by this, as he was big talk, but if you [attacked] him he would collapse. He had been publicly humiliated and wanted revenge,' Potiska said.[15]

Potiska said that Krejcir then asked him to go to Cape Town and kill Beeka. 'I said I didn't want to arrange this, and Krejcir told me not to worry and that he would arrange other people to do it.'[16]

Potiska said Krejcir then started talking to two Cape Town gangsters; he believed they killed Beeka on Krejcir's instruction.

The gangsters went along with Krejcir's plans. By getting rid of Beeka, it would give them access to the lucrative Cape Town club security scene, so they could control all the nightclubs and drugs in the city. Krejcir had promised that, in return, he would invest in some property for them as part of the deal. 'However, Krejcir did not invest because he had no money, and then there was bad blood between them,' said Potiska.[17]

Potiska's statements had provided sensational information about Krejcir's activities. In an attempt to counter this, Krejcir did something he had never done before: he released a media statement accusing Potiska of having made everything up. Previously, no matter how serious the allegations, Krejcir had made no more than offhand comments reiterating his innocence. But Potiska must have really got under his skin. Krejcir's six-page press statement showed all the signs that he was fed up – and very, very angry:

> … I wish to state that I truly frown on the manner and extent that the
> state has now on several … instances, embarked upon various different
> avenues, in an attempt to hold me hostage to their conspiracy theories,
> cunningly invented fiction, make-believe evidence, exhausting millions of

rands of the tax payers money, in their obsession in wrongfully persecut-
ing me.[18]

Krejcir said that O'Sullivan had paid false witnesses and that the media were
accusing him of various crimes in a sensational campaign. He said the stories about him were 'strangely compelling', but he believed the truth of his
innocence would prevail.[19]

He insisted he was a victim of a gross, malicious and vexatious invention
of events. He told the world he was the subject of a conspiracy made real by
a sensation-driven press, by Paul O'Sullivan, who used witnesses to concoct
events, and by the South African Government and the police: 'I can only
appeal to you to remain objective of the facts, and not to allow yourself to
be deceived, by the make-believe contrivance sensations ... orchestrated by
the state, abusing their powers to cover up a conspiracy of crimes against
humanity ... and depriving you the public of sound judgment, and from
being presented with the facts of the truth.'[20]

He said that by the 'state' he was referring to high-ranking government
officials, the police commissioner and her specially elected task team.

In his media statement Krejcir then went on to give his version of what
happened with Potiska and Shield, whom Potiska had meanwhile married in
the Czech Republic. He said that Potiska had been introduced to him in 2005
when he was in Prague. A friend, Jan Charvat, had then contacted Krejcir in
South Africa informing him that Potiska wanted to explore business oppor-
tunities in South Africa and asked if he could accommodate him.

Krejcir said he was surprised to find that when Potiska arrived he had less
than €5 000 and could not afford to invest in South Africa, that he could not
speak English, was an obsessive drug addict and alcoholic, and a fugitive
running from the police.[21]

He argued in his statement that Potiska was completely incompetent and
incapable of even simple tasks, like filling up the petrol tank or shopping,
because he could not speak English properly.

Krejcir maintained that Potiska spent 16 months in South Africa, that he
travelled to other countries 'exporting non-existent jewellery' and that he

was unaware of 'any events of my life and or my business dealings here in SA'.

He also said that Potiska had invited 'another drug addict', a man called Vit, to South Africa. Krejcir said he learnt that both were convicted criminals who had served time behind bars for drug dealing. Krejcir said that he learnt that Potiska and Charvat conducted VAT fraud involving jewellery: 'Milos was traveling and exporting jewellery, for [which] he claimed VAT abroad … (I have in my possession invoices, bills, documentation written in Milos own handwriting, which he left behind on his departure back to Czech.)'[22]

He said that Potiska and Vit were often under the influence of drugs. Krejcir said he broke all ties with Vit when the latter allegedly stole R60 000 from his safe and movable assets from his storage, such as furniture and electronics. Before Potiska left South Africa, Krejcir said he had signed a loan agreement to the effect that he had borrowed money from Krejcir's family. 'To date Milos … neglected to uphold his undertaking and did not pay back the money,' he said.[23]

In his media statement, Krejcir said that, on one occasion, they had to rescue Potiska from a fight at the Nicci Beach club with the self-confessed murderer of mining magnate Brett Kebble, Mikey Schultz.

Krejcir also said that Potiska learnt of the murder of Cyril Beeka while accompanying Krejcir to Cape Town as a driver. There was a rumour that the murder had been gang-related over jostling for power. 'I had absolutely nothing to do with the murder of Beeka, and will strenuously oppose any such allegations,' said Krejcir.[24]

Krejcir said that Potiska was attempting to turn the rumour into fact. 'He has no respect for the family of the late Beeka, publicly exploiting this tragedy and turning it into a sensation for his personal gain.'[25]

Krejcir said that Potiska was trying to implicate him in crimes in order to make money from the sale of his book and a possible movie. 'Furthermore other murders, drug dealings and extortions stated by Milos are only fantasy-related speculations created by him and Shimo, upon consulting with Paul O'Sullivan … and [remain] nothing short of a malicious act of hearsay which I reject with the contempt it so deserves.'[26]

Krejcir added that an allegation Potiska made that Krejcir had intended to murder Shield was a 'mental distorted paranoia inflicted by his drug abuse' and a delusional fallacy worthy of science fiction.[27]

In his statement Krejcir then attacked the journalist who wrote *The Godfather African*, Jaroslav Kmenta, saying he had believed unreliable sources: 'It is truly unbelievable what journalists who are engulfed in sensation are able to publish in order to gain popularity and money.

'Milos is a liar … who for income and a few minutes of fame would not have a problem to testify that I killed or gave the order to kill Elvis Presley or Marilyn Monroe,' he said.[28]

Krejcir said that he was revolted by the lies about his having been associated with business partners and friends who were victims of murder 'and/or terrorist attacks'. He said: 'I want to openly challenge the SAPS, by demanding from them, at all cost to uncover and investigate the various attempts on my life, including the numerous murders which are irrationally, and wrongfully tied to me. This is the only avenue by which I would be able to prove my innocence from the entire conspiracy aimed directly at me.'[29]

He said it was unbearable that he and his family had to face sensational media stories portraying him as a monster who had purportedly killed so many people.

'I am not the criminal, monster mobster as portrayed by the media,' Krejcir said.[30]

CHAPTER 13

THE CRIPPLE, THE LOOSE-MOUTHED SERB AND THE DRUG DEAL GONE WRONG

'You live by the gun, you die by the gun.'

It's a quote you will find among the graffiti on the walls of prison cells, and buildings and other places where gang activity is rife. It's something that men who live fast, dangerous lives are constantly aware of. If you are a successful criminal, money can flow in and life will be good. There are all the trappings of wealth – the women, the prestige.

But around every corner … 'Bam!' Chances are the last thing you will see is the barrel of a gun.

For Sam Issa, that gun was an R5 rifle and it was about to riddle his body with bullets, right outside the shopping centre where he spent most of his days.

You live by the gun, you die by the gun: the quote was whispered in fear by those who came to gawk at his murder scene. There were a lot of men who knew the dead man. They were nervous about talking and their voices were hushed as they stared.

They stared at the bullet casings that littered the road. They stared at the smashed-up car that ended up halfway across the pavement. They stared at the devastated family who huddled near by.

Issa was a regular in Bedfordview, a Lebanese drug runner whose parties with endlessly flowing champagne were legendary. He was known for his propensity to show off by shooting his gun into the air.

Those who loved him swore he wasn't a violent man, even though he shot his brother once. But most knew better: he hadn't earned the nicknames Black Sam and Cripple Sam for nothing. Black Sam because he was feared; Cripple Sam because he had a limp from an old bullet wound.

It was a beautiful, sunny Saturday, 12 October 2013. It had been quiet on the Radovan Krejcir front for a few months. There had been no murders and no remote-controlled guns firing unexpectedly. But, in true Krejcir fashion, that was about to change.

Issa had spent the evening drinking with Krejcir at Moneypoint. The two men had not got on well in recent months, so the long drinking spree until the early hours of the morning was a surprise.

Inexplicably, Issa, who lived just a few kilometres away, did not drive home that night. He slept at the Mercure Hotel, which was just moments from Moneypoint. At 5.50 am he checked out of the hotel.

He had travelled two blocks when his Audi Q7 stopped at a red light by Bedford Centre, his regular hangout. A white Ford Ranger pulled up next to him and opened fire.

Marina Valassopoulos, who lived just across the road, awoke to the sound of bullets flying. 'It was automatic. I heard bah bah bah, one after the other, then a split second of silence before it started again.'[1]

Another witness, a shaking teenager, who did not want to be named, also woke up to the sound of gunfire: 'I ran to the window and then there was a second round of gunfire,' he said.

Issa's black car was reversing away from the Ranger, in which there was a man firing the shots. The Audi crashed onto the pavement and stopped. There was no movement inside. Black Sam was dead.

'There was a white Ford Ranger that did a U-turn so fast that you could hear the tyres screeching. You can see the skid marks on the road. They put on blue lights and I heard sirens, and the Ford sped off in the direction of Eastgate,' the teenager said.[2]

The intersection was littered with bullet casings: thirty-three 5.56-millimetre cartridges lying in the road. It took police hours to circle each one in white paint. Two of them had entered Issa's windscreen; countless others went through the driver's door.

All the while, Sam Issa's body lay slumped in his Audi, his right side riddled with bullets. He lay there for three hours while forensics did their thing. His family stood nearby the whole time.

'It's a great shock,' his brother said. Police called him over to identify the bloodied corpse inside the car. He walked away, shoulders slumped, wiping tears from his eyes. Onlookers stood by and watched.[3]

Death had come to visit Issa just two weeks before, they said. But, that time – during a robbery – he had been spared. Four balaclava-clad men had entered his home, beaten him up, covered his head with a hood and cable, and tied his arms and legs, his relatives told *The Star*.[4]

Issa was no stranger to the life of crime. Paul O'Sullivan revealed to the public that the gregarious character was a middleman in the supply of drugs to Johannesburg clubs. He got the drugs mainly from Brazil.

Sally Evans from investigative-journalism organisation amaBhungane said that intelligence sources had discovered that Issa had recently been involved in orchestrating the purchase of a large consignment of cocaine routed via Kenya or Tanzania.[5] They believed concern over the payment for the consignment might have led to his murder. 'Issa was caught in the middle. In the underworld, the last man who handles the goods carries the bucket and, if something goes wrong, they also kick the bucket,' an intelligence source told Evans.

It is well known that Issa was a business partner of Krejcir's. Yet Krejcir was quick to deny he had any relationship or business dealings with him, telling Radio 702 that he didn't know Issa very well. 'He was a very private person. Nobody knew what he was doing or who his associates were.'[6]

This description of the dead man didn't fit with what everyone else knew him to be. Friends of Issa told Evans that he was a party animal who enjoyed all the bells and whistles of living the high life, including expensive champagne, which flowed at his parties where he surrounded himself with beautiful women. Sabina Essa, a model and friend of Issa's, told Evans that Issa had loved to socialise and host parties. She described him as an 'extremely passionate and positive person, who was always laughing and joking'.[7] He was also described as a loudmouth who would do things to show off, like firing bullets into the ceiling.

O'Sullivan said that Issa, who had lived in South Africa for 16 years, was in the country on a false identity document and that he had last worked in 2008: 'His credit history shows he was employed years ago at a metal company. There is no indication he has held a job since then.'[8]

Without a job, how could he afford the champagne-filled parties? It was a clear indication that Issa was very likely to be involved in crime.

Issa's friends, who spoke to *The Star* on condition of anonymity, said they had warned him that he would be killed and that he needed to leave Joburg. They said Issa was constantly complaining about Krejcir. 'Sam helped Krejcir with bail money. Sam complained about it all the time, saying Krejcir had never paid him back. He also said Krejcir owed him money from a business deal.'[9]

Chad Thomas, a forensic investigator from IRS Forensic Investigations, said he knew Issa well.[10] He said he had met him some years before at the launch of his girlfriend's beauty salon in Bedfordview. Thomas said that Issa had an extremely volatile personality. He spoke of an incident in which Issa had invested a large amount of money in a property development company. When the scheme did not render the investment results it was supposed to, Issa demanded his money back from the owner, a man called Billie. Said Thomas:

> When he wanted his payout, Billie could not pay him. So Sam kidnapped Billie and the man made all sorts of promises under duress. A few weeks later he went to a church where Billie was a pastor in the East Rand suburb of Sunward Park, and Sam held the entire management of the church hostage claiming they benefited from Billie's dishonest activities. On leaving the church, Sam fired a couple of shots into the air. That was the kind of man Sam Issa was.[11]

Others close to him said that during the robbery incident just two weeks before his death, Issa had been kidnapped. He was bundled into a car and the men said they were going to kill him. However, Issa said that one of the men went soft and decided to spare him after he begged for his life. The others wanted to kill him but, in the end, it was a burst tyre that saved him. His kidnappers left Issa and fled.

'He was told that God had given him a second chance, that he should leave Johannesburg. Because whoever had sent those men to kill him was not happy with them. A few days later they came back and finished the job,' said one acquaintance.[12]

The day after Issa's death, Jerome Safi, the man who had invited Uwe Gemballa to South Africa to discuss a business venture, received a death threat. On the Sunday morning, Safi received an SMS saying 'you are next'.

'The message could have come from anyone, but everyone knows I am an associate of Krejcir, and given that Issa was murdered the day before, I take this as a direct threat,' Safi told *The Star*.[13]

By this stage, many assumed Krejcir was in some way involved in Issa's death, and Safi, who was a witness in the Gemballa murder trial, saw the SMS as a threat from him.

Miloslav Potiska said during an eNCA *Checkpoint* documentary that he had warned Sam Issa, 'Don't push him [Krejcir] so much, okay.'[14] Potiska said in Kmenta's book that Issa had lent money to Krejcir on two occasions. The first loan was R1.2 million; the second was R500 000.[15] The second loan was used to pay Krejcir's bail in the cancer fraud case.

Issa had given the cash to Michael Arsiotis, who then gave the money to Krejcir's attorney, Piet du Plessis. 'A few months later Issa started to phone me all the time, telling me that Krejcir would not answer his phone, and that Krejcir needed to start paying back the money he had lent him. Issa was becoming very impatient with Krejcir, and Krejcir started getting annoyed with his demands,' Potiska said.[16]

Potiska said he told Issa that Krejcir would pay him when his mother sent money again. 'Issa put pressure on Krejcir to meet to discuss repayments of the money. When Krejcir received some money from his mother he gave Issa R100 000. But he did not make any effort to pay back what he owed.'[17]

According to Potiska, Krejcir asked him to call Issa several times and he warned the Lebanese man that Krejcir wanted to harm him and asked him to calm down about the money and to be careful. 'I later left South Africa, in

February 2012, to get away from Krejcir and then I heard that in 2013, Sam Issa was murdered. I am very sad about it, as he was a friendly guy and did not do any harm to anybody.'[18]

Potiska also revealed that Issa had joined a terrorist cell as a young man in Lebanon and he was sent to Europe. He had spent 18 years in prison in France in connection with a bombing in a church in Paris. 'Sam hated to talk about it,' Potiska said.[19] When he was released, he came to South Africa where he dedicated his life to the drug trade. He then latched on to Krejcir 'because he smelled his power and money. He agreed with Sam on a partner-ship. Sam Issa put his money into the business with meth and expected a lot of money coming back. After some time Sam became annoyed though. He got into trouble with a Brazilian gang he had got some cocaine from, as he could not pay for the whole consignment,' Potiska said.[20]

The Czech said that Issa then started to push Krejcir hard to pay back the money he had lent him and the two men fell out. After the robbery, Potiska said that Issa became even more annoyed with Krejcir and he tried to con-tact the cops, offering to talk. 'You know the rest,' Potiska said.[21]

Issa's murder was actually the second underworld death that week. Four days earlier, high-ranking Sexy Boys gang member Leon 'Lion' Davids had been shot dead in Cape Town.

The Sunday Independent revealed that Davids had been in witness protec-tion after allegedly fingering the masterminds behind the murder of Cape Town bouncer boss, Cyril Beeka.[22] But he left the programme. He changed his version of Beeka's murder so many times that the police decided they could not rely on what he said.

The 29-year-old was shot dead at a braai and two others were wounded. Police told the paper they believed there was a link between the two murders and they were investigating.

The smoke from the bullets had barely drifted off when another associate of Krejcir 'died by the gun'. On 2 November 2013, just two weeks after Issa's death, Veselin Laganin was killed. He was victim number ten. (Another man, a Zimbabwean debt collector, had been murdered. Police knew about his death, but the public would only hear about it in the following months.)

Laganin was a Serbian national who had been charged, along with Krejcir and former bouncer Jason Domingues, for the armed robbery of a Pakistani-owned electronics shop in Pretoria.

Gauteng police spokesman Neville Malila said that two men had climbed through an open window on the first floor of Laganin's flat, which was in the secure Wedgewood complex in Bedfordview. 'They woke the victim's wife and indicated to her to be quiet,' Malila said. Laganin woke up when they took a ring from his wife's finger. They fired shots at him, killing him. 'The wife started screaming and ran out of the flat to call security,' Malila said.[23]

The attackers fled with a firearm, cellphones and R1 000 in cash. Police later found a bag with two 9-millimetre pistols outside the flat. It was a hit staged as a robbery gone wrong, said security experts.[24]

Sameer Naik wrote in the *Saturday Star* that Laganin was taken out for having a 'loose mouth' – this according to private investigator Mike Bolhuis. 'He spoke very openly about affairs in the underworld, Veselin was a character with a very loose mouth,' said Bolhuis.[25] Potiska said that Krejcir also owed Laganin money.

Known as Vesko, he was said to be hiding in South Africa because he was an internationally wanted criminal. 'He was 53 years old and had a lot of experience with the war in the Balkans and with the drug trade,' Potiska said. 'When the war ended in the Balkans, he went to Australia, but he ended up in jail because he was involved in drugs there.' Later he moved to Johannesburg. 'For Krejcir he was as highly valuable as gold. He was his liaison in the drug trade,' Potiska said.[26] At some point, Vesko lent Krejcir money.

Behind the scenes both Vesko and Black Sam had been getting anxious over the money Krejcir owed them, Potiska said. He believed that Krejcir cut Vesko out of the drug business. Potiska also claimed that Vesko began telling people that no one would ever see money owed by Krejcir. He told them to be careful because Krejcir worked with the cops. Potiska said Vesko was right: according to him, Krejcir had a deal with cops from the narcotics unit, whereby he would tip them off when an interesting consignment came in from a competitive drug ring. The police would give some of the seized goods to Krejcir for his cooperation. Potiska said that Vesko was trying to convince people to get rid of Krejcir.[27]

Murder, upon murder, upon murder: it was too much. Krejcir was acting as if there were no laws in South Africa, as if the police meant nothing. He was becoming an embarrassment to the state.

O'Sullivan pointed it out all too plainly: 'People are dying like flies around him. ... He entered the country with a fake passport, has been involved with crime and yet the state appears to be paralysed.'[28]

Hawks spokesman Paul Ramaloko tried to defend the men in blue. He asked how the police could charge someone when every time they tried to get a witness to testify they changed their minds, intimidated and paralysed by fear. No one would take Krejcir on. 'We can't bring charges if evidence is not strong enough,' he said.[29]

They needed a better plan. Police Commissioner Riah Phiyega insisted on it. It was time to take down Krejcir.

CHAPTER 14

THE BOMB

Clyde Alley was driving past Moneypoint with his four-year-old son in the back seat. Suddenly a bomb exploded a few metres from the man's car.

His first reaction was to race away from the scene as fast as he could. 'I was so frightened that something would happen to my child because you immediately wonder where the next explosion will happen,' Alley told News24.[1]

It was 5.20 pm on 12 November 2013, a busy time of day at the intersection opposite the Eastgate mall, where Moneypoint was situated. The bomb blast was heard up to two kilometres away. It blew out all the windows in the business and half the roof collapsed in.

Two people were dead; three were injured and taken to hospital with critical injuries; two sustained mild injuries.

Police and emergency personnel first on the scene ascertained that someone had walked into the gold and diamond exchange in Bedfordview with a tog bag. He put it down, walked out and a few minutes later the bomb went off.[2]

At first, the authorities weren't sure if Krejcir had been inside. The bomb squad first had to secure the scene before they could try to find out. They were aware there might be a second device. The bomb unit with their sniffer dogs emerged from the blackened building only at 8 pm. There had been no second device. Forensic investigators could now move in.

Police spokesman Neville Malila was outside the scene. He told journalists they were still in the early stages of their investigation and had not made any arrests.[3] Police did not yet know the identities of those who were killed and injured, nor did they know Krejcir's whereabouts, Malila said. Police would interview those in hospital for more information.

By the next morning, it was clear that Krejcir had not been at the business at the time of the bombing. He was safe in his Bedfordview mansion.

Residents of Bedfordview had had enough. The explosion came barely a week after Veselin Laganin had been shot dead in his Bedfordview home and just a month after Sam Issa was gunned down in the same area. A bomb was the last straw. They told *The Star* that events linked to Krejcir had made them fearful of living in the area. 'I've lived in this area all my life. My children come to the mall at night. Now I'm very worried,' one woman said.[4]

The community spoke out: they wanted Krejcir out of their once-quiet suburb. There was a petition being signed, but some people were reluctant to put their name on it. 'People are scared. They don't want to be seen as speaking out against such a dangerous man. Twelve people are already dead,' said the DA ward councillor for Bedfordview, Michele Clarke, who planned to table the petition before Parliament on behalf of the Bedfordview community. Clarke told the *Saturday Star* that the complex where Laganin was killed was next door to a retirement home, Arbor Village. Every year they hold a Christmas fete, their biggest fundraiser, which is normally well attended. 'But not this year: people didn't want to come out.' Estate agents also said there was a drop in demand for houses in the usually popular suburb.[5]

By the next morning the names of the two men who had been killed were released. They were Ronny Bvuma and Jan Charvat. Bvuma was an employee of Krejcir's. Moneypoint had been 'sold' to him by Katerina Krejcirova and he was the sole director of the business. Charvat, a close friend of Krejcir's, was a convicted tax fraudster in the Czech Republic.

Krejcir and his associates lay low for a few days, as speculation about what had happened did the rounds. There was a sense of shock among those who dallied in the underworld. If someone was robbed, they acted like it was nothing. A kidnapping – they smirked. A murder – the reaction depended on who the victim was, but they were generally blasé in their reaction. A bomb was different, however. The bravado slipped. It wasn't in the normal realm of their worlds. They didn't know what act to put on. They truly had no idea what had happened, and they were scared. It took a few days for reality to set in, then the speculation started flying around.

O'Sullivan was at the scene of the blast. He said that ten of the people who had been murdered until that point had one link or another to Krejcir – 'and tonight's casualties adds to 12'.[6] O'Sullivan said it was premature to assume the bombing was intended to kill Krejcir. He pointed out that the lease at Moneypoint was about to expire at the end of the month and the owners of the building had indicated they would not be renewing the lease. They had plans to turn the piece of land in the sought-after area of Bedfordview into a block of flats.

O'Sullivan's revelations begged the question, could Krejcir have been angry enough with this news to blow the place up? O'Sullivan implored the authorities to act once and for all, and to extradite Krejcir to the Czech Republic.

Forensic investigator Chad Thomas said Krejcir needed to be taken into protective custody if the explosion had not been staged 'until such time as his refugee status is either confirmed or he gets deported to the Czech Republic'.[7] Thomas later said that he believed the bomb had been arranged by Krejcir, that he knew the net was closing in on him and he was worried that his closest allies would spill the beans. So he delivered a bomb with a zero timer.

There was also a rumour that a suicide bomber had set off the device. 'I'm finding this bizarre,' said Thomas, 'because a suicide bomber normally has a passion for a cause or is a fundamentalist. This is the first time in my life that I've heard of a suicide bomber being used in organised crime,' adding that this version of what happened was unlikely to be true.[8]

O'Sullivan said it was likely that the bomb had been detonated remotely. Many suggested that Krejcir himself or a group trying to lessen his power base was murdering people close to him. Some said it was a Cape Town gang involved in a turf war; others that it was rogue police officers or an international hit squad; meanwhile, others said the blast might not have been intentional and that the explosives may have accidentally detonated while being transported with a shipment of weapons delivered from Cape Town to Moneypoint.

Sally Evans wrote in the *Mail & Guardian* that one of the speculations was that the bomb was a revenge attack by Serbian gangsters for the death of Laganin.[9] But others said the bomb was too amateurish for them.

The truth was, nobody really knew what had happened.

Those close to Krejcir revealed that he had meant to be at the shop when the bomb went off. A meeting had been meant to take place, but Krejcir was late. They said he was a shaken man.

In his book, Jaroslav Kmenta says some thought the target of the bomb was Bvuma. He wanted out of Moneypoint, and was asking Krejcir for the money back that he had put into the business.[10] Kmenta also writes that Krejcir allegedly had someone inside SARS helping him. The intention, Kmenta says, was to deliver the bomb there and take out all the servers at the taxman's Pretoria head office, thereby effectively erasing a tax case against Krejcir, but it accidentally went off at Moneypoint.

Kmenta says that Krejcir had called a meeting with all the people closest to him. It was meant to start at 5 pm. At the meeting table were Jan Charvat and Bvuma, and a number of other Krejcir employees. Twenty minutes went by and Krejcir had still not arrived.

Then the shop door opened: it was a customer. Bvuma asked where Krejcir was. Three minutes later there was a blast.

A week later, the business manager at Moneypoint, Ivan Savov, was arrested by the Hawks for alleged fraud of millions of rands. The Bulgarian was allegedly the mastermind behind the looting of millions from the accounts of multinational security firm G4S Secure Solutions, which had a contract guarding Bloemfontein Correctional Services. G4S director Lourens Smit told *The Star* that the money had disappeared from the company's ABSA account.[11] A bank employee, Vuyolwethu Koboka, who, according to the police, allegedly stole the funds, was also arrested. They were charged with fraud, money laundering and theft.

Prosecutor Richard Tshabalala said Savov, Koboka and Charvat (who had died in the blast) had allegedly fraudulently transferred R12 million from an account at ABSA. He said the money had then gone to a firm of attorneys,

Faber Goërtz Ellis Austen, under the pretext that it was for buying gold commodities.[12]

The charge sheet, which contained an affidavit by investigating officer Humbelani Jonathan Makhado from the Hawks, said that Koboka was an ABSA bank teller at the Maponya Mall branch, whose duties included helping clients make withdrawals from their bank accounts. He also had access to the treasury room where cash was kept.

The affidavit said that Bloemfontein Correctional Contracts (Pty) Ltd (BCC) was a client of ABSA and between 26 January and 2 February 2013, 'the applicant processed withdrawals and transfers from the account of BCC to the total amount of R12.8 million. BCC neither authorised [nor] performed the transactions.'[13]

In a separate case of fraud, for which Savov was charged, Savov was accused of unlawfully transferring money between a company known as Scara Technologies and Charvat. Piet du Plessis, who represented Savov, said that when it became clear the money was unlawfully transferred, Savov assisted the investigation and paid the money back. Scara Technologies was the 12th respondent in court papers, which would had been filed by SARS in an attempt to get a preservation order granted on Krejcir's assets.[14] The taxman believed the company was used as a front to fraudulently claim VAT on non-existent sales between fraudulent companies. Savov was one of the men closest to Krejcir, and his arrest, so soon after the bomb blast, indicated the net was closing in.

It seemed the time for silence was over. Krejcir needed to make it clear: he wanted to tell the world he was a victim, that the bomb had been meant to kill him. Nadezda Krejcirova sent out a press release offering a R2 million reward for information that could lead to the arrest or arrests of the people trying to kill her son.[15] She said she was looking for information provided to the police that would lead to the arrest, prosecution and conviction of those responsible for the two attempts made on Krejcir's life. She referred to the first attempt as a 'car that had been rigged with crude guns and operated by remote control' that had been shot at Krejcir. The second was the bomb blast. Krejcirova said she was offering a reward of R1 million for each incident.

Krejcir gave an interview with Mandy Wiener from Radio 702, which also appeared in *The Star*, telling her that he thought the bomb had been meant for him: 'I believe I'm under attack, because so far there is already two attempts to murder me,' Krejcir said. 'I lost two of my closest friends and I'm very sad about it. We are not talking now about any hit on the person. We're talking about [a] serious terrorist attack. They don't care if there are 20 people or kids there. They will blow all these people up ... We're talking about al-Qaeda style, about terrorism.'[16]

In a prepared statement, he told Wiener that he had no involvement in any of the 'underworld killing': 'I want to categorically state that I have had no involvement in any of the killings [of the 12 murders of people with links to him] that the media have been so freely speculating about. I am sure that if there was any evidence of my involvement, the South African police would have found such evidence by investigation.'[17]

He said South Africans needed a bogeyman and they had found it in him. 'I will be happy if somebody [takes] my place.'

He said people should not fear him: 'Do I look evil? I've done nothing wrong in my life.'[18]

CHAPTER 15

THE ARREST

Police Commissioner General Riah Phiyega was furious. Sam Issa's blood had flowed on a street where people did their grocery shopping. Bullet casings from his shooting lay outside a beloved Methodist church. Eyewitnesses were traumatised – right outside the windows of their homes they saw the man being gunned down.

And now a bomb. It was outrageous. It was time to put her foot down. She was determined. These underworld assassinations would stop.

Krejcir had become an embarrassment for the police, one man flaunting his power with such impunity. Krejcir didn't seem to care about authority. He appeared to think he could get away with anything. Phiyega, it seemed, had had enough: she was determined to show who the law was in this country. The bloodletting would stop.

Within days of Issa's murder, the police commissioner had called a high-level meeting.[1] The Hawks chief, Lieutenant General Anwa Dramat, the head of Detective Services, Lieutenant General Vineshkumar Moonoo, the Deputy National Police Commissioner for Policing Operations, Lieutenant General Khehla John Sithole, members from the Crime Intelligence Division and various brigadiers and generals all made their way to the police headquarters in the Wachthuis Building, Pretoria.

It was early in the afternoon when they assembled in Phiyega's boardroom. The commissioner started the meeting with two questions: why were people being killed in Bedfordview and what was being done about it?[2]

An insider revealed that those questions were not quickly answered and it took hours to thrash through them. Every person gave their own view on Krejcir and why it was so difficult to get any results from their investigations. It was not that the police had not been trying. The difficulty, they said, was the fact that the main person behind the killings was not getting his hands dirty and it was other criminals taking each other out.

The officers told Phiyega how Krejcir had got into the country and how they believed he was bribing almost everyone. They explained that it was almost impossible to have a watertight case against him because no one was willing to testify against him.

The police's top brass walked out of the meeting at 1 am, nowhere close to reaching a conclusion on how to solve the Krejcir problem.

Phiyega was told in that meeting that Sam Issa had been operating a scrap-metal business. She was told that Ekurhuleni Metro Police Department officers used to provide him with an escort when he went to bank his money. On one particular day, there was a robbery outside Issa's business and a crime intelligence agent was killed in the shoot-out that ensued.[3] Phiyega demanded to know why she had not been told about this. The police commissioner had recently introduced a new procedure whereby a report had to be sent for each incident involving the death of a police officer. She asked crime intelligence managers if they had attended the funeral. They said they hadn't because the officer was a Muslim and was buried the same day. She asked if they had been to pay respects to the family. They said no. She asked them what the crime intelligence agent had been doing there and how he got involved in a shoot-out. They didn't know.[4]

After the meeting Phiyega met separately with Sithole and Moonoo. They promised Phiyega that if there was a docket, an open case, they would have Krejcir behind bars within three months.

But the Hawks and national police units clashed over the case, insiders said. The Hawks refused to disclose their dockets. It seemed they were close to a breakthrough and didn't want to share the glory with other law-enforcement units.

Phiyega wanted one docket, that one case against Krejcir that would nail him and where witnesses would not be scared to testify – that one case that would stick. The police suspected that once they had Krejcir behind bars, the witnesses would start to talk.

A few days later, Phiyega was at a management meeting at the Southern Sun Hotel at OR Tambo International Airport, insiders revealed to me, when a tough, seasoned, no-nonsense Crime Intelligence Division officer with the nickname 'Killer' was snuck in.[5] Phiyega, Moonoo, Sithole and acting head of crime intelligence, Major General (Dr) Bongiwe Zulu, sat and listened to Colonel Nkosana 'Killer' Ximba. He told them about an incident he knew about in which Krejcir was involved in a drug deal that had gone wrong and a man was burnt in the process.

In the meeting, the police top echelons once again heard about corruption within the police, and how Krejcir had bribed officers whose interference made cases difficult to solve. They quickly realised they needed to form a specialised Krejcir task team with officers from various key police departments led by the national office. This dream team was made up of Tactical Response, the Hawks, Crime Intelligence and detective officers.[6]

The challenge was to identify the right investigating officer for the task ahead – a detective who could work with Ximba and his crime intelligence colleagues. Insiders revealed that Phiyega wanted someone who could not be corrupted and who had experience of organised crime. Sithole came up with a suggestion. He recommended for the job Captain Mashudu Freddy Ramuhala, whom he knew from his days as provincial commissioner of the Free State.

As Thanduxolo Jika wrote in the *Sunday Times*, Ramuhala had quietly made a name for himself cracking a heist case in Limpopo a few years earlier targeting security-services company SBV. Four security guards had been burnt alive in the back of their cash-in-transit vehicle.[7] Later Ramuhala was lead detective in the Free State's organised-crime division. He was a career policeman, a 37-year veteran, and he was up for the job. He was not scared to take on this case. In Ramuhala's words, being scared of the challenges would imply that he wasn't protecting his country or serving the victims out there.[8]

As time went on, Ramuhala was to be surrounded by equally hard-working men in blue, among them Bongani Gininda (who had travelled to the Czech Republic to get statements from Miloslav Potiska) and captains Walter Mabuti and Henry Ndinisa. In court this impressive team, and a number of tactical response members, would soon be recognised as a fearsome group – dedicated, determined and fearless.

The police had their docket on the kidnapping case where the victim had been burnt, which 'Killer' Ximba had provided. And they had their men. It was now time to arrest Radovan Krejcir.

On 22 November 2013 the police made their move. It was a Friday, around 6 pm, when they entered Krejcir's mansion. This time, the only media cameras were outside the property. Krejcir was at home with his girlfriend, Marissa Christopher. His wife and sons were on holiday out of the country.

Sameer Naik from the *Saturday Star* witnessed a handcuffed Krejcir being taken out of his house. He was wearing a white hoodie that covered his face.[9]

Naik wrote that the police's blue vehicle lights flashed in Krejcir's face as he was led by six officers armed with assault rifles to an unmarked white BMW. Two officers sat on either side of him in the back seat.

'The convoy of police vehicles crammed with heavily armed officers had surrounded Krejcir's mansion in Bedfordview for more than an hour, then sped off,' Naik reported.[10]

National police spokesperson Lieutenant General Solomon Makgale said that Krejcir had been arrested on charges of attempted murder and kidnapping. Makgale said that Krejcir's arrest had been executed by a specialised multidisciplinary team appointed by Phiyega, who had worked day and night to nab him. He was taken to an undisclosed location.

The *Cape Argus* reported that Krejcir's arrest came as a surprise to the Hawks, who were also on the point of arresting him.[11] It would later emerge that some Hawks members had been corrupted by Krejcir, making any case they had against him difficult to stick. There had been dedicated officers in the unit, however, who had been working hard on the case for years. One officer said they had amassed more than 60 cases against the men surrounding Krejcir. They saw him as the head of a criminal syndicate and they had been trying to steadily cut off his tentacles.

But, in the end, it was to be Phiyega's special task team, with skilled members drawn from all the law-enforcement units, who made the big arrest.

Paul O'Sullivan was relieved. Finally, his calls on the police to do something about Krejcir had borne fruit. He had accumulated thousands of pages of witness statements against Krejcir over the years and had been getting increasingly frustrated that nothing was being done to hold him to account. He seemed to have achieved what the police until that point had not: he got witnesses to talk.[12]

O'Sullivan also revealed that the arrest had come just in time: if police had waited any longer they might have had no one to arrest. The investigator said Krejcir had been planning to flee the country. He had arranged to fly from Lanseria Airport to Windhoek, Namibia, and thence to Buenos Aires, Argentina. 'He had already paid for the whole journey, but he hasn't made it, so he's going to lose that money,' O'Sullivan told the *Cape Argus*. O'Sullivan explained that Krejcir had been planning to join his family, who had left South Africa for Argentina earlier in the week.[13]

A press conference was held the day after the arrest, during which Phiyega said that Krejcir had initially been charged with intent to do grievous bodily harm, but this had been changed to attempted murder, given the severity of the assault.

Sources close to police Crime Intelligence said the arrest was connected to an alleged drug deal that was supposed to happen at OR Tambo International Airport.[14] The deal went bad: a man was supposed to deliver a consignment of smuggled drugs to Krejcir's associates, but instead disappeared. In response, the brother of the man had been kidnapped and severely burnt to induce him to reveal what he knew about the incident.

Meanwhile, Krejcir had not been the only target of the police. A Sandton businessman who nobody had heard of before, Desai Luphondo, was arrested along with Krejcir.

Later that week, four days after Krejcir and Luphondo's arrest, police moved in again – this time on their own people. Police spokesman Solomon Makgale revealed that two Hawks warrant officers had also been arrested in connection with the crime. 'It is always disappointing when we have to act in this manner against our own members but we cannot just shrug our shoulders and not act against those who are alleged to have contravened the laws of this country,' he said.[15] The first man they arrested was an officer known as Saddam, *The Star* revealed.[16] His real name was Samuel Modise Maropeng, and he was a man known to love the high life, the paper said. He drove many cars and had many addresses. A few hours later, fellow Warrant Officer Machache George Jeff Nthoroane was arrested.

Saddam had earned his nickname because of his bad-boy reputation. He had been seen driving in Joburg in a red Ferrari, a Maserati and a Range Rover. When police raided his home they attached a Range Rover Super Charger and a Mercedes-Benz SLK. His vehicles were completely unfeasible for what a police officer earns: a warrant officer takes home a salary of about R160 000 a year.[17]

Sources close to the investigation said that cellphone data and surveillance linked the two officers to the kidnapping case that Krejcir had been arrested for.

'He's a real bad dude,' said Paul O'Sullivan of Saddam. 'He's been in the [police] payroll for the last three to four years, but working for the gangsters. His takedown is long overdue.'[18]

At the time of their arrest, the *Mail & Guardian* reported that the head of the Germiston Priority Crime unit, Colonel Francois Steyn, had received a loan of R408 000 from Groep Twee Beleggings.[19] Steyn admitted receiving the loan but denied he knew that Krejcir controlled the company. He worked in the same unit of the Hawks that the two arrested officers belonged to.

At the press conference, Phiyega said that Krejcir's arrest was a major breakthrough for the police and followed lengthy multi-team investigations. 'There are many investigations that are taking place, even on the charges that the suspects have been arrested for. We hope to arrest more suspects as the investigations unfold. We will also be looking at any involvement of our own members,' she said, referring to the police officers who had been corrupted.[20]

Police Minister Nathi Mthethwa commended the police for the arrest and said there was a watertight case against Krejcir.

Phiyega said the police feared for Krejcir's safety. 'We're taking precautionary measures to ensure his safety and [that] of those around him,' *The Sunday Independent* reported Phiyega as saying.[21]

Krejcir's legal team immediately flew into action. At midnight on the Friday he was arrested, BDK Attorneys applied for a High Court interdict, forcing the police to disclose where their client was being held. They claimed he had not been taken straight to a police station, but had been driven around and tortured.

On the Sunday night, the legal team brought another urgent application before the court. They asked for Krejcir to be removed from the police's holding cells and taken to a hospital. They said he needed urgent treatment because he had allegedly been tortured after his arrest.[22]

The police watchdog, the Independent Police Investigative Directorate (IPID), confirmed to *The Star* that they had launched an investigation into allegations that Krejcir had been tortured at the hands of the police.[23] Krejcir's lawyers claimed that their client had been tasered and nearly suffocated with a plastic bag after his arrest. Subsequently, charges of assault with intent to do grievous bodily harm, and attempted murder, were laid against the police at the Protea Glen Police Station.

Ulrich Roux, a director of BDK, said in a statement: 'At least five vehicles were in the motorcade which pulled over in a rural isolated area where our client was forced out of the vehicle by an officer electrocuting him with a [Taser] gun. After being forced to his knees and asked several unanswerable questions, our client was tortured by having a plastic bag placed over his head and being [almost] suffocated until he lost consciousness.'[24]

The attorney said that about 20 police officers had witnessed the alleged assault. Roux said when Krejcir had regained consciousness he was tasered again and a chemical was poured on cuts he had on his wrists and forearms, causing him 'severe pain'. IPID spokesman Moses Dlamini confirmed the directorate was investigating the matter.[25]

The legal team said that although Krejcir had been arrested at 6 pm on Friday, he had been placed in a police cell only six and a half hours later. Said Roux: 'It is clear that the police officials denied our client his right to legal representation in order for them to torture him, and in so doing, force him into making some sort of confession.'[26]

In their urgent application, Krejcir's legal team said they feared he would suffer renal failure because of the condition of his kidneys. Just after 10 pm on Sunday, the lawyers put Krejcir's doctor on the stand in the Johannesburg High Court.[27] A gastrointestinal surgeon who had been in private practice since 1995, he had examined Krejcir the morning before.

According to an eNCA report, the doctor said Krejcir's blood-test results could prove his claims that he had been repeatedly tortured and subjected to electric shocks by the police.[28] The doctor said Krejcir's body showed signs of 'significant muscle damage'. He told the court that unless there were healthcare personnel present at the cells where Krejcir was being held, he should be moved to a hospital. According to the medical form read out in court, Krejcir had reportedly sustained multiple cuts and scratches to both hands, and he had burns to his wrists, showing that he had been through 'a trauma of sorts', the doctor said. The doctor said Krejcir must have been tasered repeatedly, causing muscle trauma, which could have damaged his heart.[29]

The doctor insisted Krejcir might suffer cardiac and renal failure, and needed medical attention, that he would need to be observed for 48 hours and be seen by a heart specialist.

As far as he knew, Krejcir had no history of chronic medical conditions, only that he had high blood pressure. The doctor said Krejcir's blood tests showed high levels of creatine kinase that had resulted from trauma. Such raised levels of the enzyme usually mean there has been an injury or stress to muscle tissue or the brain. The doctor said Krejcir needed a drip to rehydrate him and to avoid renal failure.[30]

In response, state prosecutor Gustav Lekade said there was no confirmation from the laboratory of Krejcir's condition, adding that comprehensive tests needed to be done. He questioned the medical report, saying the doctor hired by the defence was manufacturing evidence. Lekade said a doctor hired by the state pointed out the bruises (to the forearm, wrist and thumb), and his numb wrist joint and painful neck were probably caused by the handcuffs. He also pointed out that the raised creatine kinase levels could be from a pre-existing chronic condition that Krejcir had, meaning it could be managed with medicine. It could also have been caused by drug use.[31]

Mpiletso Motumi from *The Star* reported that the application continued until the early hours of the morning and that judgment was reserved until

11.30 am the following Monday – the same day that Krejcir had to appear in the Palm Ridge Magistrate's Court for the charge he had been arrested on.[32]

After a break, a police officer told the court that he had been told by Krejcir that he had neck and chest pains, and had expressed a need to take his medication.

Judge Monama told the state that the issue was not what had caused Krejcir's injuries, but rather whether he needed medical attention. 'We are looking at the facts, not at the human being concerned,' said the judge.[33]

The next morning, the Monday after the arrest, Monama ruled that Krejcir should be taken to hospital. The judge found Krejcir's private doctor's testimony to be credible.[34] Monama said the issue of the application was not to determine whether Krejcir had been assaulted – that would be up to police investigators to determine. The issue was whether he needed urgent medical attention or not. Judge Monama decided that Krejcir had the right to receive proper medical treatment, and even the state's expert doctor had conceded that the Czech businessman should be admitted to hospital if Krejcir's private doctor's testimony was to be believed. 'It is in the interests of the state that [Krejcir does] not go into renal failure, to ensure he has his day in court,' said Monama.[35]

The judge ordered the state to pay costs. The state was also ordered to pay the costs for the application two days earlier by Krejcir's lawyers to see their client, whom they said they had not been able to consult since his arrest. According to Roux, five lawyers at BDK Attorneys were brought onto the case and had worked through the weekend, meaning costs could run into hundreds of thousands of rands.

After his first court appearance for the charge of kidnapping, which took place that same Monday, Krejcir was transferred to Linksfield Hospital, where he spent a few days under 24-hour surveillance before being transferred to the hospital wing of Kgosi Mampuru Prison in Pretoria.

CHAPTER 16

KREJCIR IS AL CAPONED: WHEN ALL ELSE FAILS, CALL THE TAXMAN

The jail cell is small, especially for a big, six-foot man like Krejcir. It's 61 square feet, just enough room to take a few steps in either direction. It's cold, the walls a musty yellow. And there are definitely no views.

But this is Krejcir and he managed to wangle his way into getting a kettle inside his prison cell, and a hotplate and a flat-screen TV – or so it is rumoured.

But, no matter how much he kitted out the cell, there were still bars on the door and nothing to see but yellow walls.

No doubt he lay on his single bed and thought back to the days when he slept in a king-size bed with its white leather headboard. In front of him a large TV screen and a disturbing picture of a ship run aground in a storm, lightning blazing across the darkened sky. It was a picture that seemed to capture the essence of the man: dark and dangerous with troubled times always on the horizon.

As he lay in his tiny jail cell, journalists walked through the mansion he once lived in, gawking at everything that had once been his.[1] Next to the bed he had once lain in was his son Damian's camp cot, the only sign of domesticity in his room. To the left were walk-in closets, made of dark wood and overflowing with designer clothes. One for him and one for Katerina.

His enormous bathroom had been built of cold stone, the sunken bath was the size of a small swimming pool. It looked painfully uncomfortable to sit in. But maybe its aim wasn't to have a relaxing soak brimming with soapy bubbles. The bath faced northwards, as did the rimflow pool on the floor below. In every main room in the house there was only one thing to see: the whole of Johannesburg, its north, its east and its west, in all its frenetic steel and green glory. The entire north-facing structure of the four-storey mansion was floor-to-ceiling windows. Even the lift was see-through. You could never forget where you were in this home, with Johannesburg lying open before you at every turn.

Inside, Krejcir must have felt like the king of all he surveyed. Lying in the bath, in bed, or swimming laps in his pool, he must have felt literally on top of the world.

And, for a time, he was king – but not of the fertile greenness of this big urban forest, or of the glinting steel of the Sandton skyscrapers. But of what was below: king of the city's dark and glittering underbelly. Its crime and its nefarious characters. The world where money means more than anything, especially human life.

Krejcir had been arrested, but he had been arrested before. And each time he had walked away unscathed. His purportedly vast wealth and ingenuity meant he had found a way out of every situation, no matter how dire it seemed.

Would he walk free again?

It was one of the oldest tricks in the law-enforcement books, and for a man who seemingly loved anything gangster, it was something you would have thought Krejcir would see coming.

Yet he didn't. Perhaps being so on top of the world blinkered his view slightly. He could only see into the shimmering distance, he was blinded by all his riches. The taxman, however, was already at his door. Krejcir was about to be 'Al Caponed'.

Alphonse Gabriel 'Al' Capone was a famous 1920s American gangster involved in a whole batch of illegal activities, including murder, smuggling, prostitution and bootlegging liquor. He became famous during the prohibition era as the co-founder and boss of the Chicago Outfit and seemed safe from law-enforcement because of his relationship with mayor William Hale

Thompson and the Chicago police. The people of the city loved him because he made various donations to charities, but his methods became increasingly violent, culminating in the Saint Valentine's Day massacre, in which seven men from a rival gang were gunned down in broad daylight. That is when federal authorities moved in and successfully prosecuted Capone for tax evasion. His seven-year crime spree ended when he was sentenced to 11 years in prison.[2]

Nobody, it seemed, even the seemingly invincible, could escape tax law – something Krejcir was about to learn first-hand.

It was an obvious tactic, and yet it worked. The first indication that SARS was taking a closer look at Krejcir was during his arrest in March 2012 during the Marian Tupy bungle. Hours after the Hawks had gone in, busting down gates, finding hit lists and making arrests, SARS simply opened the door. The SARS team wrangled with lawyers the whole day and won – the proof clear for everyone to see when two of Krejcir's luxury sports cars were towed away.

'That car is worth more than my house,' one Kloof Road neighbour had laughed as SARS took away the spoils. Shaun Smillie from *The Star* said people swarmed outside with cellphones and cameras taking pictures of the sports cars.[3]

A Ferrari F340, was destined for the back of a flatbed truck, and then off to a warehouse in Pretoria where the taxman stores 'all those boy's toys and other luxury stuff impounded from alleged criminals,' Smillie wrote.[4]

A Lamborghini Murcielago then joined its mate, destined for the same fate. The Lamborghini's V12 engine roared to life and the car idled its way down the driveway, the driver wearing wraparound sunglasses even though it was night-time, Smillie reported.

The spectators oohed and aahed. 'Don't get too close, boet, they will probably shoot you,' laughed one.[5]

The cars were driven away under police escort, their combined value between R5 million and R6 million.

Behind the scenes, Paul O'Sullivan and SARS officials were hard at work watching everything Krejcir and his associates did, and gathering evidence. When Katerina arrived at court in her expensive car and designer clothes, they were there writing it all down. When Nadezda Krejcirova arrived in the country allegedly with a bagful of cash, SARS officials were in the background, watching it all. When Krejcir told the court he had millions in assets, and therefore was tied to the country and would not flee during his bail application, SARS officials silently stood in the court and recorded it all. They noted down the number plates of the cars that the people he knew arrived in, they traced who owned them. They built a map of his associates.[6]

The SARS officials were part of the High-Risk Investigations Unit, an investigative arm of the taxman that some media have come to label the so-called rogue unit. The unit was eventually disbanded and some of its members suspended or fired. However, the unit's last great coup before the public scrutiny into their actions started happening, was to unravel the illegal business empire that was the heartbeat, the powerhouse of Krejcir's existence.

Researcher Simone Haysom wrote in a report published by amaBhungane that the SARS team's intelligence gathering even took them to the Czech Republic to find out about Krejcir's past and his networks in Eastern Europe.[7] Even his Facebook profile, in the name of Russell Knight, yielded information.

Krejcir hadn't exactly been hiding his wealth. He loved to talk about his money. Back in 2010 he boasted to journalist Julian Rademeyer that the reason that so many of South Africa's most controversial businessmen and notorious underworld figures, like Lolly Jackson, George Louca, Cyril Beeka, Glen Agliotti, Alekos Panayi and previous Gauteng police Crime Intelligence head, Joey Mabasa, were friends with him was because of his money. 'People find me,' he said, 'because they believe I've got money, that I'm an opportunity for them, that I can do some business with them. So the people are coming, especially to this restaurant [the Harbour], like a bee on honey.'[8]

Everyone believed Krejcir owned the Harbour, where he held court, and perhaps he did – through one of his notorious loan agreements, which, as SARS would finally uncover, was part of his modus operandi to hide what was really in his name.

In the parking lot at the shopping mall, in a private, roped-off bay near the front door, Krejcir would park one of his two Porsches, or a Lamborghini, a Ferrari or a Mercedes.

Krejcir had no qualms about showing the world he had cash. It was part of his allure. It brought the people he needed to do his work to his side and kept them there, sometimes against their own better judgement. But just how wealthy was he and where was all this wealth coming from? SARS meant to find out.

Between September 2012 and January 2013, the revenue service made their second move after having removed the two sports cars. This time it was a full-scale offensive, to reel Krejcir in with a tax-income inquiry. A summons was issued and a whole batch of people who had worked with and were close to Krejcir were called in to give evidence in a closed and secret inquiry.[9] They weren't happy and there was much grumbling about being called to Pretoria to testify. But they had no choice.

At the core of his empire was Groep Twee Beleggings (which SARS referred to with the acronym G2B). G2B had been established in April 2006, when Krejcir was in the Seychelles. Officials believed it was a conduit Krejcir used to set up a money-exchange scheme that involved Lolly Jackson, among others. Jackson 'lent' money to G2B, and Krejcir paid him in euros or dollars in Greece using his foreign bank accounts. SARS believed this was a scheme to avoid tax and launder money, known universally as hawala. G2B also borrowed money from Nadezda Krejcirova, to create the impression it was in debt.

The list of people called in by SARS was long and included some whom the public had never heard of. As well as Krejcir himself, it consisted of close family members, Katerina and Denis. Krejcir's girlfriend, Marissa Christopher, was also called. Those closest to him in his business activities were also summonsed, including Ivan Savov, G2B's manager and the owner of another business called Scara Technologies, and Ronny Bvuma, who had bought Cross Point from Katerina Krejcir in September 2012.[10]

There were also accountants, business partners and attorneys, among them Juan Meyer, the owner of Pan African Refineries, and Djordje Mihaljevic, the director of Sandton Gold and Diamond Exchange, who had helped Krejcir set up Cross Point in Bedfordview. Even convicted drug lord

Glen Agliotti, who had borrowed R400 000 from Krejcir to pay his legal fees, was called as a witness.[11]

The inquiry revealed that Krejcir had set up an intricate business empire made up of at least 15 companies, whose sole existence it seemed was to move cash around and hide its origins. SARS said many of Krejcir's companies were not bona fide businesses, but entities through which to launder money.

In a preservation order that was finally served in November 2013, SARS said it had reasonable grounds to conclude Krejcir used the companies as fronts through which to channel and hide income and assets to evade tax.[12]

Krejcir stood before the inquiry and claimed innocence. Not one of the businesses was in his name. The director listed on most of them was Katerina. Krejcir claimed he was an unemployed man who lived off the money his wife and mother gave him.[13]

Nobody bought his story.

When it was Katerina's turn to give evidence she could not answer a number of questions about the day-to-day activities of G2B and the other related entities. She told the panel to please direct the questions to Krejcir.[14]

The inquiries eventually led to a case heard at the Pretoria High Court in November 2013 when SARS asked for a preservation order be granted. Johann van Loggerenberg, then group executive of Tax and Customs Enforcement Investigations at SARS, deposed an affidavit before the court that uncovered exactly what Krejcir had been up to. SARS wanted R114 million, which they said Krejcir owed in personal income tax as well as R59 million that G2B owed. Krejcir was said to be worth R130 million.[15]

Van Loggerenberg named a number of people and companies as respondents in their action. SARS identified no fewer than ten companies, two trusts and four individuals – all associated with Krejcir – as respondents. SARS indicated that all these entities had been used in a tax-evasion scheme. One of them was Crosspoint Trading 242 (Pty) Ltd, whose trading name was Moneypoint, the business that would be blown up a short time later. Krejcirova was the sole director of Crosspoint, until it was sold to Ronny Bvuma.

Krejcir did not operate any personal bank accounts in South Africa but he used the bank accounts of the various respondents to receive money.

'SARS believes that if either the first respondent [Krejcir] or the third respondent [Katerina] are involved in an entity, it is reasonable for SARS to believe that that entity's tax affairs are not in order,' Van Loggerenberg said in his affidavit.[16]

Aside from Krejcir's complex web of business ownership in South Africa, the court application revealed that he still owned an extensive business empire in the Czech Republic, including 98.86% of the shares in DKR Investments Praha SPOL.S.R.O, which was used in the acknowledgement of debt claim against Lolly Jackson's estate. Krejcir also owned 98.8% of the issued shares in TT Real Services, and 52.44% of the issued shares in K Plus G Invest SPOL. He is also a shareholder in the company DKR (Pty) Ltd, registered in the Seychelles.

G2B was listed as the owner of the Kloof Road property, which Krejcir had bought in 2007 for R13 million, as well as a home in Bloemfontein, purchased for R4 million, and a house on the Vaal River, purchased for R4 million in 2008.[17]

There were eight sources of income for the company: foreign transfers, interest income, rental income, management fees, proceeds of the sale of a diamond, sale of spare parts and R30 million received from a Mr Haimann. In 2012 the accounting records reflected the following balances:

- DKR Investments Praha: R11.4 million
- TT Real Services: R15.9 million
- N Krejcirova: R20.8 million
- K Plus G Invest: R2.8 million[18]

There were numerous loans reflected in the accounts. One was a loan to George Smith (Louca) of R3.7 million. Louca allegedly pledged to pay R3.5 million to G2B and left a number of assets as security for the loan in the form of vehicles and boats, which Krejcir had acquired when he lived in the Seychelles. One of the inter-entity loans was an amount of R10.2 million owing by DKR Auto for the purchase of vehicles transferred by G2B to DKR Auto in August 2009.

Said SARS: 'It appeared that G2B was used by Radovan Krejcir as a conduit through which monies could be received and disbursed, various transactions could be concluded, and various assets could be acquired, all for the ultimate benefit of Radovan Krejcir, his wife and sons. The company had no genuine and bona fide business of its own.'[19]

The taxman said that almost all of the business dealings had been conducted by Krejcir himself and many of the people the company loaned money to had no idea of G2B's existence.

DKR Auto CC was the company used by Krejcir to acquire his cars, which he used in his personal capacity. The long list of over 30 vehicles revealed just how much he loved his engines. Among them was a Porsche 990 tiptronic sports car and a Mercedes-Benz CL 63 AMG.

Other assets were acquired from Louca when he defaulted on his R3.5 million loan. Among them were yachts, a Yamaha Superjet, motorbikes, a Porsche Cayenne and a Lamborghini Murcielago.[20]

SARS said that the vehicles appeared to be used mainly by Krejcir and his family, and the people working for him. A nice perk of the job, it seemed.

The court action also revealed that Krejcir had a plan in place when he made his move to come to South Africa. Just a few weeks after arriving on South Africa's shores, he bought Intaglio Trading CC. Its main business was the cultivation and sale of instant grass. It was bought to show he had a business interest in South Africa in support of his application for recognition as a refugee. But, as soon as he bought the company, it ceased trading. Nevertheless, between September 2007 and July 2009, R4.4 million was transferred from G2B to Intaglio, with the name 'Radovan' in the accounting records. Of this, R4.1 million was withdrawn on the same day the deposit was made. The bank account reflects further deposits of R3 million.[21]

The cheque withdrawals from the company amounted in total over time to R4.8 million – payments to credit cards of R67 200; payments of R99 100 to G2B; payments of R28 000 to 'KK' (Katerina); payments of R70 520 to 'Matispa' or 'Salon'; and payments of R237 900 to 'Radovan'. There were also withdrawals for 'salaries' of R392 138; 'rent' for R660 867 and 'water and electricity' for R74 022, even though the business had no premises.[22]

No tax was ever paid.

Although Crosspoint Trading 242 (Pty) Ltd had been sold to Bvuma in

2012, SARS believed Krejcir had remained in full control of the business. When questioned, Bvuma said he did not have any real knowledge of the day-to-day operations and that it was under the management of Savov. The business, conducted through subsidiary companies, was involved in money lending and the purchase of gold.

The SARS investigators found there was a substantial flow of funds into and out of the bank account, but Crosspoint submitted an income tax return of only R169 563 for 2010 and nothing in subsequent years.

'Crosspoint has been used by Radovan Krejcir, either wholly or in part (which I believe the case to be) as a conduit or front for income accrued to Radovan Krejcir and disbursement of funds for the benefit of Radovan Krejcir and his family,' Van Loggerenberg said.[23]

Tiger Falls Diamonds (Pty) Ltd was the only business owned by Denis Krejcir. It traded from an office in the Rand Refinery under the previous director, PH Hopley. Before the 2010 Soccer World Cup, Tiger Falls required funding of R5 million for a business deal that it wished to do with FIFA. Negotiations were conducted between Krejcir and Hopley, and G2B subsequently provided security for the R5 million. The business deal, however, did not materialise and the money was repaid. But Krejcir negotiated the acquisition of the controlling shareholding in the company, as he believed it possessed an import-and-export licence for gold and because the premises were secure and not easily accessible. The company then ceased trading and there were no assets in its name.[24]

Scara Technologies CC was used in an elaborate scheme to try to claim non-existent VAT returns from SARS. Evidence provided by Yiannakis Louca (George Louca's cousin) during the tax inquiry and a subsequent affidavit revealed that dud spare parts for motor vehicles would be used to make the claims.

Yiannakis Louca was a motor mechanic who owned Silverstar Auto CC. He had met Krejcir through George Louca in 2007. George told his cousin that Krejcir was in the process of importing spare parts for motor vehicles into South Africa and suggested that he became involved. Yiannakis Louca said he met Michael Arsiotis at a warehouse in Germiston, where they made arrangements to rent out the premises to Silverstar Auto for the storage of the spare parts. But when he unpacked the parts, he saw they were for vehicles not available on the South African market and were therefore useless.

Krejcir invited Louca to a meeting at his house with Savov. They suggested they use the parts in a VAT scheme, Louca said. The idea was simple: they would sell the parts from one company to another and claim a VAT refund on the sale. Louca agreed on the basis that he would receive 25% of the money made. Louca said he gave Savov company letterheads of Silverstar Auto, and Savov fabricated invoices indicating that Silverstar had sold parts to Scara at a price of R17.8 million (excluding VAT) and R20.3 million (including VAT).[25]

Louca was contacted by SARS at one point indicating that Silverstar owed SARS approximately R2.5 million in taxes. He said that Savov then came up with a scheme whereby Scara would provide diamonds to Silverstar in part payment for the spare parts (the sale of which was a sham) and that Silverstar would then sell the diamonds in a similar VAT refund scheme. Louca again agreed on condition he got 25% of the money made. The documents were created and VAT was claimed. SARS, however, did not make payments on the claim.

Van Loggerenberg's affidavit indicated that to create the appearance that Scara had made payment to Silverstar for the spare parts, Scara entered into a loan agreement with G2B for an amount of R20 million, and funds were transferred to Scara's bank account and then to Silverstar. Each time money was transferred, the money was withdrawn and handed to people representing Krejcir. As security for the 'loan' Scara pledged a 2007 model Lamborghini Murcielago to G2B, which was forfeited to SARS in June 2012.[26]

But these were all side shows compared to G2B.

SARS found that the company's outstanding income-tax debt stood at R59.8 million, including interest of R15.3 million.

'Evidence at the inquiry supports SARS's contention that Mr Krejcir used G2B as a front and as a conduit to transact in his personal capacity. These amounts will now be raised against Mr Krejcir personally,' the court concluded.[27]

'SARS contends that Radovan Krejcir used his wife, the DKR Share Trust, the DKR Property Trust and the corporate entities of the other respondents to hide the income that accrued to him and his assets, with the intention of evading payment of tax. ... Radovan Krejcir is clearly the person in control of all the other respondents, including his wife,' the court papers stated.[28]

The court issued a preservation order, which stated that all of Krejcir's assets be placed under the control of a curator, Murray Cloete of the Sechaba Trust, who preserved all the assets, including shareholding in companies, loan accounts, members' interests in close corporations, movable and immovable assets, and funds held in their bank accounts.

Krejcir's personal tax bill was estimated at R114 million. His worth in South Africa was estimated to be R130 million, but it was held in properties and trusts. The order rendered him insolvent.

The affidavit by Van Loggerenberg was used in court to stop Krejcir's bail application on the kidnapping charges. He could now no longer argue that he was a wealthy businessman with enough assets in the country to keep him on South African shores. He now owned nothing.

Katerina and Denis, who were in the Seychelles when the preservation order was granted, found themselves stranded, with cancelled credit cards and no access to funds. The curator had to pay for their flights back to the country and their hotel bill.

'Czech mate. The corrupt machine that is Krejcir has come to a grinding halt,' said O'Sullivan. 'This is the culmination of two years of hard work by SARS and my four-year investigation.'[29]

The ultimate humiliation came in December 2014 when the curator put Krejcir's mansion up for auction. A few days before the hammer went down, Sechaba Trust and the auction house, the Michael James Organisation, allowed journalists to walk through the four-storey faux-stone house that the hacks nicknamed 'gangster's paradise'. They played in the glass lift, going up and down the four floors staring at the magnificent views.[30]

The clothes and personal effects had been packed away in storage. Only a few items of furniture were left. Wires protruded from the walls where multiple flat-screen TVs had once been mounted. Denis's girlfriend, Marlene

'Molly' Nezar, had been living there for a few months. O'Sullivan said she had removed all the electronics and other items of value.

An empty fish tank, dog kennel, aviary and a few items of furniture were all that was left of the family that had lived there. Two pictures were still on the walls: in the main room, the ship run aground in a storm, and a framed photo of a fingerprint, which hung in the second room upstairs, where Denis had slept.

Behind the main house was an incomplete second building, which Krejcir had been building for Denis and his girlfriend to live in. There was going to be a cinema and a bowling alley. Now it was just an abandoned construction site.

The third room on the fourth floor was for Damian, where a mural of a car racing away from a crashing wave took up one wall and a Nemo underwater theme graced his en-suite bathroom.

It was a magnificent home, with its tinted floor-to-ceiling windows displaying what must be the best views in the whole of Johannesburg. But everyone cringed when looking at the faux-rock walls. If they could talk, would they reveal the truth about what had happened inside? It was a disturbing thought.

In one fell swoop it, and the millions in cash that had helped prop it up, was taken away. All that Krejcir had left were his clothes and personal belongings in storage somewhere – and the walls of his prison cell.

Without his money, Krejcir was crippled. His allies had either been arrested alongside him or they had melted away, no longer drawn to the lure of easy money.

Without the crutch of wealth, Krejcir was no longer on top of the world. He was suddenly just a man, his hair greying, wearing the same once-fashionable jeans and black leather jacket over and over again to court. The only clothes he had left.

He refused to show this was getting him down. Every so often, his charming sense of humour emerged, revealing that perhaps there was more than just the wealth that had drawn people to him.

He wasn't about to give up. He always was a man who had a plan, and he had one now. He was about to play his next card.

CHAPTER 17

KIDNAPPING AND TORTURE OF BHEKI LUKHELE: KREJCIR'S ACHILLES HEEL

The corridors of the Palm Ridge Magistrate's Court were so packed a sardine wouldn't have been able to fit between all the journalists, photographers, officers from the Tactical Response Team and curious members of the public.

It was Radovan Krejcir's first court appearance for the kidnapping charge and everyone wanted to be there. The press wanted to find out the details of the case. Even journalists from the Czech Republic had flown in to see the man who, years after fleeing his country, was still making headlines there.

Everyone wanted to get a glimpse of the man whose name had been linked to 12 deaths and whose business had just been bombed. They wanted to look into Krejcir's eyes. Perhaps they thought it would be like watching a real-life horror movie and they were thrilled at the thought of getting a cold shiver down their spine.

Krejcir had been in the Johannesburg High Court the day before, where it was argued that he had been so badly tortured he might die of renal failure if not taken to hospital. Yet here he was in court, surrounded by his police escort, very much alive. The cynical among us couldn't help wonder if his health problems had all been a sham, although, later, Judge Colin Lamont said in his judgment that he did believe Krejcir had been tortured by the police.

Judgment in that application was taking place at the same time in the other court. Only when he finished with this first appearance in Palm Ridge would he find out that his lawyers had been successful in that application and instead of being whisked out of court to a jail cell, he was taken to a private hospital for treatment.[1]

Krejcir was being charged with attempted murder and kidnapping – not murder, like everyone had expected. What on earth had he been up to, they wondered?

But everyone was going to be disappointed: heavily armed police chased the crowds out of the courtroom, leaving behind only those directly involved in the case. This was 'for security reasons', explained Senior State Prosecutor Kenny Ramavhoya.[2]

Unlike during Krejcir's previous court cases in 2012, the security in and around the court was overwhelming. There were about two dozen police officers inside the court, some of whom were heavily armed with R5 rifles and Uzis. Outside, several members of the Tactical Response Team and police officers kept guard, all heavily armed.

Krejcir's legal team, including Piet du Plessis and Ulrich Roux, were in the courtroom. They slammed the state for holding Krejcir's first court appearance behind closed doors. 'The whole scene was over the top,' said Roux, adding that there was no security threat that they knew of.[3]

The journalists had to wait for Krejcir's bail application before they were allowed into court. Then they were allowed to enter if they presented their IDs and press cards, if they walked through a metal detector and agreed to be body-searched. Fancy pens were not allowed – they could be used to hide a gun, it seemed. All technology was to be switched off during court proceedings. There were to be no Twitterati commenting on this case.

The case started with Krejcir telling the court he was being vilified by Paul O'Sullivan. He slammed O'Sullivan, labelling him an 'unstable vigilante and a self-appointed white knight'. He was convinced that the investigator was behind his arrest.[4]

Krejcir said that he would not flee if he was granted bail. 'I am the very opposite of a flight risk,' he said. He said the fact that he was fighting an extradition order to the Czech Republic indicated that he wanted to stay in

South Africa. 'I enjoy living in South Africa and want to stay here for the rest of my life,' he said. 'The SAPS conducted a military-style raid at my home,' Krejcir said. The court didn't appear impressed by this argument.[5]

The court then learnt about the kidnapping and torture of a man named Bheki Lukhele. An affidavit by investigating officer Captain Ramuhala opposing bail revealed for the first time the details of the case. He said that Krejcir had allegedly organised a shipment of 25 kilograms of crystal meth – valued at R24 million – to Australia. The affidavit said that Krejcir organised this through his drug pusher, his co-accused, Desai Luphondo, who knew Bhekisizwe Doctor Nkosi (someone referred to at this stage only as 'Doctor'), who worked at the clearance agency at OR Tambo International Airport.[6]

'Doctor' gave Luphondo a receipt with a serial number as proof that he had shipped the drugs, as per the arrangement, but Krejcir and Luphondo later discovered the drugs had not been shipped, so the two began searching for him. Krejcir ordered the two Hawks officers, Maropeng and Nthoroane, to help them find Doctor.

The state's case was that on 25 June, Krejcir had ordered the three co-accused – and others, who had not yet been arrested – to kidnap any member of Doctor's immediate family should they not find the man himself.

The man they came across was Bheki Lukhele, Doctor's younger brother. They persuaded Lukhele to open the gate to his home in Katlehong, saying they needed to see his grandmother, and when Nthoroane produced his police identification card he did not hesitate. They beat him up and took him to Moneypoint, where they held him captive and tortured him, Ramuhala said.

'Applicant 1 [Krejcir] poured … boiling water over his head,' Ramuhala's affidavit said. Lukhele was also forced to divulge where his family home was in Ermelo. Luphondo, Maropeng and Nthoroane went there with the victim hidden in the back of the car, but they could not locate Doctor. 'His ordeal lasted for four days after which he was dumped near the Huntersfield Stadium in Katlehong,' said the affidavit.[7]

'Prove it,' the accused's legal team challenged the state. Luphondo's advocate, Andre Steenkamp, said that police had beaten a confession out of his client. In a reference to apartheid-era police tactics, Steenkamp said: 'With due respect, it sounds like the olden days.'[8]

Krejcir denied it all and claimed he knew Luphondo only because they were opening a curio shop together in the duty-free section at the airport. In his version, Krejcir claimed that he had been introduced to Luphondo two years previously and he had negotiated to acquire a 40% share in Luphondo's company if he won the tender to get the curio shop.[9]

The state came forward and said they had been receiving threats. It would not be the first time their lives were allegedly threatened over the coming months. Ramuhala told the court that Krejcir and his three co-accused had threatened state prosecutor Louis Mashiane and a witness.[10] They laid complaints with the police.

The investigating officer told the court that the case against the four had not originally been investigated by the police and had been closed, but it was reopened in October after it was referred to the national task team that had been established by Phiyega to investigate Krejcir. Krejcir's claim that he was being vilified and had no intention of leaving South Africa did not win over the court. He was denied bail.

Krejcir's history of falsifying passports, committing fraud and absconding from prison in his home country had now come back to haunt him. That, and his inclination to intimidate witnesses, had thwarted his bid for freedom. 'It's ridiculous,' Krejcir told the media after his failed bail bid, before being led away to the cells below the courtroom.[11]

Magistrate Reginald Dama referred to 'damning evidence' from Johann van Loggerenberg's SARS affidavit, which had been used in court to show Krejcir's fraudulent business dealings in South Africa and the Czech Republic, and his huge debt to SARS.[12]

Luphondo was released on R10 000 bail; Maropeng and Nthoroane had theirs fixed at R5 000 each.

Krejcir's team didn't give up. They tried two more times to get him out of jail by appealing the bail decision.

On 3 January 2014 an urgent application was made before the High Court in Johannesburg.[13] The city was still in a sleepy festive mode and the halls of the venerable court building were empty. Katerina and Denis sat in the front row as defence lawyer Francois Roets launched a desperate High Court bid to have Krejcir freed.

The lawyer said police investigators had failed to prove that the injuries to the victim were of a serious enough nature to constitute grievous bodily harm. He said the burn wounds were not serious enough to make the victim spend any time in hospital. Prosecutor Mashiane retorted with emotion: 'The victim was burnt with boiling water. Boiling water was poured over his head.'[14]

Roets argued that Krejcir had been out on bail before and had never fled the country. 'Ignore the press. They have made dark aspersions on the character of Radovan Krejcir. He is a suitable character for bail,' he argued.[15]

Judge Leonie Windell asked the defence if Krejcir had not fled the Czech Republic. 'He got on a bicycle and cycled to Poland,' the judge pointed out. Roets replied that Krejcir had fled because his life was in danger. 'His father was killed. He was put in a tank of acid,' said Roets.

'But is he not fearing for his life at the moment?' the judge retorted, querying the bomb attack at Moneypoint and the shots fired at him by remote-controlled guns rigged in a car.

'There have been attempts but he does not fear that he will be killed if he is released on bail,' said Roets.[16]

Judge Windell said that, according to his past, every time things got too hot for Krejcir he leaves the country. She also pointed out that Krejcir had indicated he did not believe he would get a fair trial in South Africa. She turned down the application.

In the meantime, a third police officer had been arrested. Warrant Officer Jan Lefu Mofokeng had fled, but police tracked him down. During Mofokeng's bail application, the state revealed again that witnesses in the case had received death threats. 'The witnesses have already been intimidated and could be killed,' said an unimpressed Mashiane. The state opposed bail because Mofokeng had tried to elude arrest by going to Bloemfontein, where he had been tracked down. Mashiane told the court the witnesses in the case had now entered witness protection. Mashiane from then on had two bodyguards flanking him at all times.

Despite this, Mofokeng was granted bail of R5 000.[17]

The third attempt to get Krejcir out on bail took place in February 2014.[18] This time, unlike his previous assertions that he was extremely wealthy, Krejcir now revealed he was in trouble financially. He told the court he and his family would become poor if he were kept behind bars.

He also said Katerina was relying on financial support from his mother while he was in custody. 'If I do not stay in this country and fight for what is rightfully ours, we will lose everything we have built up in this country over many years and we will be left totally destitute,' Krejcir said in an affidavit.[19]

Another accused, a man who would be revealed as Krejcir's alleged hit man, taxi boss Siboniso Miya, now stood in the dock. A total of six men now faced the court.

Krejcir said the SARS affidavit used to oppose his bail was highly irregular, as it was a document used by SARS to get a preservation order against Krejcir's assets. He told the court it should have been kept secret because of confidentiality clauses between SARS and those being investigated, as per the Tax Administration Act.

Instead of granting him bail, in a surprising move the state then arrested his wife. Plain-clothed policemen arrested Katerina Krejcirova right there in the court building, where she had come to support her husband.

She was arrested in connection with a stolen car and an alleged fraud scheme, police said. They also announced they were looking for 21-year-old Denis in connection with the case. Later that day Denis handed himself over to police. They were in possession of a stolen vehicle seized the week before, police said. Piet du Plessis said the arrest was malicious. Nadezda, who had been sitting with her daughter-in-law, returned to court looking dejected.[20]

Krejcir's defence lawyer, hired by BDK Attorneys to argue the case in court, Annelene van den Heever, asked Krejcir in the court if there was anyone to look after his four-year-old son, Damian. He said there wasn't. But Mashiane pointed out that the boy's grandmother was sitting in court and there were four security guards and two domestic workers at the house. Krejcir said his mother could not look after his son, as she spoke only Czech and the child spoke English. She had also recently had a heart attack, he said. The court was not impressed and Krejcir was denied bail for the third time.[21]

It seemed the arrest of Katerina and Denis had been done as a precaution in case Krejcir was granted bail and they took the opportunity to flee the country *en famille*. When Krejcir was denied bail, his wife and son were released on a warning and the case against them quickly fizzled away.

If Krejcir's arrest had not been ample enough indication of their intent, the arrest of his wife and son at that precise moment revealed just how serious the police were about keeping him behind bars. They meant business. The Krejcirs now realised they were in real trouble.

The court drama didn't end that day, however. On 5 May 2014 Paul O'Sullivan made an appearance. Brendan Roane described in *The Star* how the two arch-rivals greeted each other through gritted teeth and fake smiles.[22] Everyone stopped and stared. What would happen next?

'Hi, Paul O'Sullivan, how are you?' Krejcir asked, locking eyes on the investigator.

'Fine, I've come to see justice,' said O'Sullivan. 'You didn't fix me,' he added, an obvious reference to Krejcir's repeated threats to kill him.

'You must wait,' Krejcir said as he was led down to the cells below. A furious O'Sullivan said it was a threat and he would take it further.[23]

Finally, the nitty gritty of the case got under way, and the trial proper started. Journalists were raring to go, believing it would take a week or two of fascinating testimony and the case would be done. They wanted to know exactly what had happened. Was Krejcir a drug dealer on top of everything else? How was a man kidnapped and tortured? It had been about six months since his arrest and everyone was dying to know more.

Everyone was more than eager to hear what the state's first witness, Peter Msimango, had to say. Msimango had been a part of the group who had kidnapped Lukhele, it seemed, and had turned state witness in exchange for immunity from charges. The self-confessed drug dealer took the stand for five days.

The state's case was that it was a drug deal gone wrong. The man tasked with ensuring the safe delivery of 25 kilograms of crystal meth to Australia, Bhekisizwe Doctor Nkosi, had disappeared into thin air. Krejcir therefore ordered a manhunt for him and when he could not find him he took out his rage on his brother, kidnapping and torturing him by pouring boiling water over him.

The state said that Doctor had been paid R70 000 to ensure the delivery of the drugs; it was not the first bag he had been given to deliver for Krejcir. Doctor had informed Krejcir that the bag had been confiscated by the police.

Brendan Roane reported that Msimango testified that he had gone to Krejcir's business, Moneypoint, where he saw a man facing the wall with a bag over his head and his hands tied.[24] Krejcir ordered that the bag be removed from his head. 'They all took part in asking him where his brother, Doctor, was. He told them he did not know,' Msimango said in court.

According to Msimango, Krejcir said to the victim, 'Look at me ... do you know who I am? Why are you lying about your brother? You want to die like a soldier? Well, that's fine then.' Krejcir then poured boiling water over his head. 'The boy gave out an excruciating scream, stopped and then started shaking.'[25]

Later, they drove Lukhele to a place near Alexandra, assembled a cellphone and made him call his brother. He pleaded with his brother, Msimango said: 'He said, "Doctor, my life is in your hands. Return whatever you owe these people. If I die, this is all in your hands."'[26]

Luphondo then took the cellphone and told Doctor to make it easy for everyone and return the consignment. Doctor promised he would return the drugs the next day. Msimango said the skin on Lukhele's head was now peeling because of the boiling water.

Msimango admitted to the court that he had been brought in to work for Krejcir because he was an expert in crystal meth. He had been promised 2 kilograms of the drug in return for locating Doctor. He expected to make R600 000 after selling the drugs, he said. (A gram of tik has a street value of R300.)

Lukhele was in the stand next. He revealed in graphic detail the horror he had been through. He said that the policemen hired by Krejcir burst into his home brandishing police badges. They bundled him into the back of their car, blindfolded him with his own T-shirt and bound his hands behind his back with cable ties. The policemen who abducted him used his phone to call Doctor.

'They said I must tell him that my life is in his hands. He [Doctor] responded that he will make their lives difficult,' Lukhele said.[27] They tried to call Doctor again but his phone was off.

Lukhele was then taken to an unknown location and forced to sit facing a wall. He was repeatedly asked where Doctor was and when he said he did not know, one of the men poured boiling water from a kettle over him. 'I felt pain. I gave out a scream,' he said.[28] He was also kicked in the mouth and stomach.

When asked by Mashiane if he could identify the man who had poured the boiling water on him, Lukhele locked eyes with Krejcir. He pointed at Krejcir: 'It is the gentleman over there wearing a white suit.'[29]

Under cross-examination by Krejcir's advocate, Van den Heever, Lukhele was asked about the doctor's report of his injuries and when he made his statements. He said that after he had been freed from his ordeal, he went to see a doctor. He did not immediately go to the police because he did not trust them because police had been involved in his kidnapping. When he did speak to the police, months later, they gave him a J88 medical certificate, which they asked him to get the doctor to fill in. Van den Heever said the signature on the certificate had an uncanny similarity to that of the investigating officer.[30]

Van den Heever asked him why he had not opened a case after his kidnapping. Lukhele told the court he had been too weak and confused to tell the police about his kidnapping and torture right away. 'When I was initially taken from my home, my family had already laid a complaint with police,' he said.[31]

Two weeks later, a policewoman came to his home, but he did not describe to her what had happened. 'I had no strength, no power. I was still under a state of confusion,' he said.[32]

Lukhele told the court he would not forget what Krejcir had said to him before the torture began. Krejcir said: 'Look at me. Do you see me?' Then he poured boiling water over his head. 'I turned to look at him. He was on my left-hand side.' Lukhele had been looking down because his captors did not want him to look at them. His hands were tied behind him.

'[Krejcir] poured it over my head little by little,' Lukhele said. 'He would pour the water and then stop and ask me where is my brother. I said I did not know and he would pour the water again.'[33]

He screamed in pain. He was also hit and kicked, he said.

Krejcir's defence team suggested again that it was in fact the investigating officer who had signed the medical report about Lukhele, rather than a doctor. Van den Heever accused Lukhele of either changing his testimony or concocting it with police. However, he stuck to his story, never cracking under the pressure of cross-examination.

The third witness was a Krejcir employee who, like Msimango, had also agreed to work with the state in order to get immunity from prosecution. Paul Mthabela said he had been called by Msimango to help look for Doctor. Mthabela revealed just how close Lukhele was to being murdered during the four days he had been held captive, with the men arguing whether he should be killed or not. He said a man called Mike said they should kill Lukhele. He told the group of kidnappers that the police feared Krejcir.

Mthabela said he did not want Lukhele killed because he believed the police would find and arrest them. 'This is South Africa, this is not Bosnia,' Mthabela told Mike. 'Police officers do their work, they arrest people.'[34]

Miya argued that Lukhele should be killed, Mthabela said. '[In the taxi industry] they kill a person for a taxi for about R20 000 and here you are looking for drugs worth millions? You are just playing games,' Miya told him.[35]

According to Mthabela's testimony, it was Luphondo who convinced everyone not to kill Lukhele. He was vehemently against the murder, the witness revealed. 'This youngster is not the one who took the bag,' Luphondo told the group.[36]

Mthabela said that Msimango had devised a plan to steal some of the drugs if they found the bag, sell them and split the profits. Mthabela's job was to guard Lukhele when Luphondo was not there. He said that after the drugs had gone missing, Luphondo met Doctor and said Krejcir wanted him to undergo a lie detector test to see if police had really confiscated the parcel. If he did, Krejcir would not hurt him.

'Out of desperation, Luphondo said to Doctor: "Look, man, you will get me into trouble. That person will kill me [if I don't get him answers],' said Mthabela.[37] Doctor said to Luphondo that he refused to explain himself to this white person. Mthabela said he was called the day after Lukhele had been snatched to relieve Luphondo of his duties as his guard.

Mthabela said that Luphondo told him how cold-hearted this white person [Krejcir] was, describing him as a criminal. Luphondo told him that boiling water had been poured over Lukhele's head. Mthabela said he could see his injuries. He said Luphondo got pills and ointment to treat Lukhele.

The trial was then suddenly brought to a halt at the beginning of May 2014 by Van den Heever.[38] She had subpoenaed the phone records of the police commissioner, Phiyega, Crime Intelligence boss Chris Ngcobo, Colonel Ximba, Mthabela, Msimango and Paul O'Sullivan. Ximba was also told to produce his vehicle tracking records. Van den Heever was trying to prove that the witnesses knew Ximba: the defence's angle was that they had all collaborated to create the case.

Van den Heever said she could not continue her cross-examination of Mthabela until she had received all the documents. The subpoena served on the investigators required them to produce all documentation linked to their investigation. If the court granted the application, it would mean the police commissioner and police Crime Intelligence officers would have their cellphone data publicly revealed. O'Sullivan's cellphone operator was also subpoenaed to provide all his call and text records from June the year before until February.

O'Sullivan vowed to fight back, saying the defence was just trying to fish for sensitive information from his investigation into Krejcir and that it could put the lives of his sources in danger. In an affidavit, O'Sullivan told the court that since May 2012 he had been assisting the Hawks in their investigation into Krejcir.[39] 'Furthermore, owing to the fact that Krejcir is still attempting to have me murdered, I submit it is lawful for me not to appear in the above honourable court by prior arrangement, unless the State first notifies me and supplies me with armed escorts,' he said.

O'Sullivan said the legal team already had access to some of the phone records and he brought an urgent application to the court to have the records destroyed. He accused the SAPS of failing to act on his investigation's findings for some time, as Krejcir 'had senior police officers, to the rank of general, in his pocket'.[40]

Attorney Piet du Plessis said the phone records were sealed and lodged with the registrar of the High Court, and the defence would not touch them until given the green light.

After weeks of wrangling, Judge Colin Lamont found in favour of the investigators, saying access to the information would infringe on their privacy; the cellphone data was destroyed.

Looking clearly annoyed, Lamont said the application had been a waste of the court's time and Krejcir was ordered to pay the costs of counsel.

This would be a substantial amount. O'Sullivan said he had spent R1.5 million in legal fees; the state's attorneys representing the police would also have to be paid. None of them ever saw the money, however, and they are still out of pocket from the application to this day.

A few days later the case got under way again. The fourth witness, Bhekizitha Khumalo, took the stand. He described how he had been one of the men who helped transport Krejcir's drugs. Khumalo said he had fetched the drugs from Kempton Park and had been paid R10 000 for doing the job. He said there were 25 packets of drugs in total and that Doctor had accompanied him to collect the bag from Luphondo.

Then, it seemed that the man everyone had been searching for had finally been found. Bhekisizwe Doctor Nkosi took the witness stand. He too would testify for the state in order to avoid prosecution for the role he had played in the drug deal. He admitted to the court that he had in fact stolen and sold the consignment of drugs destined to be shipped to Australia. He said he had been picked for the job because he worked for a luggage company at the airport. He said there had been some trial runs to see if the drugs would make it to their final destination. The first two trial runs had failed, and the recipient in Australia did not get the drugs. The third shipment worked and Doctor was paid R70 000 for his role in having it delivered. Even though he

Ian Jordaan (left) and Lolly Jackson out on bail, outside the Johannesburg Magistrate's Court, 1 March 2010.
Mujahid Safodien, *The Star*

Paul O'Sullivan celebrates the arrest of Radovan Krejcir at the Harbour Cafe in Bedfordview, Johannesburg, 25 March 2011.
Cara Viereckl, *The Star*

Krejcir's wife, Katerina, and son Denis, 26 March 2011. De Wet Potgieter, *The Star*

Krejcir's mother, Nadezda Krejcirova, arrives at OR Tambo International Airport, 6 April 2011. Phill Magakoe, *The Star*

Krejcir coming out of the Johannesburg Magistrate's Court after his bail application, 8 April 2011. Sizwe Ndingae, *The Star*

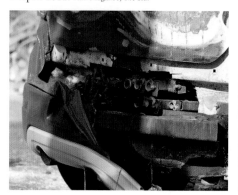

A VW Polo Cross was used to conceal and release several projectiles that lodged in Krejcir's black Mercedes CL66, parked near Eastgate, Johannesburg, 24 July 2013. Timothy Bernard, *The Star*

Ballistics investigators gather evidence at the scene after an attempt is made on Krejcir's life, 24 July 2013. Timothy Bernard, *The Star*

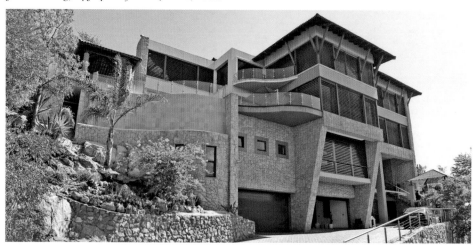

Krejcir's home in Bedfordview, 24 November 2015. Antoine de Ras, *The Star*

LEFT: Krejcir outside the Kempton Park Magistrate's Court, Johannesburg, while fighting attempts by the National Prosecuting Authority to extradite him to the Czech Republic, 21 August 2013. Itumeleng English, *The Star*

RIGHT: Krejcir looks worried during his bail application at the Palm Ridge Magistrate's Court, 11 December 2013. Timothy Bernard, *The Star*

Local and international media gather at the Palm Ridge Magistrate's Court, 25 November 2013. Antoine de Ras, *The Star*

Forensic officers gathering evidence after three suspects were arrested for conspiracy to murder
Paul O'Sullivan in Rivonia, 9 January 2014. Matthews Baloyi, *The Star*

Katerina Krejcirova is arrested at the Palm Ridge Magistrate's Court, 28 February 2014.
Antoine de Ras, *The Star*

LEFT: Krejcir at the Palm Ridge Magistrate's Court, 12 August 2014. Nokuthula Mbatha, *The Star*

RIGHT: George Louca, accused of murdering strip-club boss Lolly Jackson in 2010, leaves the Kempton Park Magistrate's Court after his case is postponed, 8 December 2014. Itumeleng English, *The Star*

Krejcir at the Palm Ridge Magistrate's Court, 18 February 2015.
Chris Collingridge, *The Star*

Diagnosed with cancer, George Louca appears at the Palm Ridge Magistrate's Court in a bid to convince the state that he is too sick to be in jail, 21 April 2015. Nokuthula Mbatha, *The Star*

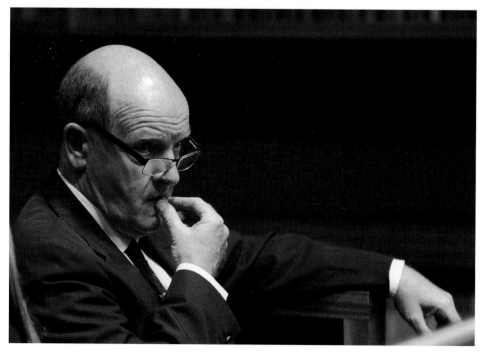

Paul O'Sullivan in the Palm Ridge Magistrate's Court to discuss subpoenas received from Krejcir's lawyer, 16 March 2015. Chris Collingridge, *The Star*

Krejcir's alleged hit man Sakhile Bhengu (on the ground) is arrested when the police detain him in possession of a stolen BMW, 25 June 2015. Motshwari Mofokeng, *The Star*

Krejcir and his co-accused are found guilty of kidnapping, attempted murder and drug dealing at the South Gauteng High Court, 24 August 2015. Nokuthula Mbatha, *The Times*

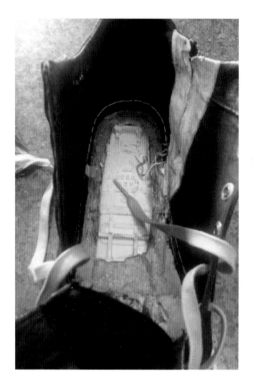

LEFT: A shoe found in Krejcir's possession in jail has a cellphone concealed inside the sole, 26 October 2015. South African Police Service

RIGHT: A frying pan found in Krejcir's possession in jail has several cellphone batteries concealed inside it, 13 November 2015. South African Police Service

A gun found hidden in Krejcir's prison cell in preparation for his escape attempt, 13 November 2015. South African Police Service

was paid another R70 000, Doctor decided to steal the fourth consignment to make a bit more money. So, instead of delivering them, he sold the drugs for R100 000, *The Star* reported.[41]

After these revelations there was a sudden halt in proceedings. Judge Lamont told the court he feared for his safety. Lamont said that during a lunchtime break a knife had been discovered in the presence of Krejcir and his lawyers in a consultation room. The knife was the third security breach he had been told about, the judge said.

Van den Heever said the knife was a harmless mistake: she had brought cake in a container from her birthday celebrations the previous day for her client and was unaware that a bread knife was in the box.

'What would've happened if that knife had been used by somebody? It's a dangerous weapon,' Judge Lamont said.[42] Lamont also said something had happened the day before that made him fear for his personal safety. 'It constitutes a serious attack on me personally or it's an accident, but we don't know which it is.'

Makgale, the police spokesman, later explained that Lamont had been driving home when he heard a loud bang outside of his car, and saw that his windscreen had been cracked. Police were investigating whether someone had shot at his vehicle. Either way, it meant Lamont would be given round-the-clock bodyguards during the trial, like witnesses in protection.

There was another incident: a kettle heating element had been discovered in a parcel given to Krejcir at the court. Lamont said he would tighten security measures for packages from then on. Van den Heever objected to being 'chastised' in an open court and asked for a postponement, so she could defend herself and her client. Lamont refused and she had to continue her cross-examination of Doctor.[43]

Van den Heever began by saying that it would not have been possible for Doctor to circumnavigate security at the airport. Lamont then ordered journalists to stop taking notes and for TV cameras to be switched off, so that Doctor could reveal how he did it. He gave a full explanation to a very interested courtroom. It could be done, it seemed. Airport security could be bypassed.

Seemingly, to prevent the case from proceeding smoothly, the defence introduced more and more applications, delaying proceedings. Three months into the trial, Lamont said that the repeated delays and stalling were becoming 'problematic'. The trial had initially been set for one month.

A trial within a trial had just started, whereby Van den Heever asked the court to rule that Luphondo's confession when he had been arrested was inadmissible because, she claimed, it had been beaten out of him. She failed in her bid, however, and the court ruled that nothing untoward had happened and his evidence was admitted.

Lamont's patience was to be tested further that day.[44] When the court convened after the break for lunch, Miya said he hadn't eaten all day and Krejcir was slumped forward in the dock. Van den Heever told Lamont that Krejcir had not eaten either, and that he was diabetic and was about to faint. The trial was postponed again so that the prisoners could be given food.

Ramuhala, the investigating officer, was next up in the hot seat. He was asked why he did not have an official police diary, why it looked like his signature was on the J88 medical form and why witness statements had some facts that were different from their testimony. Ramuhala responded to the effect that he remembered events perfectly, did not have to write them down and had 37 years' experience as a policeman.

Lamont was not impressed with all of his answers and later chastised the police officer for what he said was shoddy work. He said that Ramuhala was found to have given false testimony and was deemed to have been devious in his conduct during the investigation and arrests.

Van den Heever claimed that Krejcir's arrest was part of an overall conspiracy by top police officers to remove her client from society, as they believed he was a local underworld kingpin.

Meanwhile, Paralympian athlete Oscar Pistorius, who had shot his girlfriend, Reeva Steenkamp, on St Valentine's Day, joined Krejcir at Kgosi Mampuru Prison. The two, alone in their section of the prison, became unlikely friends. Reports emerged that when Pistorius's family came to visit, they always brought a small something, a snack or drink, for Krejcir and a video was later released of the two men playing soccer in a prison courtyard.

But it seems their relationship may not have been that cosy at first. In a letter of complaint, Krejcir wrote that he had asked for a bicycle and a treadmill, so that he could exercise: 'My equipment was offered to Mr Oscar Pistorius ... on his arrival at this facility without my knowledge.' He said he did not object to this and the two started training together. But then the equipment was moved somewhere else.[45] Krejcir said he had been deprived of his ability to train, which he said was a form of mental and emotional torture.

He also complained that his TV was removed, following media reports that he had access to DStv, and that memory devices containing entertainment in his mother tongue, as well as reading material and trial notes, had been taken away.

It was to be the first of many complaints Krejcir made about the way he was being treated by correctional services. It was all part of the conspiracy by the government to bring him down, he believed.

Months of plodding arguments went by. The public lost interest for a while, and even the number of journalists still covering the trial had dwindled to just a few. Their disgruntled faces when entering the court told their own story.

Shain Germaner from *The Star* wrote that the novelty of the trial had long faded for Krejcir too.[46] Even when it was time for closing arguments, he had stopped focusing on his lawyers' passionate speeches in his defence. Instead, he would play on an iPad. Journalists asked him what he was playing. 'Zuma,' he replied with a smirk.

On one occasion, during Mashiane's closing arguments, he said, 'I don't want to hear that crap.' It seemed Krejcir had tired of the endless court arguments, and a cynicism had crept in. His face looked drawn and he was clearly tired of jail and the courts.

It had now been 20 months since his arrest. Germaner recorded Krejcir's words in July 2015: 'It's the neverending story. This is my Rivonia Trial. It's like Mandela,' Krejcir said. He used the opportunity to complain about his health. He said he had had toothache and that he had been forced to use a 'shitload' of painkillers to dull the pain and had to see a dentist. 'They are clearly trying to torture me,' Krejcir said.[47]

In the early court appearances, Krejcir appeared relaxed, sharing jokes with his lawyers and smiling at his elegant wife, who sat in the gallery. Katerina, Denis and Krejcir's mother were often in court, always well-heeled and never revealing their emotions. They were a solid block of support – at least in the beginning of the case.

His son Denis's girlfriend, Marlene Nezar, was the only family member who now still came to court. Krejcir often sat and spoke to her quietly, all signs of his jokes and humour gone. In contrast to the way everyone perceived him, when he spoke to Nezar, Krejcir looked like a doting dad, Germaner wrote.[48]

The rest of his family had by now fled to the Czech Republic and had been barred from entering South Africa again. And, soon, Marlene too was wanted by the police and fled the country to be with Denis. His only tie to his family had gone. Krejcir was now completely alone.

Before the court could rest, Van den Heever put in another application,[49] this time before a Pretoria court. It was to have her client moved to a medical facility. She said Krejcir had been isolated and for two months had not been allowed to interact with other prisoners. His friend Pistorius had been released.

Van den Heever said Krejcir was suffering from depression and a new disease was named: epilepsy. He was also under 24-hour surveillance, which meant he had no privacy, she said.

The lawyer representing the Department of Correctional Services, Marumo Moerane, said Krejcir had been placed in a single cell in a new wing of the prison because he had been in the hospital wing with prisoners with contagious diseases, like tuberculosis. His cell had access to hot water.[50]

The court dismissed the defence's application. Krejcir was to stay where he was.

Finally, after more than 140 days of court proceedings, judgment day, 24 August 2015, had arrived. Both sides were convinced of a victory. But it was the state who won the day.

Radovan Krejcir, Desai Luphondo, Siboniso Miya, and Germiston Hawks officers Samuel Maropeng, Jeff Nthoroane and Jan Mofokeng, were found guilty of kidnapping. Only Nthoroane escaped a charge of attempted murder. Instead, he was found guilty of common assault. Krejcir and Miya were convicted of a third charge: drug possession.

It was the first time in a South African court that Radovan Krejcir had been found guilty of a crime. He could now officially be called a criminal.

Judge Lamont said that any discrepancies in the state witnesses' testimony were due to shoddy work by the investigators and did not indicate any untruths by the witnesses. He said there was no conspiracy against the accused, as Krejcir's defence team had believed. Lamont discounted Luphondo's claims that the men were searching for Nkosi to reclaim money he had borrowed from him and Krejcir's version that even though the torture took place at his business, he was not present.

A shocked Krejcir said 'lies and hate have won over truth and the love'. He told journalists he would appeal the judgment.[51]

The state was ecstatic: it was a huge victory for them and for society at large. NPA spokeswoman Phindi Louw expressed what many were thinking: 'It has been a long journey. It stretched the State's resources, but we are glad we are close to the end,' she said.[52]

Phiyega was joyous. This case had been her one big victory in her time as police commissioner. 'After years of terrorising people and being assisted by criminal officers, Radovan Krejcir has finally been convicted. I wish to thank the investigating team for the hard work. I know that it was a difficult undertaking and a huge risk to their personal safety, but nonetheless they didn't let that deter them,' she said.[53]

The commissioner said the conviction of the three Hawks members was a matter of serious concern. She also hinted that there were more police officers involved in criminality with Krejcir. She said that the conviction should send a message to people from anywhere in the world that South Africa could not be used as a backyard for criminal activities and for fugitives to run to.

'We believe that once his trials are over, Bedfordview and the circles he was moving in will be much safer places for law-abiding people to move, and that the horror stories so often mentioned in the same sentence with his name will be a thing of the past,' said Phiyega.[54]

This case was just one court battle that the state had to fight against the wily Czech criminal. He was about to face an onslaught of charges. The police had been right, though: once Krejcir was arrested all those scared witnesses would begin to talk. Krejcir's house of crime was crumbling around him.

The police investigators couldn't rest just yet, however. Krejcir had a few more tricks up his sleeve.

CHAPTER 18

CONSPIRACY TO MURDER

It was a sunny Thursday, back in January 2014, when Paul O'Sullivan and crime intelligence officer Colonel Nkosana 'Killer' Ximba were meant to die.

The assassins were primed, the woman set to watch the two targets was awaiting instructions and the R5 rifle was stored in the boot of the BMW ready to be used. Their boss, Krejcir, was awaiting word of their deaths from his prison cell, police said.

But Ximba, Colonel Gininda and their colleagues in blue were a step ahead. They had a man on the inside and knew the alleged killers' every move before they made it. This would be no bungled raid. Lessons had been learnt, and these cops had the measure of the men they were about to pounce on. They were too smart, too on the ball and their information was solid. The hunted had become the hunter.

Before any bullets flew, the specialised police task team swooped in and caught three of the would-be killers.

Police spokesman Makgale said officers had been following the accused for days, aware that they intended assassinating O'Sullivan and Ximba at their homes that Thursday morning.

O'Sullivan, who had no idea what was about to go down, told *The Star* he almost shot three police officers after he caught them tailing him.[1] He said he had gone for a walk when he saw three men in a black BMW following him. Feeling that his life was in danger, he drew his pistol and challenged them. 'They said "Please, Paul, don't shoot. We are police and we are here to help you",' O'Sullivan said.

The officers told him they were following him because they were aware he was in danger and that a hit had been taken out on his life. O'Sullivan said the police told him that the planned hit was to take place between 10 am and noon, when he was going to leave his house on the way to a meeting. The men would first target Colonel Ximba and then him.

'They said a Fortuner was going to be the spotter vehicle and they would call men who would wait for me in another car with the R5 rifles and they would plug me,' O'Sullivan said. He was told to leave his cellphone behind, as it was being traced.[2]

A heavily armed police team arrested the first suspect at a Sandton restaurant around noon. The information they gleaned from him led them to a man and a woman at the Road Lodge in Rivonia. Officers uncovered three vehicles: a Nissan van, a silver Toyota Fortuner and a BMW X6. Inside the BMW they found an R5 assault rifle, two 9-millimetre pistols, blue police lights, five balaclavas, gloves, six cellphones and numerous number plates.

Makgale said the two men, aged 32 and 33, and the woman, aged 23, would appear in the Alexandra Magistrate's Court to face charges of conspiracy to commit murder.[3]

This arrest was a massive breakthrough and would uncover other crimes that this gang had allegedly been involved in. It appeared the men were not just ad hoc appointments to Krejcir's team: they were an integral part of what had been happening around him for years and, with their arrest, a number of skeletons were about to fall out of the closet.

O'Sullivan thanked the police for a job well done, but said he was ready for any eventuality. 'I don't believe I am infallible or invincible, but if [the assassins] had tried to shoot me, they would have been the ones taken away in body bags,' he said.[4]

Once again, there was a swarm of media at the Alexandra Magistrate's Court where in fact three men Siboniso Miya, Jacob Nare, Owen Serero and a woman, Zoe Biyela, stood in the dock.[5]

Magistrate Renier Boshoff looked annoyed when he entered the heavily guarded courtroom. Police armed to the teeth with R5 rifles lined the walls.

The accused were charged with conspiracy to commit murder, two counts of robbery of motor vehicles with aggravated circumstances (armed hijacking), two counts of theft of motor vehicles, and two counts of possession of illegal firearms and ammunition.

Miya and Biyela's attorneys told the court their clients had been assaulted while in custody. NPA spokesman Nathi Mncube said the state planned to oppose bail because of the seriousness of the charges. He said police took the security of the case very seriously because it involved a conspiracy to kill a very senior police officer.[6]

Of the accused, it appeared that Serero was a seasoned criminal. With his arrest, the police said they had solved a string of other crimes. He had previously been arrested for armed robbery, but had escaped from custody.

He appeared later in the Johannesburg Magistrate's Court after police had connected him to a string of hijackings. In that court he faced three charges of robbery, two of possession of illegal firearms and ammunition, three of motor-vehicle theft, one of contravening road traffic laws, one of interfering with an investigation and one of escaping from custody. The state believed he would also be connected to other crimes.

He apparently planned to escape again. Prison warders found him in possession of five cellphones and two hacksaws while in custody, when he appeared in the Johannesburg Magistrate's Court, investigating officer Sifiso Xulu told the court.[7]

Prosecutor Penny Pillay asked the court to allow Serero to be moved from Johannesburg Prison to the more secure Kgosi Mampuru Prison in Pretoria. He was a high-risk detainee and a list of family members who he would want to visit him would have to be supplied because they would need to limit the people who could visit him.

Serero pleaded not guilty, but six witnesses testified against him, three of whom identified him as a man who had pointed a firearm at them during a hijacking and robbery. One witness, Frederik Coetzee, said Serero had been wearing the same smart shirt that he had on in the dock when he had hijacked him on 7 November 2012. Serero had allegedly stolen a BMW from Coetzee in the Roodepoort area.[8]

In another incident, in Boksburg in 2013, Serero and two accomplices allegedly held up two people at gunpoint and stole items worth R35 000 from them before speeding off in a BMW.

And Simon Kekana testified that Serero was the man who had pointed a gun at him and hijacked two BMWs he was delivering in January 2014.

The police weren't done. The next arrest was to take in an officer working in the same office as Colonel Ximba. Nandi Nkosi was a sergeant who worked in Crime Intelligence. She allegedly supplied GPS coordinates to the hit men who were going to kill O'Sullivan and Ximba. Nkosi allegedly sent a picture of her boss, Ximba, and downloaded state GPS cellphone tracking technology on the targets. She also gave the men details of Ximba's new car. She was allegedly paid R30 000. When Nkosi was arrested, police confiscated nine cellphones from her.

In the Alexandra Magistrate's Court none of the men tried to get bail. But the two women wanted to get out of custody. Everyone was wondering what Biyela's role had been. She was the youngest person arrested and her Facebook profile, before it was taken down, revealed that she was a student who liked 'romantic comedies'. The state, however, said she was very aware of what she had been involved in. The court was told that she had been spotted attending a meeting where her co-accused allegedly discussed plans to kill O'Sullivan and Ximba, and she was seen exchanging sports bags with the other accused.

Biyela claimed she knew nothing of the assassination plot and was just at the wrong place at the wrong time.[9] Biyela and Serero were a couple; they were arrested together at the Road Lodge. Her attorney, Titswa Modise, claimed that Biyela had arrived in Joburg from KwaZulu-Natal the day before and had been picked up by Serero in the BMW. He had allegedly invited her to the hotel for the weekend, claiming he was moving house.

The state, however, said Biyela had been seen driving the BMW containing the rifle on the day of the arrests. Modise denied this and said that at no point had she been driving the car.[10]

The court also heard that Ximba had overheard Nkosi on the phone discussing the plot with Serero. State prosecutor Lawrence Gcaba said that
Nkosi had sent photos of Ximba and O'Sullivan to the other accused, and
that SMSes exchanged between the accused allegedly showed that Nkosi
wanted her boss to be 'removed' earlier.[11]

Magistrate Deon Schnetler denied the two women bail, saying they had
failed to prove that their release would be in the interests of justice. Gcaba
described Nkosi as dangerous in terms of her skills because she knew the
witnesses and had the means to track them down. She had been suspended
from her job in the Crime Intelligence Division.

Schnetler said it was clear that Biyela's claims of innocence were false. He
said it was possible that the two women might inform those syndicate members who had not been arrested and, worse still, could attempt to perform
the assassination themselves. Biyela, in particular, was a flight risk because
she lacked a permanent address, he said.

Police revealed they had found information on a cellphone discovered in
Krejcir's prison cell, allegedly instructing the hit men to kill O'Sullivan. He
was formally charged and stood in the dock with the other accused.

Police believed that Krejcir had hired Serero to drive the vehicle that was
going to be used for the hit, while Miya and the man they would soon arrest,
Nkanyiso Mafunda, were going to shoot the targets. Jacob Nare, it would
later turn out, had been a police plant in the gang and had been arrested just
to protect his identity.

Siphiwe Memela was the next person to be arrested. Memela had fled
Gauteng and was a fugitive when he was shot in the leg during an armed
robbery in KwaZulu-Natal.[12] 'At the time of the shooting, this suspect was
found in possession of a vehicle reported stolen from Bayview in Chatsworth,
just outside Durban,' said Makgale.

Memela limped into court looking upset as he struggled to manoeuvre
his crutches in the narrow dock. Writing in *The Star*, Germaner said that he
almost fell over and Magistrate Boshoff told him to keep his balance.[13] The
magistrate warned Memela that the conspiracy charges carried a minimum
of 15 years' jail time.

Weeks later, police revealed another assassination plot when they arrested Krejcir's accountant, Lubomir 'Mike' Grigorov. Police believed he was in charge of paying alleged hit men. They arrested Grigorov at Benoni Police Station when he appeared as part of his bail conditions over a separate matter he had been arrested for. The Bulgarian was out on R5 000 and R25 000 bail on two charges of fraud not linked to the Krejcir probe.

According to *The Star*, Grigorov allegedly arranged for two hit men to fly from the Czech Republic to kill O'Sullivan.[14] 'He sat at a coffee shop and was heard talking to someone in English, arranging the hitmen who were going to kill me to get weapons and the phones,' O'Sullivan claimed. 'There was someone undercover at the coffee shop who managed to position himself next to him and overheard all of his conversation. After that, we started watching him.'

O'Sullivan said that Krejcir was 'a walking evil': 'He is planning the hits while behind bars.'[15]

And it wasn't the last allegation of attempted hits either. In May 2016 Krejcir and a new friend he had made while in jail, police impersonator William 'King of Bling' Mbatha, allegedly planned to have five people murdered, starting with O'Sullivan.

The suspected plot was uncovered after middlemen went shopping for the hit man. Mbatha, who received a jail sentence of 113 years for a spate of house robberies, while dressed as a police officer, allegedly helped Krejcir to plan the hits. He and Krejcir were incarcerated at Zonderwater Prison together at the time.

The Star revealed that an undercover agent was contacted by a middleman who wanted him to carry out the killings.[16] The agent posed as a hit man and met the man in Pretoria, where he was shown photographs of O'Sullivan. While the fee of R200 000 was discussed between the two men, a cigarette packet was handed over with O'Sullivan's location scribbled on it. O'Sullivan was warned of the plot and contacted the police.

There were four more who needed to be killed, the middleman revealed, unknowingly, to the police. The price for the hits had increased to R250 000 each. Investigators were also told another team had been put on the job, and whoever carried out the hit first would get the money.[17]

Police confronted Krejcir with the fact that he was going to be charged (for a third time) for conspiring to have O'Sullivan murdered. Krejcir's new lawyer, defence attorney Cliff Alexander, was quick to dismiss the allegations, saying it would have been impossible for the Czech to make such a plan, as he had no contact with other prisoners. 'The allegation is that he approached an inmate at Zonderwater [to arrange the hit], but this would be impossible, as he is kept in isolation. Radovan Krejcir emphatically denies this,' said Alexander.[18]

In between all the alleged attempts on O'Sullivan's life, Krejcir, along with Miya, Nkosi and Mafunda, was also charged with the murder of a man the public had never heard of before: Phumlani Ncube.

The murder case was linked to the conspiracy-to-murder charges. Solly Maphumulo revealed in *The Star* that Ncube had been an employee of Krejcir.[19] Ncube's family believed he was a debt collector. A state witness later claimed, however, that he had been Krejcir's hit man but had started talking to police and was discovered to be an informer.

Ncube's brothers told Maphumulo that Ncube had planned to take his son for lunch on the day he was murdered. Instead of spending the day with his child, the Zimbabwean man was kidnapped and shot to death. His bullet-riddled body was found dumped in a field outside a farm in Heidelberg in July 2013. Miya allegedly took over the role of hit man after Ncube's death.

Investigators said Krejcir had sent Ncube to Sandton to sell krugerrands for him: 'Instead of delivering the R50 000 he got for the Kruger Rands, Ncube did not go back to give Krejcir the money, as agreed. Krejcir instructed his people to hunt him down and kill him. As he approached Louis Botha Avenue in Hillbrow, he was stopped by a police officer under the pretext that he was under arrest.'[20]

Ncube's car was found abandoned in Pretoria; a message had been sent from his cellphone to one of his friends, informing him he had been arrested. Ncube, who lived in Norwood, was allegedly shot and killed at a house in Joburg before his body was dumped in the veld near a farm.

Maphumulo spoke to Ncube's family outside the Alexandra Magistrate's Court after Krejcir was charged with his murder: 'He wanted to take his kid to lunch; instead we received this news,' said a relative. 'Every day the wound is opened, it's painful.'[21]

The arrests of the alleged hit men also led to the solving of another crime: one of the firearms, an AK-47 found during one of the arrests, was forensically linked to a high-profile murder.

With this, the men in blue were ready for their next offensive. Krejcir was about to be charged with the murder of Sam Issa.

CHAPTER 19

A WITNESS DROPPED FROM STATE PROTECTION

Jacob Nare was gambling with his life. He knew it, but he had no choice: it was either talk to the cops or die in a shoot-out when the police come knocking.

He had to act. So he contacted Colonel Bongani Gininda. He prayed he had made the right choice, that this cop was clean. That he wasn't one of the many in Krejcir's pay.[1]

He had no way of knowing. So, every day after he met Gininda, he waited for the call to come revealing that he had sold out his best friend. He listened every time he heard his friend's phone ring. Was this the call that would finally end it all? Would his duplicity be revealed? Would he die that day?

He listened to everything the men living in his flat said – the gang that worked for Krejcir, who were in the bedroom next to his. They were armed to the teeth, AK-47s at the ready in case the police showed up. They were determined they would not be arrested. Rather die in a shoot-out.[2]

At night Jacob Nare could not close his eyes. He could not sleep. His mind spun with what would happen. Would he die that night?

Jacob Nare is not his real name, but it is the name you will see printed in newspapers as one of the members of the gang arrested for planning to kill Paul O'Sullivan and Colonel Nkosana Ximba. The fake name was an attempt to keep his identity hidden – because Nare wasn't one of the accused: he was the police's informer, the man who, through his bravery, saved the lives of O'Sullivan and Ximba.

Jacob Nare was the state's number one mole. He didn't set out to be a hero. He was just an ordinary man who made the wrong friends and was forced to make a difficult decision. This is his story, which he revealed both in affidavits[3] and in an interview with me.

It started in 2004 when he first met Siboniso Miya. They were teenagers, firm friends, who saw each other every day. Miya became a businessman, a taxi owner, who was becoming more and more successful. There were hints that he was becoming involved in criminal activity. But things were generally going well for both men, until Miya met a man called Phumlani Ncube in January 2013, about ten months before Krejcir and his co-accused were arrested.

The three men met for lunch. Seated at a table in a busy restaurant in Sandton City, Ncube introduced the whole business of being a hit man to Miya. Ncube said he was looking for a guy who could do a hit on 'some white guy in Bedfordview', to assassinate him.[4]

The man they wanted dead was Krejcir. The man who wanted him dead, a Sandton businessman, was paying very good money – R500 000 for the whole thing. Miya was interested. The money appealed to him.

But instead of following through on the job, Miya and Ncube went to Krejcir and told him they had been hired to kill him. Krejcir then promised them better money to take the hit back. The Sandton businessman was killed.

Nare said that Miya was open about what he was doing, that he bragged about it and would put Krejcir on speaker phone, so that whoever was there could hear their conversations. He said that Miya and Ncube did quite a few jobs for Krejcir, including a project robbing people of krugerrands, which led to a misunderstanding between them. Ncube took some of the krugerrands for himself.

Miya told his friends he wanted to take over Ncube's job. Ncube was No. 1 with Krejcir, and Miya wanted that position. It meant more money, fancier cars and prestige. Miya wanted to become the 'trusted one'. Eventually it happened when he took out Ncube.[5]

Nare said that Phumlani Ncube was killed because Krejcir found out he was talking to Colonel Ximba. He was giving information to crime intelligence. They allegedly found out from a policewoman in crime intelligence, Nandi Nkosi, who gave Krejcir information. Nkosi was later arrested with the rest of the gang.

Miya was already wanted by police at that stage for the kidnapping and torture of Bheki Lukhele. Every time the police set up a search for him, Nkosi would warn Miya about it. 'I found out that Phumlani had been killed when a friend of his called me, asking if I knew where Siboniso was. He told me Siboniso had killed Phumlani the day before.' Nare said he then realised how dangerous his friend was.[6]

Nare also found out about other killings. On one occasion, Miya was calculating how much money Krejcir owed him. He was working from a list that Nare could see and the name Zak was on it. He heard Miya telling fellow gang member Nkanyiso Mafunda that he had sent a coloured guy called Ziggies to kill this guy Zak, but that 'they had not done the job properly as they had not killed him'. Said Nare: 'I heard Mafunda say, "You should have given the job to me, it would have been done properly." I also remember Miya saying to Mafunda that a certain car, a white Ford Focus, had to be parked up and not used, as it had been used in the "Sandhurst job". I took that to mean the car had been used to try and kill Zak, by Ziggies.'[7]

Nare also heard about the plan to kill Sam Issa. The car that was used in the murder, a white Ford Ranger, was one of the cars Miya used regularly. He had parked it at Nare's flat in Sandton when Nkosi tipped off Miya that the police were about to raid his house. Miya asked another friend to drive the Ranger to Nare's place. This friend took a gun from the car and put it in Nare's bedroom. The following day, someone broke into his apartment and stole the gun, along with some household items.

'I opened a case of house robbery and I told the police about the gun. When I told Siboniso about the police report, he almost died. He said if police ever find that gun, they will charge me [Nare] with a murder,' said Nare.[8]

These kind of incidents began to escalate and Nare was becoming increasingly involved in Miya's world of crime.

Miya told Nare that a man would be coming to put a tracker into the Ranger. 'I came down to check on him and I saw the car flashing. I asked the man what the lights were and he told me he had just installed blue lights in the car, in my basement, where anyone could have seen.' Nare said that Miya used the blue lights regularly. 'We passed cops and he flashed the lights to the police,' he said. They would wave at him. 'Siboniso had everything that made him look like police. He got the police appointment cards from Durban, bulletproof vests and bullets from a TRT [Tactical Response Team] officer girlfriend and the blue lights.'[9]

Just before Issa's murder, Nare said that Miya asked him if he could buy two SIM cards for him. He put one in a small machine and one in a Samsung S4. Nare was told the machine was a tracking device that synced the phone. It had been supplied to Krejcir by crime intelligence, Nare said. The tracker was attached to the petrol tank of Issa's car with a magnet. It was used to track Issa.

After Issa was killed, Miya went to Nare's house. 'You could see something had happened. … He said they had just done a job for the boss and he went to sleep.'[10]

At 3 pm Nare heard about Issa's murder on the news. Miya told him they would never find the Ranger. They had parked it at the house of a cop.

Miya and two other men he worked with then moved in with Nare because they were wanted by police. 'I had a two-bedroom apartment and I was accommodating all of them. I would wake up and go to work, leaving them in the house.' The men were taxi bosses and their drivers would arrive to hand them the day's takings. Nare said the security guards at his complex were asking who these guys were because men were continually coming and giving them money. 'I had a problem with that. I told Siboniso that I could not live with his friends.'[11]

They reacted angrily, telling Miya that if Nare wasn't their friend they would give him an AK-47 – meaning they would kill him. 'They came back to the house every day carrying bags with their AK-47s inside. They said they would never be arrested. Those AKs were for the cops. I kept on thinking that I could get caught in the middle of a shoot-out.'[12]

Unsure what to do but increasingly worried that he might be caught in a shoot-out, Nare went to speak to another friend of his to ask for his advice. 'These people were very connected. I couldn't just go to a police station and report it. Krejcir knew the cops. Siboniso would even take certain routes when he drove, simply because he knew that if he was arrested, he knew this was the police station he would be taken to, and Krejcir had people there.'[13]

Nare said they operated in Sandton, Bedfordview or Rosebank because Krejcir had connections there. He was also privy to the plans being made to kill O'Sullivan and Ximba. And he knew that if he did not act, the two men would die.

His friend told him about a police officer whom he knew in Lenasia. He vouched for him and said he did not take bribes. It was Colonel Gininda. Said Nare:

> It took me about three weeks after our first meeting to tell him every-thing. The assassination of Paul and Ximba was coming closer. They were going to use my house as a hide-out after the murder.
>
> That put me under pressure to speak out. I was reporting on people that lived in my house. I knew that at any point, if that information came back to Krejcir, they would kill me like a fly.[14]

Nare said he knew what these men had done, they were not rational, not like normal human beings. 'It was so hard to trust this policeman. After speak-ing to him, I had to go back to those people, sleep in the next bedroom. Every time Siboniso got a phone call from Krejcir, I didn't know if he was telling him what I had done.'[15]

Nare explained how he would be sitting near Miya, hearing about his plans, and how he would then message Gininda at the same time, keeping him informed of every step of the way.

He wrote in an affidavit afterwards that through his friendship with Miya he had managed to penetrate a syndicate around Krejcir and was giving the police information in December 2013 and January 2014. 'To be clear, I never engaged in any criminal conduct myself, but was a "plant" in the syndicate and was regularly feeding back information. It was very dangerous, as the guys in the syndicate were bragging all the time about how many cops were on the payroll of Krejcir.'[16]

Nare said the plan was that Miya and the others were going to kill three people for Krejcir. The first to be killed was a state witness, who was a victim of Krejcir's previous crime of kidnapping, attempted murder and torture, Bheki Lukhele. He had been placed in witness protection.

The next person to be killed was Colonel Ximba and then O'Sullivan. O'Sullivan's coordinates were sent to Miya by police officers. Miya had also received an email from someone, showing exactly where Lukhele could be found. Nare had gone with Miya to an Internet cafe to print the email with Lukhele's address.

'It was by now clear to me that Krejcir had penetrated, with his corruption, every organ of State including the witness protection programme,' Nare said in the affidavit. But the plans went awry after O'Sullivan attended court where Krejcir was applying for bail and provided documents to help the state oppose his bail. When he learnt of this, Krejcir was furious and gave instructions to kill O'Sullivan first and to do so urgently, Nare said.[17]

> On the morning of 9 January 2014, when O'Sullivan was supposed to have been killed, I was with Miya and simultaneously briefing my handler [Gininda] about the operation to murder O'Sullivan. I distinctly recall Miya getting a call from Krejcir, which he put on speaker, and Krejcir complained as to why he had not heard on the radio about O'Sullivan being killed. He was desperate to hear about O'Sullivan's murder. I was shocked as to how he could be phoning and arranging hits, whilst in prison.[18]

Nare was arrested with Miya that day, but he was soon taken by the police and brought to meet senior police management. They wanted to discuss Nare's protection because he had information that would see him being a witness in the conspiracy to murder Colonel Ximba, O'Sullivan, Issa and Ncube, as well as witness to a house robbery and the attempted murder of a Hawks officer in Soweto.

Initially, the police wanted him to go into the witness protection programme. But having seen how Krejcir knew the whereabouts of Bheki Lukhele, even though he was supposed to be in witness protection at the time, Nare flatly refused to go into the programme. 'If Krejcir could succeed in killing me, most of the cases against him would simply collapse,' Nare said. Something more was needed to protect him.

Nare met with Deputy Police Commissioner Lieutenant General Khehla Sithole and Police Commissioner General Riah Phiyega. He told them of his fears. He told Sithole that he did not trust the witness protection programme. Sithole agreed and said that 'it would be better I go outside of South Africa. I went to the UK.'

At first, things ran smoothly but Nare explained that, later, the head of Detective Services, Vinesh Moonoo, cut his living allowance and then, on the pretext that he was coming for a short visit to see his child, brought him back to South Africa in December 2015. Just after landing, Nare was told that he would not be going back to the UK. 'I felt I was being taken out into the open to be killed,' he said.[19]

Colonel Gininda and provincial head of crime detection Major General Norman Taioe took Nare to meet the head of witness protection, Adam Dawood, at an office at OR Tambo Airport on 24 December 2015.

They wanted to convince him that it was safe to stay in the local witness programme. Without their knowing, Nare recorded that meeting.

Dawood said he was there to assure Nare. He boasted about the witness protection programme, saying it was one of the top five in the world. He explained that witnesses are secure, how they are given full medical care and access to counselling, and are put in houses that are fully furnished, with swimming pools and DStv They provide training for witnesses if they want to restart their lives and become self-sufficient in a new place, Dawood assured him.

'This is not Mickey Mouse, this is high level … I understand your fears … and I am not saying this to appease you,' Dawood said. To which Nare replied:

I do not want to go into our local Witness Protection Programme. First it was safety, by safety I mean I have been in a position where I saw one of the people that you are protecting being compromised. And he was actually about to be killed, something just happened there, but his location and everything was given up or it was identified. The address and everything was sent as a form of an email with the drawings of the surroundings and everything ... It was actually given to Krejcir.[20]

Dawood replied that Lukhele's safety had never been compromised and said that Nare would be safe. But Nare was not convinced: 'I've been brought where I was to be dumped ... and forced into a very dangerous situation ... I'm not going to fall asleep if I know that there is somebody who knows where I am sleeping ... it seems too high risk for me.'[21]

Nare refused to enter the programme. Not knowing what to do with him, the police then took Nare to O'Sullivan, who was asked to take him in.

Attorney Darryl Furman sent a letter to General Sithole saying it was essential that Nare was looked after by the state 'given Krejcir's previous propensity to murder witnesses'. Furman pointed out that Nare's evidence was crucial in securing convictions against Krejcir. Because of Nare, the syndicate around Krejcir was completely broken and most of the people were arrested.[22]

'I have to throw myself upon the mercy of Paul O'Sullivan, or find myself on the street, or in the witness protection programme, either of which would be a death sentence,' Nare said in an affidavit in 2016. He could not understand why he was now in this situation when the top police officers in the country had personally promised him protection.[23]

'I asked Sithole and Phiyega two years ago [in 2014], what if I testify and you people just drop me in the street? I would be killed. They promised me it wouldn't happen. They said: "We will protect you until the end."'[24]

But the affidavits were written in February 2016, and times had changed. Phiyega had subsequently been suspended and new police bosses were now in her place – bosses who had never made that promise to Jacob Nare. He would continue to be left out in the cold.

CHAPTER 20

THE FINAL TAKEDOWN: KREJCIR CHARGED WITH SAM ISSA'S MURDER

There was no way Krejcir was getting out of jail any time soon. He was facing two trials in two different courts. Now he was about to have a third charge flung his way. Police had him cornered. But they weren't taking chances.

In February 2015 the state announced that they would be charging Krejcir with the murder of Sam Issa. With the announcement of the charge, police also allowed the public a glimpse into just how much work they had put into the case.

Krejcir, it seemed, hadn't just allegedly been ordering hits left, right and centre. He and his gang of criminals, corrupt cops and fugitives had also been robbing and defrauding people.

The Star revealed that the Krejcir specialised task team had opened more than 100 cases against the Czech.[1] These included more than 20 cases of murder, 15 cases involving drug trafficking, five cases of robbery involving krugerrands, 30 cases of house and business robbery, 15 fraud cases and many hijacking cases.

All of them featured Krejcir as the main suspect. He was well and truly caught. If one charge was dropped, the police would choose others.

Giving us a glimpse into what had really been going on behind closed doors at Moneypoint, investigators told the public that the gold and diamond pawn shop was merely a front to clean money. Krejcir had allegedly taken over the business from someone without their permission and it was used to sell high-value items, krugerrands, firearms and drugs, many of which were stolen during business and house robberies.

Krejcir would allegedly sell someone krugerrands, and then steal them back, investigators explained. For instance, a buyer would buy R10 million worth of the gold coins and on their way home they would either be hijacked or their home would be robbed later that night and all the krugerrands would be stolen.[2]

Sometimes the item sold was drugs and then a hijacking or arrest would happen, allegedly by the Hawks officers who were Krejcir's accomplices in the kidnapping and torture case.

When arrested, the drug seller would be taken to Germiston Police Station and the officers would get the man to confess that he had allegedly sold the drugs to Krejcir. They would then call Krejcir, who would arrive at the station, speak to the officers and then tell the seller that he had organised for his release, but that he had paid the police R2 million to do so.

Krejcir would then tell the victim that he owed him R2 million. So the drugs were gone, the money for them was gone and now the victim had a R2 million debt.

Police explained that one of his fraud cases involved a McLaren sports car, which Krejcir bought from someone in the Western Cape for R3 million. The money was paid into the seller's account, but once the car was delivered, the money disappeared. It was a scam that was becoming relatively common. They had been sent a fake deposit notification, the money had never been in their account.[3]

Another case involved three vehicles: a BMW M5, a Range Rover and a Mercedes-Benz, which Krejcir bought from someone in Benoni for R2.8 million in total, after negotiating hard for a cash discount. The money also disappeared from the account when the vehicles were delivered. Only R800 was left.

The gang members involved were often referred to by nicknames. Krejcir was Baas John. Siboniso Miya was known as Zulu Boy and Siphiwe Memela was Baba ka Jesu, or Jesus' father. They all appeared alongside Krejcir in the Germiston Magistrate's Court for Issa's murder, along with Nkanyiso Mafunda and Krejcir's accountant, Lubomir Grigorov. All of them were co-accused in the conspiracy to murder Colonel Ximba and Paul O'Sullivan.[4]

The police laid out their version of what happened to the Lebanese man that fateful day when 33 bullets flew at his car.

They said that Krejcir owed Issa money – R10 million for a drug consignment that had been delivered but never paid for, and this led to the two men falling out. Issa also allegedly paid Krejcir's bail money of R500 000 when he was arrested by the Hawks in 2012. They confirmed that Issa was an international drug trafficker who was angry that Krejcir had not paid him back the money he owed. 'So Issa planned to kill Baas John,' said an investigator.[5]

The police believed it was Issa who plotted to shoot Krejcir with the car fitted with guns behind the number plate outside of Moneypoint in 2013. Krejcir found out about the plot and acted swiftly. Issa allegedly worked with people from the Western Cape who wanted revenge for the murder of Cyril Beeka.

It was also revealed that the R5 rifle and a 7.65 pistol found at the scene of the conspiracy to murder Paul O'Sullivan and Colonel Ximba had been stolen during house robberies, one in Bedfordview and the other in Roodepoort. When arrested, Mafunda, Miya and Memela were found with an AK-47 and a 9-millimetre pistol. The AK-47 was positively linked to the murder of Issa: both a cartridge found at the murder scene and a projectile found in Issa's body were linked to the firearm. Police said that each hit man had been paid R250 000 for the hit.

Krejcir's attorney, Du Plessis, said his client denied committing any crime, and aside from the cases he was facing in court, everything else was rumours and speculation. 'The police must bring the proof,' Du Plessis said.[6]

In June 2015 the investigating team showed they were still on the ball with the arrest of another alleged hit man, before he could carry out his nefarious deeds. In a sting operation, a man said to be the uncle of Siboniso Miya, Sakhile Bhengu, was arrested at a petrol station on the M2 highway south of Johannesburg. Bhengu was also linked by police to another armed robbery alongside Miya, in which a child was killed.

Graeme Hosken wrote in *The Times* that Bhengu's arrest took place just hours before a series of killings were due to happen.[7] The targets were all witnesses in the Issa trial. Hoskins said the arrest of the 40-year-old man was carried out by members of police Crime Intelligence, the special investigation Krejcir team and members of the SAPS Tactical Response Team. Police spokesman Brigadier Vishnu Naidoo said the suspect had been charged with conspiracy to commit murder. 'This is a massive breakthrough in this particular case because if this conspiracy had not been uncovered in time, not only would we have struggled to secure a successful prosecution [in the Krejcir case] but, more important, many innocent lives would have been lost,' Naidoo said.[8]

Police arrested Bhengu as he sat in his car at the filling station. According to a source, he was under the impression that he was to be met by someone who would give him items to be used in the killings, which were to have begun that day.

In court the police revealed that another suspect in the Issa murder was Krejcir's son Denis.

Few believed he would ever be caught, however, as he had been declared a prohibited person by Home Affairs and denied access to re-enter the country after he left in December 2014. He had moved back to his homeland along with his mother and younger brother.

From the start, the Issa trial was filled with dramatic testimony. Krejcir, taking the stand for the first time in a bail application, used a tryst with his mistress as an alibi. It was an open secret, one that had been reported numerous times in the media, that Krejcir had been dating Marissa Christopher, of *Playboy* magazine fame. Krejcir had put Christopher up in a R15 million mansion in Linksfield, but he had not been paying the R90 000 a month rent. The owner had been too scared to do anything about it, sources told *The Star*.[9]

Shortly after Krejcir's arrest, Christopher had also allegedly had his child, a little girl. (Krejcir allegedly had another mistress, a woman known as MJ, in the Seychelles, who had a son with him.) Krejcir claimed that on the morning of Issa's shooting, he was at Christopher's Linksfield home, and not at his Bedfordview home with his wife and children.

He denied all the charges, admitted he had known Issa but denied ever having borrowed money from him. Krejcir said the R500 000 bail had been paid by his mother in the Czech Republic.

The Star's Shain Germaner wrote that Krejcir told the court he had been threatened by a police officer. He claimed 'Captain Stacey' – not her real name – had said to him: 'Either I must withdraw my bail application, or new cases and charges will be brought against me.'[10] Krejcir said it was a conspiracy.

His lawyer, Annelene van den Heever, said the state had failed to produce any evidence linking Krejcir to Issa's murder during the bail application. But his version was not accepted by the court and, just as in the kidnapping and torture case, bail was denied.

When the case was moved to the Johannesburg High Court for trial, the drama continued.

Krejcir's new lawyer, Cliff Alexander, put in applications to have his restraints in court removed and his prison conditions changed.

Germaner wrote that the case took a turn for the bizarre when Krejcir was asked to bare his midriff during the televised court proceedings and reveal a shock belt attached to him.[11] Krejcir claimed the belt – designed to electrocute and incapacitate detainees if they attempt to escape from custody – was infringing on his constitutional rights.

He had been shackled in court and surrounded by numerous armed tactical police members.

SW van der Merwe, the lawyer representing all the accused except Krejcir, said the restraints were creating a false perception of their guilt because it appeared that they had a desire to escape from custody.

Alexander asked Krejcir to lift his shirt. He said the stun belt had caused Krejcir injury and he was unable to sit comfortably because of it. He asked the court to acknowledge 'marks on the fat roll on his hip'.[12]

Prosecutor Lawrence Gcaba argued that security concerns surrounding the case meant the restraints were necessary. The state won out in the end, and the restraints – sore 'fat roll' and all – remained.

Just when the trial looked like it was set to continue, an explosive affidavit presented to the court ground the case to a temporary halt.[13] Germaner revealed details of the document. It was the testimony of an experienced house robber, Lucky Mokwena, who had worked for Krejcir.[14] Mokwena's affidavit revealed how, for years, Krejcir had been acting with impunity, doing whatever he wanted, but his ideas were becoming more and more out-landish and desperate as time went on.

There was even a crazy plot to kidnap billionaire businessman Patrice Motsepe for a ransom and then to have him murdered. The affidavit also linked Krejcir to convicted drug dealer Glenn Agliotti, the bribery of high-ranking police officials, and the murders of Gemballa and Phumlani Ncube.

Ex-head of the Hawks Major General Shadrack Sibiya, who was named in Mokwena's affidavit as a policeman on Krejcir's payroll, told Germaner through his lawyer, Ian Levitt, that the allegations against him were 'abso-lute nonsense', with no truth to substantiate the claims: 'If the authorities want to investigate it, they must do so,' said Sibiya.[15]

'It seems someone is bringing [Sibiya's] name into this for their own dubi-ous reasons,' said Levitt. Sibiya said each case connected to Krejcir would be opened at police-station level and assigned an investigating officer. He said that, logistically, he could play no role in having a case 'disappear', as Mokwena had claimed. He also noted he was aware that dozens of criminal cases had been opened against Mokwena himself.[16]

Glenn Agliotti also denied the allegations made by Mokwena. 'Mokwena still has serious charges pending against him and I believe he will say any-thing to divert attention away from himself,' said Agliotti through Levitt.[17]

Patrice Motsepe, through his spokesperson, said he had never spoken with or had any business or other dealings with Krejcir, or anyone associ-ated with him.

Mokwena wrote in his nine-page affidavit that he had first been intro-duced to Krejcir in 2009 by his 'friend' Glen Agliotti because Mokwena was selling a watch. Krejcir told Mokwena to bring any stolen jewellery to him, as Krejcir dealt with stolen jewellery at his pawn business, Moneypoint.[18]

Mokwena said he later discovered that a house robbery that he had been asked to do by Agliotti had in fact been a job for Krejcir; he hadn't known that at the time. The robbery was at a house in Norwood where a German person lived (Gemballa). Mokwena had been told to steal any laptop or computer he found at the property. Mokwena said he had been paid R200 000 by Agliotti to carry out the robbery. Krejcir allegedly later told Mokwena that he had paid Agliotti R500 000 to get the job done.

This wasn't the last house robbery he did for Krejcir. Mokwena said that at a meeting with Krejcir, a certain Kabelo and Mike (Grigorov) had asked him to rob someone in Atholl. 'Krejcir said I should go with Nkanyiso Mafunda and Siboniso Miya, nicknamed Zulu, to do the robbery.'[19]

Mokwena said that in 2011 they had gone to a double-storey yellow house, entered it during the morning hours and held everyone at gunpoint while they robbed all the jewellery. 'We found the said man [owner] in the house as well as two elderly people, a guard, a female helper and two children,' Mokwena said.[20]

He said that at that time he was driving a silver BMW 330, which he bought from Thabo and K in Soweto, who did fraudulent car buying for those who wanted luxurious cars for cheap.

Mokwena said the BMW was seized by the police, as it was at Moneypoint when the bombing occurred there.

He said Krejcir asked him about the car and he then set up a meeting between him and Thabo and K. 'The two guys told Krejcir that at the time they were busy with the paperwork to defraud the following vehicles: a white Ford Ranger, a white Range Rover, a white BMW M3 and a blue VW Scirocco [Mike Grigorov was found in possession of this car and charged].'[21] Mokwena said Krejcir gave Thabo and K R20 000 in cash to speed up the paperwork. He paid R50 000 for the Range Rover and R30 000 each for the BMW and the VW, Mokwena said.

But Krejcir's requests went further than robbery and fraud, according to Mokwena. In his affidavit he said that Krejcir told him he wanted to kill Phumlani Ncube because he had found out the Zimbabwean man had robbed Moneypoint and that he was a police informer: 'I was ... at Moneypoint on one of the days when a certain police officer driving a VW Jetta from the Hawks came to inform Krejcir that Phumlani was indeed working with the police.'[22] He said that Krejcir referred to Phumlani as a cockroach and Krejcir told him that he had had him killed. Mokwena said that Krejcir gave Phumlani krugerrands to sell. This was done to draw him closer to him, so that Siboniso, Nkanyiso and Baba ka Jesu could kill him.

Mokwena also revealed in his affidavit that the bomb had gone off in Moneypoint by mistake. The device had been intended for the SARS offices, a desperate attempt to make their case against him go away:

> Somewhere during November 2013 I was at Money Point when Krejcir ordered a bomb from Vatchie of Cape Town. The reason for this was that Krejcir was under investigation by SARS and Desai Luphondo told him that there is a person in SARS who can smuggle the said bomb into the SARS offices in Pretoria, in order to destroy all the documents including the computer servers that were going to be used in the Krejcir investigation by SARS.[23]

Mokwena said he was driving towards Moneypoint as the bomb went off.

He also revealed just how desperate and outlandish Krejcir's criminal antics had become with the plans to kidnap Motsepe: 'Before Ronny [Bvuma] died in the bombing I was in Money Point when Krejcir told Ronny to arrange some business contact with Motsepe regarding some mining projects in Lesotho. The whole intention was to bring him closer to us so that he could be kidnapped and forced to transfer money from his accounts to fraudulently opened accounts and then be killed.'[24]

Mokwena said he was asked to do surveillance on Motsepe's house and he spent one night outside counting all the cameras, and noting the security systems and how many security personnel there were guarding the inside yard. He said he was told that there was a police officer on Krejcir's payroll who would track Motsepe's cellphone. The plan was that, after the murder, Krejcir and his gang would run away to Turkey, as it would be too 'hot' for them in South Africa.

Mokwena had also been witness to plans to kill O'Sullivan and Ximba. He said he had heard Krejcir ordering Miya, Mafunda and another unknown man to go and kill O'Sullivan. He said when the men returned they said they had not been able to access the place where O'Sullivan was meant to be, 'but that they managed to kill someone else'.

It was September 2013 when Krejcir asked him to enter Sam Issa's home, rob him of all his jewellery and cocaine, and then kill him, according to Mokwena. Krejcir told Mokwena that Issa had robbed him and that the assassination attempt using the remote-controlled gun mounted on the VW Polo had been arranged by Issa.

Mokwena said he was not willing to kill anyone, but that he would burgle Issa's property. He entered Issa's estate, next to the Bedfordview Life Hospital, and damaged two of Issa's vehicle tyres as confirmation of his presence there. 'After Krejcir saw this he was very happy and pushed me to do the robbery and kidnapping.'[25]

Mokwena entered Issa's home during the night and found him asleep in his bed. He woke him up at gunpoint and then tied him up. He and a friend from Mamelodi then ransacked the house and stole 20 watches, 2 kilograms of cocaine, R600 000 cash, a box of cigars and a Glock pistol with a silencer. He gave all the items, except the cash and cigars, to Krejcir.

'We drove out of the complex with Issa and dropped him off next to the N3 highway. We left him inside his car.'[26]

He said that Zulu (Miya), Nkanyiso (Mafunda) and Baba ka Jesu (Memela) were told in his presence to kill Issa.

'I do know that my friend Glen Agliotti was present at Money Point the night before Sam Issa's death and he also knows that Radovan ordered the killing of Sam Issa. This is because Krejcir was bragging and telling the people that he trusted that he "killed the cockroach". He did this so that people in the underworld would fear him,' said Mokwena.[27]

And the scheming did not stop after Krejcir was arrested, according to the witness. Mokwena said that he was smuggling cellphones to Krejcir in prison in Pretoria through corrupt prison officials.

'At that stage Krejcir told me that when he comes out on bail he is going to kill everyone who betrayed him and bring a reign of terror to his enemies. He said that it will be a clean up campaign.'[28]

Mokwena said Krejcir had told him that he wanted to rule the whole of South Africa by having all the high-ranking officials in his pocket, and those he couldn't control he would kill.

After Mokwena's affidavit was revealed in court, he started receiving death threats. Prosecutor Lawrence Gcaba asked the court to warn Miya that he must not interfere with witnesses linked to the case, and it was disturbing that he had tried indirectly to contact Mokwena.

Fearing for his life was a reality that Mokwena knew he would face when he started talking to the police, but he knew he stood a better chance of staying alive if he was protected by the state. He had been living with the fear of death for months, his affidavit revealed.

Mokwena said that, even after Krejcir had been arrested, he continually called Mokwena asking him not to reveal everything he knew to the police. He threatened him with death if he crossed him.

'I have made peace with that because I know he will want to kill me, whether I talk or not.'[29]

After Mokwena's affidavit was produced in court, there were a number of postponements. One of the major reasons for the delays was that Krejcir lost another lawyer because of non-payment. Towards the end of 2016 the case repeatedly stopped and started, and there was every indication that it was going to take months before it was concluded.

CHAPTER 21

KREJCIR TRIES TO ESCAPE

Krejcir had just been found guilty of kidnapping, drug dealing and attempted murder and, with new cases stacked up against him, things weren't looking good. His hot-shot legal team weren't getting him off the hook like they had in the past: the police had piled up too much evidence against him.

It was time for another plan, one that needed time to execute. But time was something Krejcir had lots of, locked up in his cell at Zonderwater Prison.

One of the only people who still came to visit him, before she left South Africa, was his son's girlfriend, Marlene Nezar. She had been living alone in his mansion. She and Marissa Christopher were frequent names on the prison's visitors' register.

Nezar, 22 at the time, had earlier in 2015 brought an urgent application against the Minister of Home Affairs before the High Court in Pretoria. Zelda Venter wrote in the *Pretoria News* that Nezar described herself as Denis Krejcir's life partner. She wanted an order permitting Denis to return to South Africa.[1] He had been either deported, expelled or excluded from South Africa in December 2014, as he, his mother and Nezar were due to leave for a holiday abroad, the court was told.

Nezar, a South African citizen, said she had been living with Denis for two years at his parental home in Bedfordview and they intended to get married soon. According to Nezar, an immigration officer at OR Tambo Airport informed Denis that he had been classified as a 'prohibited person' in terms of the Immigration Act. He was told he had to leave South Africa and was not permitted to return. An immigration officer said Denis's permanent residence permit was fraudulent.

Nezar said they had not been given any explanation for this decision. 'Since leaving in December, Denis has been forced to remain in the Czech Republic,' Nezar said. This infringed on their rights, she claimed, as they were unable to see each other or live together. 'Denis does not have a home in the Czech Republic ... or anywhere other than with me in South Africa.'[2]

Nezar said she was not employed, but that she did help Denis's mother to run the household and to look after his five-year-old brother, Damian. His grandmother gave them an allowance to cover their living expenses.

She said her relationship with Denis was serious and that they had 'experienced more stress and personal tests than many other couples experience in a lifetime'. The couple had wanted to get married in Las Vegas, but given the 'difficult circumstances of Denis's family' had decided to postpone their marriage plans 'until a better time in the future'.[3]

However, according to the police, Nezar wasn't languishing in the Bedfordview mansion, feeling depressed about her challenging circumstances. She had been very busy: inside the 'care packs' that she brought when she visited her future father-in-law in prison was more than just food, it seemed. Somehow – but nobody is sure how – the police believe she smuggled in phones and numerous other items to help Krejcir escape. Police believed that, between her and Christopher and other visitors, a gun and ammunition were sneaked into Krejcir's cell. Nezar subsequently fled the country at the end of 2015 to join Denis.[4]

Krejcir hid the pistol, along with several rounds of ammunition, inside his exercise bike. He also found other little hiding places inside his electric frying pan and kettle, for a stun gun, a pepper-spray gun, a screwdriver, a knife, ten cellphones, SIM cards and memory sticks. He was also in possession of a Correctional Services officer's uniform. Krejcir was getting ready to bust out of prison.

But what he didn't know is that intelligence officers were listening in on his calls. The police were one step ahead of Baas John.

On the morning of his planned dramatic escape on 26 September 2015, Correctional Services warders entered his cell and turned it inside out.

'A number of illegal items were discovered in different cells during the search operation,' said Correctional Services Deputy Commissioner of Communications Manelisi Wolela. 'Preliminary investigations reveal three inmates were involved.'[5]

Solly Maphumulo, writing in *The Sunday Independent*, said there was a screwdriver, steel blades, a memory stick and a diary containing the names of witnesses and investigators involved in all Krejcir's criminal cases.[6]

Police spokesman Solomon Makgale said that Krejcir was also found in possession of a detailed sketched plan of the prison building. Makgale revealed that there were two women involved in the escape plot, one of whom was a prison warder. 'The threat is in prison. There are inmates and prison officials that are helping him. There is absolutely no way prison warders would not have been involved,' Makgale said.[7]

Maphumulo revealed that a staggering R246 million had been made available to ensure his smooth escape and that three prison warders were paid R1.5 million each to help expedite the prison break. Some of the huge budget had been allocated to hire a helicopter to spirit Krejcir away once he had escaped and to pay for the landing rights for a chartered plane to fly him out of the country.

Maphumulo wrote that cops were also involved in the plan to spring him from jail.[8] Krejcir's notes detailing his escape plans revealed that he wanted to be escorted by a certain female officer to see a doctor. He then intended to overpower her and escape, after which he would be transported in a Mercedes-Benz across the border into Swaziland, where he planned to stay at the Royal Swazi Sun in Ezulwini. It was unclear how long he planned to remain there. He would then cross into Mozambique, from where he planned to be whisked away in a chartered plane to Argentina.

'Once he's in Argentina, he's a free man,' a source told Maphumulo.[9]

National police spokesman Vishnu Naidoo said a case of possession of an unlicensed firearm and ammunition, as well as conspiracy to escape from prison, had been opened.

When the escape plan was uncovered, Krejcir was transferred to an underground isolation cell after it had been established that a helicopter was going to be used in the daring raid to free him.[10]

The *Sunday World* revealed that fellow prisoner William Mbatha, who was linked to one of the conspiracy-to-murder plans, had allegedly been involved in Krejcir's escape plot.

The paper said that the Department of Correctional Services was probing allegations that Mbatha had drawn up a plan that included the layout of and escape routes around Zonderwater Prison, where both men were imprisoned.[11]

A prisoner allegedly told authorities that Krejcir had asked to be taken to Mbatha's cell because he wanted to consult Mbatha on how to interdict the department from transferring him to another correctional centre. 'When there, Krejcir asked Mbatha ... to help him draw a plan [of] the surrounding environment of the prison as he wanted to escape and he obliged,' said a prison official.[12]

At least four prisoners were involved. A prisoner who was supposed to escape with them allegedly leaked the plan to the authorities, as he believed Krejcir would kill them while they were escaping custody. The official said that the prisoner who had revealed the escape plan 'expressed his concerns after Krejcir told them he was going to wear a warder uniform while they should remain in their prison uniform when they escape[d]. He said he suspected Krejcir was going to use them as human shields.'[13]

Another alarm bell for the prisoner was the fact Krejcir planned to use a helicopter to escape, which could accommodate only a small number of people. He believed the helicopter would not carry all five of them in total.

Krejcir's lawyer, Van den Heever, said her client had never tried to escape and she declined to comment further.

In court for conspiracy to murder O'Sullivan and Colonel Ximba, Krejcir said the raid on his cell had been part of a plot. It was a conspiracy against him, he told *The Star*.[14]

The size of the police team watching Krejcir was then doubled.

It turned out this was not the only escape attempt Krejcir had planned. Makgale said some of the plots involved a dramatic escape from court. There were bomb sweeps done after that, so one can only assume the escape involved a bomb being detonated.

'He realises the court proceedings have come to a certain point, and he believes his only option is to escape,' said Makgale.[15]

A few weeks later, an estate agent from Bedfordview, Amanda Papaotois, was arrested while visiting Krejcir. Makgale said the 45-year-old woman had gone to Zonderwater Prison to visit Krejcir in 2015, supposedly to discuss the sale of his property in Bedfordview. The property had already been attached as part of Krejcir's SARS preservation order and was about to go on auction. 'She alleges that someone gave her food and Krejcir's old running shoes to give to Krejcir. However, inside the sole of the shoes, a cellphone was hidden,' he said.[16]

Police said that while Papaotois was walking to Krejcir's cell, the iPhone inside the trainer rang, alerting the prison authorities to its presence. Prison warders answered and on the other end was Krejcir's son, Denis, calling from Poland.

The woman was charged with defeating the ends of justice and she was given bail of R3 000 in the Cullinan Magistrate's Court the next day. It is believed she had been in touch with Krejcir's family and had been asked to take him the shoes.

The police clearly needed to tighten security around their prisoner – and ensure he stayed behind bars. Krejcir became the first-ever prisoner to be sent to the country's most secure prison, C-Max, before even being sentenced.[17] He spent Christmas and New Year in the high-security facility in Kokstad, KwaZulu-Natal.

This 1 400-inmate institution is home to South Africa's most hardened criminals, in particular escape artists, such as the notorious Annanias Mathe, who memorably escaped from the 'inescapable' Pretoria C-Max after smearing himself with petroleum jelly to help him squeeze between the prison bars. The super-maximum prison is also home to Sibusiso 'Tilili' Mzimela, who had escaped from prison nine times. He was sentenced to 89 years in jail in 2011.

C-Max is run off an integrated system that includes pneumatic sliding doors, an electrified security fence with detection alarm systems and CCTV cameras throughout. Access control is a combination of digital and bio-metric. There is a special national panel convened to decide which convicts should be sent there.

Sources told *The Star* that members of the SAPS elite task force escorted Krejcir to the prison in an armed convoy, monitored overhead by a police helicopter: 'Krejcir intended to escape during the festive season. Kokstad was the last resort. Security around him had to be beefed up to ensure he did not get the slightest chance to escape. That is why he was moved to that prison because he cannot escape from there.'[18]

In February 2016 police uncovered another Krejcir plot. This time, he alleg-edly planned to have the High Court judge who had convicted him murdered, as well as the investigation team and his nemesis, forensic investigator Paul O'Sullivan.

Judge Colin Lamont had found Krejcir guilty of kidnapping, attempted murder and attempted possession of drugs. Krejcir had apparently hired a European hit man to come to the country to finish him off, wrote Maphumulo.[19] Officials allegedly stopped the hit man from visiting Krejcir at Kokstad C-Max, where a plan to execute the hit was going to be hatched. The alleged hitman, who had pretended to be Krejcir's brother, was accom-panied by a police officer to visit him in prison. Krejcir was an only child – he had no brother – so alarm bells went off.

Krejcir could not be kept in the maximum-security prison indefinitely, how-ever. He had to be moved back to Zonderwater, in Pretoria, early in 2016, so that he would be closer to the Johannesburg High Court for the sentencing in his kidnapping case and for the start of the Sam Issa murder trial.

His plans to escape escalated but, once again, the police were one step ahead. In April 2016 Correctional Services official Solly Metlae and a pris-oner, Sandile Mdumbe, appeared in the Kempton Park Magistrate's Court for aiding Krejcir with yet another escape plot from Zonderwater Prison.

They were charged, along with Krejcir, with corruption, conspiracy to commit an offence and defeating the ends of justice. Metlae was guarding Krejcir when he tried to aid his escape, the state alleged.

Germaner wrote in *The Star* that Mdumbe was in tears telling his family in the public gallery that he didn't know who Krejcir was, or the warder. An unsympathetic officer told Mdumbe he should rather tell that to his lawyer.[20] At their next court appearance, police told the court they had video footage allegedly catching the accused in the act.

Colonel Gininda took the stand and said that Denis Krejcir was also implicated in the scheme to bust his father out of prison. Gininda said that Denis had been in phone contact with undercover officers and had offered to pay them millions of rands to help with the escape plot.

Gininda revealed just how ambitious this escape attempt was; he said it would have been a 'full-on war' against Zonderwater Prison, with plans for about ten assault-rifle-wielding thugs to storm the jail and free Krejcir, Germaner wrote.[21]

Krejcir then allegedly planned to be transported to a safe house in Mamelodi. He was allegedly willing to pay about R30 million for a series of 'strategic executions' in the area, which would have allowed him to escape undetected while the police services were distracted, mobilised to attend to the flurry of murders. Gininda was testifying in order for Mdumbe's bail to be denied. He said that the plan was that Mdumbe would be in charge of the safe house.

Gininda revealed that on 31 March 2016, a group of nine or ten men armed with R4 rifles were expected to arrive at Zonderwater Prison, where the Czech was being held. Having allegedly been briefed by Metlae on the weaknesses in the prison's security system, including who was on duty and the number of officers they would need to evade and/or kill, the group were expected to extract Krejcir from his cell, Germaner wrote.

According to Gininda's testimony, Krejcir would be taken from the prison to the nearby Pick n Pay in Cullinan, where he would meet with Mdumbe and be taken to the safe house. From there, an associate of Krejcir was expected to arrive with R5 million to distribute among the group to pay for their assistance and subsequent silence. According to Gininda, after the cash was handed out, the group would then conduct 'strategic executions' of residents in the area, to ensure that police were too busy to notice that Krejcir was being removed from the area.

The plot was uncovered, however, because nine of the hired guns were in fact undercover Cape Town Special Task Force police members. Gininda told the court that some of the members were trusted enough to be brought in to assist in the escape plot, and it was one of these agents who made audio and video recordings of his interactions with Mdumbe when they met a few days before the planned escape.[22]

Mdumbe allegedly told this undercover officer about how the money would be divided and the plan to meet Krejcir and his group at the Pick n Pay, and he gave out his cellphone number freely.

Police then planned their own takedown operation, and arrested Mdumbe and Metlae on the morning the escape was due to take place.

Mdumbe had a long history of armed robbery, the court heard, and the police discovered after his arrest in the Krejcir plot that he may have escaped custody from a case in Newcastle, KwaZulu-Natal, and helped another suspect to escape from custody years before.

Weeks later there were two more arrests linked to the case. Zonderwater Prison warder Marthinus Johannes Herbst and Krejcir's former mistress were also charged with taking part in the escape attempt.[23] Christopher was arrested when she went to visit Krejcir at Zonderwater Prison with their now two-year-old daughter. Police had been looking for her for three months, but after she had been booted out of her R90 000-a-month mansion in Linksfield for not paying the rent, the police did not know where she was staying.

They arrested her as soon as she arrived at the prison, removing the child, who was handed over to her grandmother. The police believed Christopher had sold a luxury Mercedes-Benz, bought for her by Krejcir before he was arrested in late 2013. O'Sullivan said cash from the sale of the car was used to pay certain known individuals to help Krejcir in his escape bid. 'It is also believed that she helped with plans to arrange a helicopter,' O'Sullivan said. 'Krejcir's "playmate" could become his cellmate,' remarked O'Sullivan.[24]

Christopher was charged with defeating the administration of justice, conspiring to allow a prisoner to escape from custody, and corruption. In the bail application, which was denied, Christopher told the court she had broken up with Krejcir months before, had no money and was dependent on her family for her survival.

On the stand, Germaner reported, Christopher revealed more of her relationship with Krejcir. They had started dating in 2010 and she gave birth to his child in 2014, several months after his initial 2013 arrest.[25] While she had continued to visit him during his incarceration, she was detained at the prison in 2015 for questioning by the SAPS.

The lead investigator had informed her that her brother's ex-girlfriend had also been having a sexual relationship with Krejcir and may have been helping smuggle contraband into the prison. After this revelation, her relationship with the Czech deteriorated. They broke up around April 2016, Christopher said.

However, prosecutor Lawrence Gcaba was unconvinced that Christopher no longer had feelings for Krejcir, arguing that she would probably do anything to help him escape. He said the reason for their supposed break-up was to allow herself to publicly distance herself from him and the escape plot, which was planned at around the same time. Christopher admitted that she had taken phone calls from Krejcir over the previous few weeks but denied any involvement in the plot. The court was not convinced. Her multiple passports led to the decision to keep her in jail.[26]

Outstanding warrants of arrest were also out for Krejcir's son Denis, his wife, his mother and his son's girlfriend, who is believed to have married Denis to avoid being deported from the Czech Republic as an overstaying visitor, O'Sullivan said.[27]

Krejcir, and all those close to him, had now been well and truly cornered by the police. There were no jokes at his next court appearances. He would sit in the dock hunched over, in his now tired-looking black leather jacket. He had lost an enormous amount of weight, had a bad cough and there were no more cold, menacing stares across the courtroom. He looked like a man lost. You couldn't help but look at him now and wonder, had he lost hope? Was Krejcir's scheming at an end?

Perhaps not yet. There were probably still one or two more plans tucked up his sleeve.

CHAPTER 22

KREJCIR'S LUCK RUNS OUT

Things were not looking good for the man who had always seemed to be able to overcome anything.

None of the alleged murder plans for O'Sullivan and Ximba had worked out. He kept on hiring undercover police officers. None of his attempted escapes from prison had worked. His partners in crime kept on running to Correctional Services officials to tell them what he was up to.

None of his court cases were panning out either. He had been found guilty of kidnapping and attempting to murder Bheki Lukhele, and he had numerous other trials still to face.

His fight to get access to his money had not worked out for him either. The SARS preservation order had strangled all of his funds, and his business associates had melted away. Without money or connections, Krejcir didn't stand a chance. He could very easily become just another number on an orange prison uniform. There was no doubt: Krejcir had been backed into a corner.

In 2014 he had tried to change the public's perception of him. Before then he had never seemed to mind being portrayed as a mafia boss. That people feared him probably helped him in all his alleged criminal endeavours. You are less likely to argue or run to the police when the person who has just defrauded you of a vehicle or walked out of a restaurant without paying a bill of hundreds of thousands of rands after an all-night party is Radovan Krejcir.

His quips to the media every time he gave an interview showed not only an intelligent sense of humour, but also a man who believed he was invincible.

But, now, that bad-boy image wasn't doing him any favours any more. He needed to try to convince the world that there really was a grand conspiracy against him. He was a victim, a man who was ill, and he was suffering terribly at the hands of senior state agents who were out to get him.

He created a Facebook account: Radovan Krejcir – Official, and numerous Twitter handles suddenly emerged defending his name, attacking police and sending a string of abuse towards Paul O'Sullivan.

One of the first things he did in his new foray into social media was post a letter online that he had sent to the chairperson of the Portfolio on Correctional Services, the Commission on Gender Equality, the Human Rights Commission, the Public Protector and Amnesty International, among others.[1]

In it, he complained that in prison he was suffering human-rights violations because his TV and exercise equipment had been taken away from him:

> I have exhausted various attempts and methods in solving these matters to no avail, and as a last resort I am now forced to appeal to you in my state of vulnerability.
>
> I have now been housed in this facility for a period exceeding more than 11 months ... proving that I remain a victim of vexatious and [malicious] attacks successfully executed by the notion published in the media.
>
> There were several untrue rumours previously brought to your attention by various unreliable sources to which you remain witness that [these were] just a poor attempt to discredit me and utilise the situation as a marketing strategy for their personal gain ...[2]

He then complained about his exercise bicycle and treadmill, which he had been allowed on condition that he would donate it to the correctional facility when he left. He said that, without his permission, the equipment had been offered to Oscar Pistorius to use and that, subsequently, he had not been able to use it.

He also complained that an article published in the *City Press* that revealed he had access to DStv had led to his television being removed, as well as memory sticks, which contained entertainment in his mother tongue.[3] He complained that he was kept in a single cell and that he was allowed no interaction with other prisoners. 'I experience these actions as a personal attack directed to me and believe this to be an infringement on my human and constitutional rights, not to mention that these actions are unfounded, unfair and psychological and emotional torture.'[4]

On top of it all, his family had been barred from the country. If they returned, they would all be arrested.

Marlene and Denis had also set up Twitter accounts to defend Krejcir's name. In a series of Tweets they claimed that the police were incompetent, that they stole from Krejcir, made up charges against him and tortured him. Public sentiment wasn't swayed, however, and the Tweets stopped.

His dire financial situation also became fodder for the public just in time for sentencing in the Bheki Lukhele trial.

Right near the finishing line, the case suddenly came to a grinding halt. Krejcir's lawyers, Du Plessis and Van den Heever, revealed that they had not been paid by their client and they threatened that, if they did not get their money, Krejcir would have to represent himself during the sentencing procedures and that he would have no lawyer defending him during his upcoming trials.

It emerged that Krejcir had been paying not only for his own legal representation, but also for the lawyers representing all the men in the dock alongside him. Each lawyer stepped down before sentencing could begin.

Du Plessis told Germaner that they would not assign counsel to Krejcir until his financial situation had been resolved and he could place a down payment on their future services for his upcoming trials.[5] Germaner speculated that the bill ran into millions of rands. Krejcir still faced sentencing on the attempted murder conviction, two murder trials, for Sam Issa and Phumlani Ncube, numerous conspiracy-to-murder charges, as well as charges for attempting to escape from prison. If you added up all the hours of preparation, an average trial can cost R60 000 a day. The attempted murder trial went on for more than 140 days, racking up a bill of about R8.4 million. It was not clear how much of this bill had been paid.

A source close to the investigation into Krejcir told *The Star* that Krejcir did have access to large amounts of money through his mother, but had been redirecting the funds from his legal fees towards his numerous escape plans.[6]

The funding problem meant that every time Krejcir came before the court, sentencing was postponed. At the fifth postponement, Judge Colin Lamont had had enough.

The alleged attempts and threats on Lamont's life meant the judge had to have bodyguards. Krejcir's prison-escape attempts meant there were more than 20 Tactical Response Team officers armed with high-calibre rifles at each court appearance, while parts of the street outside the court were cordoned off. It must have cost the state a fortune. Everyone wanted this case to end. But, instead, the new lawyer whom Krejcir was trying to get to represent him, Attorney Nardus Grove, told the court that a woman who had been sent money by Krejcir's mother to pay his legal fees had been arrested by police.[7] Lamont had no choice: he had to postpone again.

Grove brought an application before the High Court to have some of the funds from Krejcir's estate released to pay his legal fees. The court ordered that the curator bonis in charge of his assets, Cloete Murray, pay over R700 000 to Nardus Grove Attorneys. Grove brought the application when money sent by Krejcir's mother to Edenvale resident Pushpaveni Naidoo to pay Krejcir's legal fees was seized by police when they arrested Naidoo. Police subsequently dropped all charges against her.[8]

At the sixth sentencing appearance, Krejcir had to represent himself. The Czech said he had fired his new defence lawyer, Grove, for his alleged failure to request Judge Lamont to recuse himself for alleged bias, unfairness, lack of objectiveness and allegedly being part of a conspiracy against him.

Krejcir stood up and placed application after application before Lamont, who swatted them all down, one after the other. Krejcir asked Lamont for more time to find a new lawyer, for a Czech interpreter, access to a phone in prison, to have his chains removed and for the judge's recusal.

After Lamont turned all these applications down, it finally looked like sentencing was about to go ahead. But, this time, the court had to be evacuated. There was a bomb threat. Prosecutor Louis Mashiane told the court there had been a security breach. Germaner reported in *The Star* that Judge Lamont immediately suspended proceedings, moving quickly out of the courtroom.[9] The bomb threat had been called in to the office of the Gauteng Judge President. Members of the police canine unit arrived, but no bomb was found.

At the next appearance, on 23 February 2016 there were no more excuses. It was finally the day of reckoning.

The Times reported that Lamont, in his judgment, castigated the police. 'The investigation by the police was poor … [they] failed to gather crucial evidence,' Lamont said, adding that it was the compelling testimony of state witness Peter Msimang that had saved the state's case. Lamont said that Msimang, himself a criminal, was a credible witness because he had been in constant contact with Krejcir.[10]

Krejcir's version that there was a conspiracy against him did not hold sway with the judge: 'There is no evidence that suggests that the police incorrectly arrested the accused. The court cannot find any evidence of tampering.'[11]

There was no mercy. Krejcir and his co-accused Desai Luphondo, were sentenced to an effective 35 years in prison. Siboniso Miya and three members of the Germiston Organised Crime Unit, Samuel Maropeng, Jeff Nthoroane and Jan Lefu Mofokeng, were all sentenced to 15 years each. Prosecutor Louis Mashiane said the police officers had betrayed their employer in the same way Judas had betrayed Jesus for his own selfish reason. 'None of them are remorseful and are still denying that they did the crime,' Mashiane said.[12]

Lamont told the court that the severity of Krejcir and the five co-accused's crimes – the kidnapping, attempted murder and attempted drug dealing – required severe punishment.

'Maybe the solution for everybody is if I was killed or commit suicide,' was Krejcir's response. His despondent remark turned into a witticism, however, when a Czech journalist asked him for comment in his mother tongue. 'Only 35 years? I expected more,' Krejcir said, smiling as he descended into the cells beneath the court.[13]

The police were ecstatic. Police Commissioner General Riah Phiyega praised the investigating team. 'The SAPS has, through a dedicated task team of detectives, ably led by Captain Freddy Ramuhala, worked tirelessly to ensure that Krejcir's criminal activities are properly investigated and that those that he is in business with also get to experience the full might of the law,' Phiyega said.[14]

She also raised the issue of corruption within the police, pointing out that the conviction of three Hawks officers was a serious concern. It appeared that good had won out over the rotten apples in the police force. But had all the mould been discovered and removed?

Paul O'Sullivan didn't believe so. Although the investigator was happy that the man he had been pursuing for so many years could finally officially be called a criminal in South Africa, he didn't think the fight against Krejcir was over – not by a long shot.

While police were still celebrating the conviction, O'Sullivan heard about another plan by Krejcir to have him killed. And another, and another. Every few weeks it seemed there was a new plot.

The investigator and the Krejcir task team were nowhere near putting their feet up and resting after so many years of hard toil trying to catch argu-ably the worst mafia boss the country had ever seen.

All of them had risked their lives to ensure justice was pursued, and yet the end was nowhere in sight.

The tide had also turned against O'Sullivan. In his pursuit to seek out the people Krejcir had allegedly corrupted in the police force, as well as the new underworld bosses who had since replaced him, O'Sullivan once again found himself in opposition to senior police officers.

He was arrested at OR Tambo International Airport in April 2016, taken off a plane that was about to depart for London in front of his two small daughters, by a large group of Hawks officers.

He was charged with contravening a section of the Citizenship Act because he had left the country on his Irish passport – something his defence team argued that he had done in an attempt to avoid detection at the height of the attempts on his life by Krejcir. O'Sullivan was the first person in the country to have been charged with this offence.

The Hawks weren't done. During O'Sullivan's trial on the Citizenship Act, they revealed a slew of cases they were pursuing against him.[15] All of them, it seemed, had been opened by people whom O'Sullivan had once investigated. Many had been arrested because of the information O'Sullivan had gathered against them.

While fighting for his own freedom, one would have imagined that O'Sullivan would take his focus off Krejcir. But giving up was not part of the tenacious character of the sleuth. He had another plan under way, one that would hopefully uncover just how deep the rot around Krejcir had gone.

And, just as tenacious, Krejcir also had no intention of giving up. He had by now managed to acquire the services of a new attorney, Cliff Alexander, who immediately cried foul of his conviction and sentencing, saying that Lamont's mistreatment of his client constituted a violation of his human rights because he had been denied access to his client.

In an appeal, Alexander said Krejcir had been given shockingly inappropriate convictions and sentences.[16] Former Wits law professor Dr James Grant was brought into the courtroom to argue Krejcir's case. Advocate Grant said Krejcir had been convicted on a weak state's case. He said Krejcir had been prejudiced throughout his sentencing by not being given access to his lawyers and put under strict time constraints to defend himself. Grant insisted the state had not proved that Krejcir had kidnapped or attempted to murder Lukhele, and that torturing him with boiling water did not amount to attempted murder, as there was no intent to kill.

Grant argued that Judge Lamont based his judgment on Lukhele being a reliable and honest witness, despite refusing to accept certain aspects of his testimony. This was incompatible, he said.[17]

In just a few minutes, Lamont dismissed the application to appeal the conviction and sentencing. 'Why didn't he just send an SMS?' quipped one of the disappointed attorneys.[18]

Krejcir also launched an urgent application to have his 'torturous' prison conditions relaxed. He asked to be transferred to Johannesburg's 'Sun City' jail, a C-maximum correctional facility, for the duration of his murder trial and that he be granted full access to his lawyer, which he claims he has never had.

Krejcir also demanded to be allowed access to a private doctor and psychiatrist at his own expense, as well as the opportunity to have access to his own personal computer and be allowed to video-call his family abroad – also at his own expense.[19]

In the papers submitted to the court, Krejcir argued that his rights of 'appeal, dignity, equality, education and the right of reasonable access to his legal representative' had been violated. Krejcir insisted he had been kept in total isolation while in custody, and that the court needed to put a stop to what he described as this 'torture'.[20]

Prison authorities, however, refused to bring him to court for the application, insisting that instead it be heard within the prison. There was no sympathy for his claims, it seemed.

Krejcir's past in the Czech Republic had also come back to haunt him. After his failed attempt, years back, to get refugee status at the Refugee Appeal Board – which failed thanks largely to the detailed affidavit handed out by O'Sullivan – his extradition case suddenly came up in July 2016 before the Kempton Park Magistrate's Court. Krejcir had long since dropped all attempts to gain refugee status. The extradition case had been postponed so many times over the years that most people had forgotten it was still ongoing. But, with all the cases stacked up against him, nobody was sure why the case was still going ahead. Krejcir had been handed a 35-year sentence, which he had to serve in South Africa, and a whole catalogue of trials was coming up. Surely, he couldn't be extradited with all the crimes in South Africa he still had to answer for?

The Star reported that the state, however, supported the extradition application and it would be up to the Czech Government to extradite Krejcir.[21]

People close to the investigations against Krejcir said the state was sick of him. With all the security and manpower devoted to this individual, he was costing the country a fortune, just to hold him to account for all his crimes.

He had allegedly committed so many offences in the nine years he had been in the country that state officials had to work round the clock gathering evidence. More and more information kept on emerging about what he had been up to. It meant more charges, more court appearances, more escape attempts and more security.

And it was a cycle that would go on for years. The police and prosecutors who had already devoted years of their time to ensuring Krejcir paid for his crimes could still not rest. They were on constant high alert. If they turned their attention away from him for even a short period of time, one of his alleged murder plots or escape attempts could actually come to fruition. It must have been exhausting.

'This case feels like it will never end,' said one of the investigators to his colleague when Marissa Christopher appeared in court. But at every court appearance they were there. The presence of these officers, who, despite threats to their own safety, would not give up pursuing justice was a reassurance to the public. Their no-nonsense approach to this case showed that not every cop was corrupt.

If the state could ensure that Krejcir paid for the crimes he had committed in South Africa back in the Czech Republic, it would be a tempting prospect – ship him off and make him someone else's problem.

'Should the court grant the extradition bid, it will then be up to the Justice Ministers of South Africa and the Czech Republic to negotiate a deal on whether Krejcir will have to stand for his multiple criminal trials in South Africa before he is returned to his home country,' Germaner wrote in *The Star*. 'A complication arises, however, as South African Justice Minister, Michael Masutha, may also have to broker a deal with the NPA to potentially suspend Krejcir's upcoming criminal proceedings to allow the extradition to go ahead.'[22]

But these negotiations were something that would be kept out of the public's eye. Nobody really knew what kind of deal the two countries were discussing, or if Krejcir would be extradited at all. The extradition case would be postponed again while the negotiations were under way.

In June 2016, Alexander arrived in the Kempton Park court for a postponement in the extradition case and, like a repeat performance by attorneys before him just a few months earlier, he then withdraw his legal representation because he had not been paid. He was the fourth lawyer who had not been paid in full by Krejcir.

Alexander also withdrew his services from the Sam Issa trial. Krejcir told journalists that his family were still requesting 'statements' from Alexander before they would continue paying him.

Germaner reported that Krejcir's mother, who had hitherto helped pay his legal fees, had chosen to no longer financially support her son in the courts.[23] It was the ultimate blow for Krejcir. His mother had been the one constant throughout his life. She had always been there to support him, both financially and with her presence. Why, now, would she seemingly abandon him?

It had seemed an impossibility just a few years earlier, when Krejcir had appeared to be invincible. It didn't matter what he did – he could get away with it. He held court in Bedfordview at the Harbour, treating the wealthy suburb as his own personal fiefdom.

The glamorous, infamous Mediterranean restaurant is now gone, replaced by a Wimpy. Families were now in the spot where men in dark suits had once sat, with children eating ice cream and running around the play area. There are no signs left of what there once was.

Moneypoint remained an empty shell for two years after the bomb blast, although the Remax office next door carried on trading. The blown-out windows were covered with plastic sheeting, which fluttered in the wind. Bullet holes still pock-mark the wall where the hidden automatic gun had blasted at Krejcir. Bulldozers arrived one day and the whole building went down. It is now an empty stand, with signs on the walls advertising new upmarket apartment blocks, which will soon be going up in the spot.

Krejcir's majestic mansion on the hill (and his holiday home at the Vaal) went under the auctioneer's hammer in December 2015. At the end of the day, it was just a home, a beautiful one, but, still, just a home, which another family will no doubt make their own one day. His luxury car collection had gone long before that.

There were no physical signs left that Krejcir had held sway in the area.

But the memories, the shootings, the corruption, the bomb blast – they all still lingered on in the psyche of those who lived nearby. Perhaps they always would.

Krejcir has no options left, it would seem. Except maybe one. Maybe it is time to listen to O'Sullivan, and the police and prosecutors who had tirelessly been pursuing him.[24] There is a lot he could reveal, they believe. Krejcir had not acted alone. All those years, during which he had seemingly done what he wanted without any consequences, meant there had to have been payments made – payments to people in high positions. These payments were not just to the police either. There was talk of prominent citizens who helped him evade the authorities and further his business empire. The state wants Krejcir to reveal all. But, at the same time, the police and the NPA are not going to let him off the hook for the crimes he committed. Whatever deal is made it would have to be carefully negotiated.

Maybe Krejcir will start talking?

It could mean a trip back to the place where it had all started, the Czech Republic. To that jail cell the Czech authorities had been wanting to put him in for more than ten years.

Krejcir had spent so much time trying to avoid being deported to the Czech Republic, but the police and correctional services' hardball approach after his escape attempts had made his life unbearable. Suddenly the option of going back there could seem attractive. His family was there, and the culture and language would make it easier for him.

But Krejcir was never going to just bow down to pressure. Germaner reported that after approaching 12 law firms, who all turned him down, Krejcir finally found another lawyer to represent him – James Grant, the man who had stepped in to argue his case during sentencing in the kidnapping and attempted-murder trial.[25]

With Grant, Krejcir carried on fighting it out in court, and the Sam Issa murder case promised to reveal lots more about Krejcir's alleged criminal world.

What was going on behind the scenes was being kept a secret, though. Whether or not Krejcir was thinking about cutting a deal with the state and whether he would be deported to the Czech Republic were up in the air.

But just imagine what Krejcir could reveal if he did start to talk. There is no doubt it would be explosive, just like the book he wrote after he had fled the Czech Republic, which set that country alight with speculation about political conspiracies. Did he have another Watergate scandal, this time about South Africa, up his sleeve?

Either way, one thing is for sure: this is not the last time we will hear about Krejcir.

ANNEXURE
GEORGE LOUCA'S AFFIDAVIT

AFFIDAVIT OF GEORGE SMITH [No.5]

I, the undersigned,

GEORGE SMITH

do hereby make oath and say that -

1. I am an adult male, with South African Identity No 6807135282087

    and South African Passport No. 4566643640 currently detained at

    Johannesburg Prison having been extradited from Cyprus to face certain

    criminal charges.

2. I therefore make this statement freely, voluntarily and without any undue
    influence in accordance with section 204 of the Act. Further, insofar as it
    may be necessary, subject to the provisions of section 105A of the Act;
    having been informed that my statement may incriminate me in various
    offences and notwithstanding the aforesaid, I may be called as a witness
    on behalf of the prosecution and further be required to answer questions
    which may incriminate me. However, if in the opinion of the court, I am
    found to have answered all questions frankly and honestly I will be
    discharged from prosecution on such charges or any competent verdict
    thereon. Further that the contents hereof may not be utilized in any
    manner or be regarded as admissible evidence in any trial against me.

1

05/11/2014

3.   The facts herein contained are, save where the context indicates otherwise within my personal knowledge and are true and correct.

INTRODUCTION AND BACKGROUND

4.   I met Radovan Krejcir ("Krejcir") in or around April 2007 when I shared a cell with him at the Kempton Park Magistrates Court.

5.   I had been arrested on charges of theft or alternatively receiving stolen property and Krejcir, as he explained to me, had been arrested upon his arrival in South Africa in 2007.

6.   Krejcir introduced himself to me as a wealthy businessman, with businesses interests in Europe. He explained that upon his release from detention it was his intention to establish himself in South Africa.

7.   He told me that because he had no experience of the South African business environment and no business connections in South Africa; and also because he did not speak English very well at that time, that he would need help from someone who could assist him generally in his business activities in South Africa.

8.   I discovered that Krejcir was a particularly persuasive person, able to make you believe virtually anything he said.

9.   I was impressed by Krejcir and saw an opportunity to advance myself.

2

10. I told him about myself and my many business connections in South Africa. And explained that I was in a very good position to assist him to start doing business this country.

11. Krejcir asked me to assist him in doing so and promised to pay me well for my services; I agreed to do so.

MURDER OF LOLLY JACKSON IN MAY 2010

12. Lolly Jackson ("Jackson") and Krejcir met and became acquaintances.

13. Krejcir was interested in Jackson's activities generally and particularly wanted involvement in Jackson's club "Teasers". He also shared Jackson's interest in fast and expensive motor cars.

14. It was known to Krejcir that Jackson was exporting millions in funds which had not been declared, through the services Mr. Alekos Panayi ("Panayi") who ran the Laiki bank of Cyprus in South Africa.

15. Panayi identified South African residents who had money offshore and wanted access to funds in this country.

16. Panayi would arrange what was called a "cash swap" in terms of which residents in South Africa who wanted to send money offshore could give it to Panayi who made it available to other local clients who had money offshore but needed their funds in South Africa.

05/11/2014

3

17. In consideration for receipt of these funds locally, the recipient would transfer an amount equal to the money received by him locally, from his offshore account to the offshore account nominated by Panayi's client who wanted money offshore.

18. In this manner Panayi transferred millions of Rands for Jackson.

19. Panayi stole funds from Jackson. Jackson approached me with the request that I recover the amount stolen by Panayi.

20. I was able to do so and in the result Jackson began to rely upon me to assist him in a number of ways.

21. Shortly before he was murdered Jackson requested my assistance in obtaining a Greek passport. Jackson was in fact of Greek origin and I was able to obtain a legitimate Greek passport for him.

22. As a result of my services Jackson and I enjoyed a good relationship and trusted one another.

23. This occurred at a time when my association with Krejcir had become strained following two instances in respect of which we had a difference of opinion and I had refused to follow instructions given by Krejcir.

24. Jackson confided to me that he was planning to leave South Africa as pressure was mounting over allegations of money laundering. It was for this reason, as noted above, that he required Greek citizenship.

4

25. Panayi had lost his job at the Laiki bank after the discovery that he had engaged in money laundering activities.

26. In 2009 Krejcir approached Jackson and advised that he and his associate Cyril Beeka were in a position to make funds available offshore using a similar arrangement to the "money swap" scheme operated by Panayi; allegedly using certain eastern European contacts of Cyril Beeka who had set up businesses in the Cape.

27. Jackson told me that he agreed to use their services and that two or possibly three transactions involving "small" sums of money, in the nature of between R80, 000 and R120, 000 had been successfully concluded.

28. In April 2010 Jackson contacted me urgently and told me that he and Krejcir assisted by Beeka had arranged a "transfer" of approximately R740, 000.00 which amount he had given to Krejcir; but that an equivalent amount of funds had not been transferred to his account despite receipt by him of a document in the form of a "swift-transfer" which he explained to me, had upon enquiry, proved to be a fake.

29. Jackson was angered by this development and in April 2010 requested that I set up a meeting with Krejcir.

30. I arranged meeting but neither Krejcir nor Beeka, despite their commitment to attend, arrived for the meeting.

5

31.   I contacted Beeka and complained that he had not arrived despite his commitment and told him that in my opinion, that this was not the behavior I expected from a grown man.

32.   Shortly afterwards Krejcir called for me to meet him at the Harbor Café. Upon my arrival I spoke with Krejcir, and during the conversation Beeka came toward me, unseen, and punched me on the side of my head.

33.   I fell to the floor and was kicked several times by Beeka on my head and face. This took place in front of Krejcir who didn't interfere in the assault or assist in any way.

34.   As a result I was hospitalised and unable for this reason to attend a court appearance.

35.   Upon my release from Hospital, I attempted once again to set up a meeting between Krejcir and Jackson.

36.   Krejcir refused to attend any meeting at Jacksons home or office.

37.   He insisted that the meeting be held at the house where I lived in Kempton Park.

38.   It was agreed that a meeting would be scheduled for the afternoon of the 3rd of May 2010.

39.   Having confirmed the arrangement with Jackson, he and I agreed to meet on the Modderfontein Road running in front of the Greenstone Shopping

6

Centre. Jackson driving his Jeep arrived late afternoon and we set off, with Jackson following me, I was driving my Peugeot van.

40. On the way along Modderfontein Road my car broke down, from what seemed to be an electrical fault.

41. Jackson stopped his car to assist me and we drove the remainder of the way together in his Jeep.

42. Upon our arrival at my house I invited Jackson into the living room and stepped behind the bar to offer him a beer.

43. Krejcir arrived some five or six minutes later and was also offered a drink.

44. Within moments Jackson had begun to shout at Krejcir and to wave the copy of the swift transfer which he said was a fake.

45. Jackson swore at Krejcir, asking him "who the fuck" he thought he was to steal his (Jackson's) money.

46. Krejcir lunged forward to grab the swift transfer from Jackson who held it out of reach.

47. At this point Krejcir pulled out a firearm and shot Jackson once; Jackson fell onto the back of the sofa positioned directly behind him.

48. Jackson looked shocked, and began to plead and beg for his life.

49. Krejcir crossed the floor toward him standing over him and kicked him in the side of his chest said the following or words to the same effect :

05/11/2014

".....you want to know who I am, I will show you who I am you fucking

cockroach..."

50. Krejcir then proceeded to fire many shots into Jackson. I don't remember how many but there were several further shots.

51. Jackson appeared to be dead, and lay in a pool of blood. I was horrified and frightened.

52. Krejcir ordered me to pick Jackson up and take him down the corridor toward the garage. He wanted me to put the body into Jackson's car.

53. I attempted to do as he said but Jackson was quite heavy. My shirt was quickly covered in Jackson's blood. I said to Krejcir "I can't do that I can't pick him up. He asked me to go and get a blanket to carry his body.

54. I ran to my bedroom, removed the bloody shirt and put on a clean one taking a duvet off my bed and returned to the lounge where I succeeded in placing Jackson's body onto the duvet and dragging the body down the passage toward the door that leads into the garage.

55. I left Jacksons body in the passage just inside the door and stepped into the garage.

56. I opened the automatic garage door on the left and noticed Cyril Beeka seated in a car just outside the garage on my right together with someone

05/11/2014

8

who I could not see clearly save to say that he had short light coloured hair.

57. I reversed the Jeep into the garage right up to the doorway leading from the passage. When I stepped out of the Jeep in order to open the back of the car I found that I had parked it too close to the door to open the boot.

58. At that moment I was in a state of shock and felt afraid for my life; I had just witnessed Lolly Jackson shot dead by Krejcir and wanted get away as quickly as possible

59. I got back into the car and drove away, exiting through the booms at the entrance to our suburb and then called General Mabasa from my phone telling him what I that I had just witnessed Krejcir killing Jackson and to ask for his help. He asked me who was present at the time of Jackson's murder and I told him that Krejcir and Cyril were there.

60. He asked me where I was. I told him that I was driving Jacksons Jeep. He suggested that I meet him at Bedford Centre, and that I should speak to Krejcir as soon as possible

61. Mabasa knew of the problems between Krejcir and Jackson; having already been approached by Jackson to intervene and assist in facilitating a meeting with Krejcir.

62. I too had spoken with Mabasa about the need for a meeting to be arranged between Krejcir and Jackson to resolve their problem.

05/11/2014

63. I didn't drive immediately to Bedford Centre but drove around for a while.

64. Radovan was calling me on the phone. I didn't take his calls at first. Later I called him as advised by Mabasa.

65. He asked me to meet with him at Jannis Louca's Engen garage near to Linksfield. We met there.

66. He got there before me and I met him behind the garage. He wanted me to calm down, but I was extremely angry with him for what he had just done and didn't want to listen to his stories. He asked me why I had driven off and left the house. He said that I was supposed to have helped him to put the body in the car and then dumped it.

67. I drove off and then headed for the Harbour Café in order to meet with Mabasa. Upon my arrival I saw several people including Cyril Beeka who was sitting with Hein Metrovich in the smoking area. I asked him whether Mabasa was there.

68. He answered that he had not seen Mabasa. I realised that I was alone and that Mabasa was not going to show up.

69. Krejcir then arrived at the Harbour Café and before speaking with me approached Metrovich who handed him two cellphones.

70. He then turned to me and said we need to talk. We got to the parking lot and he told me that I should give him my cell phone and speak to no-one.

10

05/11/2014

71. He then said that I should drive to the Nicol Hotel in Bedfordview. I went to the second floor to room 26 as instructed by Krejcir where I found Krejcir's friend from the Czech Republic by the name of Martin.

72. Krejcir arrived at 10pm and told me that I had no choice but to leave the country. As he put it: Lolly was murdered in your house. You were there when it happened. You are fucked and there is nothing you can do about it

73. He reminded me further that I was due to appear in Court the following day (on charges of theft alternatively possession of stolen property) and that Mabasa had told him that I would get between ten and fifteen years on the charges.

74. He said I should leave as soon as possible for Cyprus; which he said had no extradition treaty with South Africa.

75. He undertook to send money to me in Cyprus.

76. This was his way of dealing with the position in which he had through his actions, placed me.

77. I called my friend Yannis Louca who met with me at the parking lot across the road from the Hotel, where I parked Lolly Jackson's Jeep.

78. We left from there and while driving I told Yannis the truth about what had happened. Yannis took me across the border to Mozambique where I travelled via Lisbon (Portugal) to Cyprus.

11   05/11/2014

DEPONENT

I hereby certify that the deponent declares that he knows and understands the contents of this affidavit and that it is to the best of the deponent's knowledge both true and correct. This affidavit was signed and sworn to before me at Johannesburg on this the day 5th day of November 2014, the Regulations contained in the Government Notice R1258 of 21 July 1972 as amended having been complied with.

COMMISSIONER OF OATHS

12

Notes

CHAPTER 1

1 Affidavit of George Smith (Affidavit no. 1), 5 November 2014.

CHAPTER 2

1 Julian Rademeyer, Krejcir scoffs at 'Mafia boss' claims, *Rapport*, 29 August 2010, http://www.news24.com/SouthAfrica/News/Krejcir-scoffs-at-Mafia-boss-claims-20100829, accessed 14 April 2016.
2 Sean Newman, Peter Piegl and Karyn Maughan, *Lolly Jackson*: *When Fantasy Becomes Reality*. Johannesburg: Jacana Media, 2012, pp. 148–151.
3 Dita Asiedu, Radovan Krejcir: A fugitive businessman in a gilded cage, Radio Praha, 3 January 2006, http://www.radio.cz/en/section/talking/radovan-krejcir-a-fugitive-businessman-in-a-gilded-cage, accessed 13 April 2016.
4 Exclusive: The policeman in court with little effort, Krejcir, translated from Czech, TV Nova, 26 June 2007, http://tn.nova.cz/clanek/zpravy/zahranici/exkluzivne-policista-si-u-soudi-s-krejcirem-nebral-servitky.html, accessed 14 April 2016.
5 Julian Rademeyer, Krejcir scoffs at 'Mafia boss' claims, *Rapport*, 29 August 2010, http://www.news24.com/SouthAfrica/News/Krejcir-scoffs-at-Mafia-boss-claims-20100829, accessed 14 April 2016.
6 Daniela Lazarová, Fugitive billionaire Radovan Krejcir launches counterattack from the Seychelles, Radio Praha, 20 October 2005, http://www.radio.cz/en/section/curraffrs/fugitive-billionaire-radovan-krejcir-launches-counterattack-from-the-seychelles, accessed 13 April 2016.
7 Ibid.
8 The very latest on Radovan Krejcir – A naturalised Seychellois arrested in South Africa four weeks ago, *Le Nouveau Seychelles Weekly*, 25 May 2007, http://www.seychellesweekly.com/May%2025,%202007/Page%205.html, accessed 13 April 2016.
9 Radovan Krejcir to return to Seychelles, *Le Nouveau Seychelles Weekly*, 11 May 2007, http://www.seychellesweekly.com/May%2011,%202007/Page%206.html, accessed 13 April 2016.
10 Ibid.

CHAPTER 3

1 Coilen O'Connor, Fugitive Czech billionaire arrested in South Africa, Radio Praha, 24 April 2007, http://www.radio.cz/en/section/curraffrs/fugitive-czech-billionaire-arrested-in-south-africa, accessed 13 April 2016.
2 Ibid.
3 Alex Eliseev, Rich Czech crime suspect arrested at SA airport, *The Star*, 24 April 2007.
4 Radovan Krejcir a free man in South Africa! *Le Nouveau Seychelles Weekly*, 13 July 2007, http://www.seychellesweekly.com/July%2013,%202007/Page%206%20-%20Radovan.html, accessed 13 April 2016.
5 Spooks haunt murder probe, *The Star*, 7 May 2010.
6 Affidavits of George Smith (Affidavit nos. 2 and 4), 5 November 2014.
7 Ibid.
8 Affidavit of George Smith (Affidavit no. 1), 5 November 2014.

CHAPTER 4

1 Sworn statements by witnesses 1 and 2 in Lazarov kidnapping, taken on 6 February 2015.
2 Affidavit of George Smith (Affidavit no. 2), 5 November 2014.
3 Sworn statements by witnesses 1 and 2 in Lazarov kidnapping.
4 Ibid.
5 Ibid.
6 Ibid.
7 Ibid.
8 Ibid.
9 Ibid.
10 Ibid.
11 Affidavit of George Smith (Affidavit no. 2), 5 November 2014.
12 Sworn statement by landlord, taken on 10 May 2011.
13 Ibid.
14 Ibid.
15 Ibid.
16 Affidavit of George Smith (Affidavit no. 4), 5 November 2014.
17 Ibid.
18 Ibid.
19 Ibid.
20 Ibid.

CHAPTER 5

1 Angelique Serrao, Shain Germaner and Kristen van Schie, Mourners bid Lolly final farewell, *The Star*, 11 May 2010.

2 Ibid.

3 Ibid.

4 Ibid.

5 Strip king Lolly Jackson's round-about life, *The Sunday Independent*, 9 May 2010.

6 Kashiefa Ajam, I was framed, says Teazers boss, *Saturday Star*, 13 February 2010, http://www.iol.co.za/news/south-africa/i-was-framed-says-teazers-boss-473417, accessed 20 April 2016.

7 Shaun Smillie and Kanina Foss, 'He lived rough and he's died rough', *The Star*, 4 May 2010, http://www.iol.co.za/news/south-africa/he-lived-rough-and-hes-died-rough-482660, accessed 19 April 2016.

8 Tragic end to a life lived in the fast lane, South African Press Association, 5 May 2010.

9 Cops search for clues in Lolly Jackson murder, *Mail & Guardian*, 4 May 2010, http://mg.co.za/article/2010-05-04-cops-search-for-clues-in-lolly-jackson-murder, accessed 28 April 2010.

10 Sean Newman, Peter Piegl and Karyn Maughan, *Lolly Jackson: When Fantasy Becomes Reality*. Johannesburg: Jacana, 2012, pp. 9–11.

11 Ibid.

12 Ibid.

13 Cops search for clues in Lolly Jackson murder, *Mail & Guardian*, 4 May 2010, http://mg.co.za/article/2010-05-04-cops-search-for-clues-in-lolly-jackson-murder, accessed 28 April 2010.

14 Cops hunt for Lolly's thug, *The Star*, 4 May 2010.

15 Ibid.

16 Kashiefa Ajam, R100 000 to kill Lolly, *The Star*, 8 May 2010.

17 Ibid.

18 Ibid.

19 Graeme Hosken and South African Press Association, Shady deal fans fury, *Pretoria News*, 6 May 2010.

20 Shain Germaner, Krejcir may face extradition bid, *Pretoria News*, 31 August 2010.

21 Ibid.

22 Mobster at the gates: The ugly saga of Radovan Krejcir, amaBhungane, 10 September 2010, http://amabhungane.co.za/article/2010-09-10-mobster-at-the-gates-ugly-saga-of-radovan-krejcir, accessed 10 May 2016.

23 Ibid.

24 Zelda Venter, Media lose bid to attend Krejcir hearing, *The Star*, 7 December 2012.

25 Ibid.

26 De Wet Potgieter, 'I am no angel and no devil' – Krejcir, *Cape Argus*, 29 August 2010.

27 Louise Flanagan and Shain Germaner, 'Czech fugitive wants our gold refinery', *The Star*, 20 May 2010.

28 Arrest warrant out for police intelligence boss, *Mail & Guardian*, 30 March 2011, http://mg.co.za/article/2011-03-30-arrest-warrant-out-for-police-intelligence-boss, accessed 26 April 2016.

29 Ibid.

30 Written submission by Paul O'Sullivan to the Refugee Appeals Tribunal, 20 January 2011.

31 Sworn statement by Paul O'Sullivan, taken on 16 May 2010.

32 Ibid.

33 Ibid.

34 Ibid.

35 Statement by Alekos Andreou Panayi, taken on 1 December 2009.

36 Ibid.

37 Ibid.

38 Ibid.

39 Ibid.

40 Ibid.

41 Ibid.

42 Ibid.

43 Ibid.

44 Ibid.

45 Author's interview with Paul O'Sullivan, May 2016.

46 Ibid.

CHAPTER 6

1 Sworn statement by Christiane Gemballa in aggravation of sentencing.

2 Ibid.

3 Ibid.

4 Email between Jerome Safi and Uwe Gemballa, 2 February 2010.

5 Statement by Ludi Rolf Schnelle, taken on 25 February 2010.

6 Sworn statement by Jerome Reuben Safi, taken on 28 January 2012.

7 Ibid.

8 Statement by Ludi Rolf Schnelle, taken on 25 February 2010.

9 Ibid.

10 Ibid.

11 Ibid.

12 Sworn statement by Juan Meyer, taken on 11 July 2010.

13 Ibid.

14 Ibid.

15 Ibid.

16 Ibid.

17 Sworn statement by Christiane Gemballa in aggravation of sentencing, 3 February 2016.

18 Ibid.

19 Omphitlhetse Mooki, Final hours of German car fundi slain on African soil, *The Star*, 2 November 2010.

20 Ibid.

21 Noni Mokati, Mother laments son's taking some wrong turns in life, *The Star*, 26 March 2011.

22 Ibid.

23 Sworn statement by Jerome Reuben Safi, taken on 28 January 2012.

24 Ibid.

25 Ibid.

26 Ibid.

27 Ibid.

28 Ibid.

29 Ibid.

30 Ibid.

31 Ibid.

32 Ibid.

33 Ibid.

34 Affidavit of George Smith (Affidavit no. 3), 5 November 2014.

35 Ibid.

36 Ibid.

37 Ibid.

38 Sally Evans, Krejcir's shadow lurks over Gemballa's murder trial, *Mail & Guardian*, http://mg.co.za/article/2015-09-23-krejcirs-shadow-lurks-over-gemballas-murder-trial, accessed 10 May 2016.

39 Alex Eliseev, Gemballa case: Key witness's memory U-turn, *Daily Maverick*, http://www.dailymaverick.co.za/article/2013-08-07-gemballa-case-key-witness-memorable-u-turn#.VzHWsFUrLcs, accessed 10 May 2016.

40 Sally Evans, Gemballa trial postponed until September, *Mail & Guardian*, http://mg.co.za/article/2013-08-15-gemballa-trial-postponed-until-september, accessed 10 May 2016.

41 Gabi Falanga, Trio guilty of murdering Gemballa, *The Star*, 12 November 2015.

42 Ibid.

43 Ibid.

44 Shain Germaner, Outrage as Gemballa's killer escapes from holding cell at court, *The Star*, 9 March 2016.

45 Angelique Serrao, CCTV shows cop helping prisoner escape, *The Star*, 11 March 2016.

46 Ibid.

47 Shain Germaner, Lengthy jail terms for Gemballa's killers, *The Star*, 16 March 2016.

48 Ibid.

49 Sworn statement by Christiane Gemballa in aggravation of sentencing, 3 February 2016.

50 Ibid.

CHAPTER 7

1 Craig McKune, Sally Evans and Sam Sole, Serb assassin's shadowy associates, *Mail & Guardian*, 13 January 2012, http://mg.co.za/article/2012-01-13-serb-assassins-shadowy-associates, accessed 23 May 2016.

2 Ibid.

3 Natasha Prince and Sibusiso Nkomo, Drive-by shooting death, *Daily News*, 22 March 2011.

4 Ibid.

5 A controversial past, *Cape Argus*, 22 March 2011.

6 Marianne Merten, The Beeka case and the hit list, *Weekend Argus*, 26 March 2011.

7 Marianne Merten, Killing blasts the lid off can of worms, *Saturday Star*, 26 March 2011.

8 Sworn statement by Juan Meyer, taken on 11 July 2010.

9 Beeka's Sinatra adieu, *Sunday Tribune*, 3 April 2011.

10 Ibid.

11 Aziz Hartley and Karen Breytenbach, The Russian lived by the sword, *Cape Times*, 31 May 2007, http://www.iol.co.za/news/south-africa/the-russian-lived-by-the-sword-355433, accessed 23 May 2016.

12 Candice Bailey, Louise Flanagan, Angelique Serrao and Zara Nicholson, Hits and hoodlums, *The Star*, 23 March 2011.

13 Ibid.

14 Caryn Dolley, Sexy Boys gang leader linked to death of Beeka – cop, *Pretoria News*, 11 January 2012.

15 Ibid.

16 Candice Bailey and Zara Nicholson, War of words over Krejcir, *Pretoria News*, 28 March 2011.

17 Ibid.

18 Henriette Geldenhuys, Anti-piracy weapons deal linked Krejcir and Beeka, *Weekend Argus*, 25 February 2012.

19 Ibid.

20 Shain Germaner, Cops smash up wrong house in raid, *The Star*, 24 March 2011.

21 Graeme Hosken, Huge hunt for fugitive, *The Mercury*, 24 March 2011.

22 Graeme Hosken, Hawks uncover hit list – Two held as Beeka assassination probed, *Daily News*, 23 March 2011.

23 Shaun Smillie, SARS seizes Krejcir's luxury cars, *The Star*, 24 March 2011.

24 Krejcir bungle – Hawks fear traitor in midst, *Daily News*, 24 March 2011.

25 Ibid.

26 Candice Bailey, Shaun Smillie and Shain Germaner, Krejcir gives himself up, *Daily News*, 25 March 2011.

27 De Wet Potgieter, Czech mate, Krejcir, *The Star*, 26 March 2011.

28 Candice Bailey, Mastermind is playing a media game – Hawks, *Cape Times*, 28 March 2011.

29 Henriette Geldenhuys, Beeka driver arrested, *Cape Argus*, 18 December 2011.

30 Ibid.

31 Ibid.

32 Ibid.

33 Henriette Geldenhuys and Warda Meyer, Thugs move on city clubs, *Cape Argus*, 11 March 2012.

34 Ibid.

35 Ibid.

36 Ibid.

37 Henriette Geldenhuys, Krejcir demands his money from gangster's estate, *The Star*, 25 February 2012.

38 Ibid.

39 Henriette Geldenhuys, Hawks seize Beeka weapons from Joburg security firm, *Cape Argus*, 1 April 2012.

40 Author's interview with forensic investigator Chad Thomas, 15 June 2016.
41 Krejcir 'not involved' in Beeka's murder, *Cape Times*, 13 April 2011.

CHAPTER 8

1 Solly Maphumulo, Wedding day bloodshed, *The Star*, 12 October 2010.
2 Ibid.
3 Ibid.
4 Angelique Serrao, Gunmen waited 6 hours for Couremetis, *The Star*, 14 October 2010.
5 Ibid.
6 Solly Maphumulo, Agliotti's 'dear friend' shot dead at wedding, *The Star*, 12 October 2010.
7 Now Agliotti builds his life, Omphitlhetse Mooki, *The Star*, 27 November 2010.
8 De Wet Potgieter, Arrest of alleged Cuban gunlord could expose international cartel, *The Star*, 9 April 2011.
9 De Wet Potgieter, Underworld hit victim had told druglord he was 'on his way', *Saturday Star*, 23 April 2011.
10 Werner Swart and Isaac Mahlangu, Mr Big's fast, but short life, *Sunday Times*, 25 September 2011, http://www.timeslive.co.za/local/2011/09/25/mr-big-s-fast-but-short-life?service=print#, accessed 23 May 2016.
11 Ibid.
12 AmaBhungane, Krejcir link in huge coke bust, 1 April 2011, http://amabhungane.co.za/article/2011-04-01-krejcir-link-in-huge-coke-bust, accessed 23 May 2016.
13 Julian Rademeyer and Thanduxolo Jika, Fugitive 'mafia boss' in SA cancer con, News24, http://www.news24.com/SouthAfrica/News/Fugitive-mafia-boss-in-SA-cancer-con-20110316, accessed 23 May 2016.
14 Sworn statements by Marian Tupy, 19 May 2010.
15 Ibid.
16 Ibid.
17 Ibid.
18 Ibid.
19 Ibid.
20 Ibid.
21 Ibid.
22 Ibid.
23 De Wet Potgieter, Health insurance fraud case sets cats among pigeons of crime, *The Star*, 26 March 2011.
24 Ibid.
25 Candice Bailey and Zara Nicholson, I offered to hand myself in, says Krejcir, *Mercury*, 28 March 2011.
26 Ibid.
27 Candice Bailey and Shain Germaner, Protection for hit list prosecutor, *Daily News*, 28 March 2011.
28 Angelique Serrao, Shain Germaner and Candice Bailey, Jail the safest place for

fugitive who gave himself up, *The Star*, 29 March 2011.

29 Ibid.

30 Shain Germaner and SAPA, Krejcir a threat to witnesses, *Pretoria News*, 8 April 2011.

31 Shain Germaner and Graeme Hosken, R500 000 bail paid – 'I feel so good', *Pretoria News*, 9 April 2011.

32 Ibid.

33 De Wet Potgieter, Krejcir chills out after Hawks raid and a spell behind bars, *Cape Argus*, 10 April 2011.

34 Krejcir counsel plans interdict, SAPA, 30 March 2011.

35 Kristen van Schie and Candice Bailey, Restraining order against O'Sullivan, *The Star*, 30 March 2011.

36 Ibid.

37 Ibid.

38 Shain Germaner, Affidavit reveals Krejcir's colourful threats, *The Star*, 13 April 2011.

39 Ibid.

40 Shain Germaner, O'Sullivan sorry for threats, *The Star*, 7 June 2011.

41 Ibid.

42 Extra colour as mother flies in, *Cape Argus*, 10 April 2011.

43 Ibid.

44 Louise Flanagan, Krejcir in custody over armed robbery, *The Star*, 13 February 2012.

45 Angelique Serrao, New twist in Krejcir drama: The crime-buster, the doctor, the cancer victim, *The Star*, 19 October 2012.

46 Sally Evans, Krejcir case: Smoke, mirrors, fraud and Czechs, amaBhungane, 15 July 2011, http://mg.co.za/article/2011-07-15-smoke-mirrors-fraud-and-czechs, accessed 23 May 2016.

47 Ibid.

48 Jaroslav Kmenta, *The Godfather African*. Prague: BookBaby, 2016.

49 Angelique Serrao, Forensic investigator says he didn't get witness drunk, *The Star*, 9 November 2012

50 Sworn statements by Marian Tupy.

51 Angelique Serrao, Forensic investigator says he didn't get witness drunk, *The Star*, 9 November 2012.

52 Ibid.

53 Ibid.

CHAPTER 9

1 Docket opened in April 2012 by Kim Marriott regarding Krejcir's alleged fake acknowledgment of debt in his claims against Jackson's estate, including her sworn statement, email exchanges between Krejcir's employees and lawyers to Ian Jordaan, as well as a sworn statement by a manager at Standard Bank.

2 Louise Flanagan and Angelique Serrao, Lolly's R200m sleaze estate, *The Star*, 1 July 2010.

3 Kashiefa Ajam and Sarah Fenwick, Jackson estate faces $1m claim, *Pretoria News*, 9 June 2012.
4 Letter by Shannon Little Attorneys with Lolly Jackson's acknowledgment of debt to Krejcir, 14 December 2011.
5 Julian Rademeyer, Lolly's lawyer's teeth removed, *City Press*, http://www.news24.com/SouthAfrica/News/Lollys-lawyers-teeth-removed-20110925, accessed 30 May 2016.
6 Ibid.
7 Candice Bailey, Angelique Serrao and Thandi Skade, Teazers lawyer killed, *The Star*, 22 September 2011.
8 Ibid.
9 Julian Rademeyer, Lolly's 'protégé' feared for his life, Media24 Investigations, http://www.news24.com/SouthAfrica/News/Lollys-murdered-protege-feared-for-his-life-20110928, accessed 30 May 2016.
10 Schalk Mouton and Charl du Plessis, Murders 'all linked to Lolly', *The Times*, http://www.timeslive.co.za/local/2011/09/30/murders-all-linked-to-lolly?service=print, accessed 30 May 2016.
11 Angelique Serrao and Candice Bailey, Murders mount in strip club saga, *The Star*, 29 September 2011.
12 Candice Bailey, Angelique Serrao, Omphitlhetse Mooki and Shain Germaner, Curse of Teazers claims 7th victim, *The Star*, 29 September 2011.
13 Ibid.
14 Paul O'Sullivan's founding affidavit in a case where he and Demi Jackson were the applicants against Vodacom Limited, signed on 22 August 2012.
15 Ibid.
16 Ibid.
17 Docket opened in April 2012 by Kim Marriott regarding Krejcir's alleged fake acknowledgment of debt in his claims against Jackson's estate, including her sworn statement, email exchanges between Krejcir's employees and lawyers to Ian Jordaan, as well as a sworn statement by a manager at Standard Bank.
18 Ibid.
19 Ibid.
20 Ibid.
21 Ibid.
22 Ibid.

CHAPTER 10

1 Cops hunt for Lolly's thug, *The Star*, 4 May 2010.
2 Angelique Serrao, 'I did not kill Lolly', *The Star*, 18 April 2011.
3 Ibid.
4 Ibid.
5 Ibid.
6 Sashni Pather, Raymond Preston, Exclusive 'I will not go down alone': George Smith, *Sunday Times*, 15 May 2011, http://www.timeslive.co.za/local/2011/05/15/

exclusive-i-will-not-go-down-alone-george-smith, accessed 26 April 2016.

7 Ibid.

8 Ibid.

9 Affidavit of George Smith (Affidavit no. 5), 5 November 2014.

10 Shain Germaner, I'll never talk, Louca insists, *The Star*, 28 March 2012.

11 Ibid.

12 Ibid.

13 Henriette Geldenhuys, Louka holds key to unsolved murders, *Cape Argus*, 25 March 2012.

14 Shain Germaner, Louca blow for Jackson murder case, *The Star*, 18 September 2013.

15 Shain Germaner and Angelique Serrao, Louca's security tightened after alleged assassination plot, *The Star*, 17 July 2014.

16 Ibid.

17 Ibid.

18 Shain Germaner, High stakes in Louca's murder trial, *The Star*, 24 January 2015.

19 Ibid.

20 Shain Germaner, Lolly Jackson murder accused rushed to hospital, *The Star*, 23 February 2015.

21 Ibid.

22 Ibid.

23 Shain Germaner, Lolly Jackson murder suspect's health a concern, says lawyer, *The Star*, 12 March 2015.

24 Shain Germaner, How Lolly was killed, *The Star*, 22 April 2015.

25 Ibid.

26 Shain Germaner, Judge denies Louca's plea to die surrounded by his family, *The Star*, 22 April 2015.

27 Louca: Krejcir screamed 'you f**king cockroach' then killed Lolly, *Sunday Times*, 5 April 2015, http://www.timeslive.co.za/local/2015/04/05/louca-krejcir-screamed-you-fking-cockroach-then-killed-lolly2?service=print, accessed 28 April 2016.

28 Ibid.

29 Mandy Wiener, 'Louca cleared me of Jackson's murder', Eyewitness News, http://ewn.co.za/Topic/Radovan-Krejcir-on-trial, accessed 29 April 2016.

30 Shain Germaner and Anna Cox, Louca family demand his body, *The Star*, 12 May 2015.

31 Ibid.

32 Author's interview with Owen Blumberg, July 2014.

33 Affidavit of George Smith (Affidavit no. 5), 5 November 2014.

34 Ibid.

35 Ibid.

36 Ibid.

37 Ibid.

38 Ibid.

39 Ibid.

40 Ibid.

41 Ibid.

42 Ibid.

CHAPTER 11

1 Lerato Mbangeni, Shain Germaner and Angelique Serrao, A dozen remote-controlled gun barrels. Blazing bullets. Fiery explosion. All this, yet Krejcir was … MISSED!, *The Star*, 25 July 2013.

2 Ibid.

3 Graeme Hosken, Underworld attack, *The Times*, 25 July 2015, http://www.timeslive.co.za/news/2013/07/25/underworld-attack, accessed 2 May 2016.

4 Ibid.

5 Lerato Mbangeni, Shain Germaner and Angelique Serrao, A dozen remote-controlled gun barrels. Blazing bullets. Fiery explosion. All this, yet Krejcir was … MISSED!, *The Star*, 25 July 2013.

6 Alex Eliseev, Krejcir assassination attempt: The stuff of movies, Bond movies, *Daily Maverick*, 25 July 2013, http://www.dailymaverick.co.za/article/2013-07-25-krejcir-assassination-attempt-the-stuff-of-movies-bond-movies/, accessed 2 May 2016.

7 Lerato Mbangeni, Shain Germaner and Angelique Serrao, 007-style hit on fugitive, *The Star*, 25 July 2013.

8 Caryn Dolley, Pipe gun easy to make, *Saturday Star*, 26 July 2013.

9 Lerato Mbangeni, Shain Germaner and Caryn Dolley, Krejcir robbed of R3m, *The Star*, 26 July 2013.

10 Caryn Dolley, Pipe gun easy to make, *Saturday Star*, 26 July 2013.

11 Ibid.

12 Ibid.

13 Jaroslav Kmenta, *The Godfather African*. Prague: BookBaby, 2016.

14 Ibid.

CHAPTER 12

1 Jaroslav Kmenta, *The Godfather African*. Prague: BookBaby, 2016.

2 I have proof of Krejcir's murders – Potiska, eNCA, 1 December 2014, https://www.enca.com/media/video/i-have-proof-krejcir%E2%80%99s-murders-%E2%80%93-potiska?playlist=109, accessed 10 May 2016.

3 Sworn statement by Miloslav Potiska on the murder of Cyril Beeka, 27 February 2015.

4 Sworn statement by Miloslav Potiska on when he was asked by Krejcir to kill Paul O'Sullivan, 27 February 2015.

5 Sworn statement by Miloslav Potiska on creating fake/false bank swift transfer documents, 27 February 2015.

6 Sworn statement by Miloslav Potiska on Paul O'Sullivan's telephone records getting into the possession of Krejcir, 27 February 2015.

7 Sworn statement by Miloslav Potiska on when he was asked by Krejcir to kill Paul O'Sullivan, 27 February 2015.

8 Ibid.

9 Sworn statement by Miloslav Potiska on the relationship between Krejcir and Joey Mabasa, 27 February 2015.

10 Ibid.
11 Sworn statement by Miloslav Potiska on creating fake/false bank swift transfer documents, 27 February 2015.
12 Ibid.
13 Ibid.
14 Sworn statement by Miloslav Potiska on the murder of Cyril Beeka, 27 February 2015.
15 Ibid.
16 Ibid.
17 Ibid.
18 Media release by Radovan Krejcir following the interview with Miloslav Potiska on eNCA's *Checkpoint*, 25 November 2014.
19 Ibid.
20 Ibid.
21 Ibid.
22 Ibid.
23 Ibid.
24 Ibid.
25 Ibid.
26 Ibid.
27 Ibid.
28 Ibid.
29 Ibid.
30 Ibid.

CHAPTER 13

1 Candice Bailey and Angelique Serrao, Underworld probe after drive-by hit, *The Sunday Independent*, 13 October 2013.
2 Ibid.
3 Ibid.
4 Ibid.
5 Sally Evans, Krejcir: A dangerous man to know? *Mail & Guardian*, 18 October 2013, http://mg.co.za/article/2013-10-17-krejcir-a-dangerous-man-to-know, accessed 17 June 2016.
6 Mandy Wiener, Krejcir shaken by Sam Issa hit, 12 October 2013, Eyewitness News, http://ewn.co.za/2013/10/12/Krejcir-shaken-by-Bedfordview-shooting, accessed 17 June 2016.
7 Sally Evans, Krejcir: A dangerous man to know? *Mail & Guardian*, 18 October 2013, http://mg.co.za/article/2013-10-17-krejcir-a-dangerous-man-to-know, accessed 17 June 2016.
8 Black Sam in country on false papers, says private investigator, *The Star*, 16 October 2013.
9 Ibid.
10 Author's interview with Chad Thomas, June 2016.

11 Ibid.
12 Black Sam in country on false papers, says private investigator, *The Star*, 16 October 2013.
13 Anna Cox, 'You are next' Krejcir ally and state witness told, *The Star*, 15 October 2013.
14 I have proof of Krejcir's murders – Potiska, eNCA, 1 December 2014, https://www.enca.com/media/video/i-have-proof-krejcir%E2%80%99s-murders-%E2%80%93-potiska?playlist=109, accessed 10 May 2016.
15 Jaroslav Kmenta, *The Godfather African*. Prague: BookBaby, 2016.
16 Ibid.
17 Ibid.
18 Ibid.
19 Ibid.
20 Ibid.
21 Ibid.
22 Candice Bailey and Angelique Serrao, Underworld probe after drive-by hit, *The Sunday Independent*, 13 October 2013.
23 Sameer Naik, Serbian slain because he had a loose mouth, *Saturday Star*, 9 November 2013.
24 Ibid.
25 Ibid.
26 Jaroslav Kmenta, *The Godfather African*. Prague: BookBaby, 2016.
27 Ibid.
28 Brendan Roane, Death of Krejcir associate 'like a hit', *The Star*, 4 November 2013.
29 Ibid.

CHAPTER 14

1 Pauli van Wyk, Bomb kills two outside Krejcir's business, News24, 13 November 2013, http://news24.com/news24/archives/witness/bomb-kills-two-outside-krejcirs-business-20150430, accessed 20 June 2016.
2 Theresa Taylor and Angelique Serrao, Deadly Krejcir blast, *The Star*, 13 November 2013.
3 Ibid.
4 Sameer Naik and Kashiefa Ajam, Bedfordview 'living in fear' of underworld man, *Saturday Star*, 16 November 2013.
5 Ibid.
6 Theresa Taylor and Angelique Serrao, Deadly Krejcir blast, *The Star*, 13 November 2013.
7 Ibid.
8 Theresa Taylor, Angelique Serrao and Brendan Roane, Blast! Another Radovan ruction, *The Star*, 13 November 2013.
9 Sally Evans, Krejcir: Revenge of the Serbs? *Mail & Guardian*, 15 November 2013, http://mg.co.za/article/2013-11-14-krejcir-revenge-of-the-serbs, accessed 17 June 2016.

10 Jaroslav Kmenta, *The Godfather African*. Prague: BookBaby, 2016.
11 Shain Germaner and Angelique Serrao, Krejcir associate held over R10m, *The Star*, 18 November 2013.
12 Affidavit by investigating officer Humbelani Jonathan Makhado from the Hawks in the case against Ivan Savov 14 November 2013.
13 Angelique Serrao, SARS tells of Krejcir 'fraud scheme', Savov to seek bail today, *The Star*, 19 November 2013.
14 Affidavit by SARS investigator Johann van Loggerenberg in support of a preservation order against Radovan Krejcir, 1 November 2013.
15 Angelique Serrao, Mother offers reward of R2m, *Pretoria News*, 20 November 2013.
16 Mandy Wiener, Radovan Krejcir breaks his silence, *The Star*, 15 November 2013.
17 Ibid.
18 Ibid.

CHAPTER 15

1 Information gathered from author's interviews with police insiders who were present at the meeting.
2 Ibid.
3 Ibid.
4 Ibid.
5 Ibid.
6 Ibid.
7 Thanduxolo Jika, The mom behind Krejcir's failed escape bid, *Sunday Times*, 4 October 2015, http://www.timeslives.co.za/sundaytimes/stnews/2015/10/04/The-mom-behind-Krejcirs-failed-escape-bid, accessed 1 June 2016.
8 Ibid.
9 Sameer Naik, Krejcir arrested. Heavily armed police storm Czech fugitive's mansion, *Saturday Star*, 23 November 2013.
10 Ibid.
11 Henriette Geldenhuys, Ivor Powell and SAPA, Arrest foils Krejcir plot to flee SA, *Cape Argus*, 24 November 2013.
12 Author's interviews with Paul O'Sullivan, March 2016.
13 Henriette Geldenhuys, Ivor Powell and SAPA, Arrest foils Krejcir plot to flee SA, *Cape Argus*, 24 November 2013.
14 Ibid.
15 Brendan Roane, Hawk caught in Krejcir net, *The Star*, 26 November 2013.
16 Brendan Roane, Angelique Serrao and Solly Maphumulo, Krejcir: 'Saddam' nabbed, *The Star*, 27 November 2013.
17 Ibid.
18 Brendan Roane and Angelique Serrao, Hawks officer 'Saddam' held in connection with Krejcir attempted murder case, *The Star*, 27 November 2013.
19 Sally Evans, Krejcir's R400k loan to top cop, *Mail & Guardian*, 22 November 2013, http://mg.co.za/article/2013-11-21-krejcirs-r400k-loan-to-top-cop, accessed 5 June 2016.

20 Loyiso Sidimba and Candice Bailey, Police fear for Krejcir's safety, says Phiyega, *The Sunday Independent*, 24 November 2013.

21 Ibid.

22 Brendan Roane, Krejcir claims the police tortured him, *Cape Times*, 25 November 2013.

23 Ibid.

24 Ibid.

25 Ibid.

26 Ibid.

27 Mpiletso Motumi, Late-night Krejcir court drama, *The Star*, 25 November 2013.

28 Karyn Maughan, Krejcir in danger of organ failure, eNCA, 24 November 2013, https://www.enca.com/south-africa/krejcir-danger-organ-failure, accessed 20 June 2016.

29 Mpiletso Motumi, Late-night Krejcir court drama, *The Star*, 25 November 2013.

30 Ibid.

31 Ibid.

32 Ibid.

33 Ibid.

34 Shain Germaner and Theresa Taylor, Judge sends Krejcir to hospital, *Cape Times*, 26 November 2013.

35 Ibid.

CHAPTER 16

1 In pictures: The fall of Krejcir's Bedfordview palace, eNCA, 25 November 2015, https://www.enca.com/south-africa/pictures-fall-bedfordview-palace, accessed 6 June 2016.

2 Wikipedia, https://en.wikipedia.org/wiki/Al_Capone, accessed 25 May 2016.

3 Shaun Smillie, SARS seizes Krejcir's luxury cars, *The Star*, 24 March 2011.

4 Ibid.

5 Ibid.

6 Simone Haysom, Krejcir and the destruction of state capacity, amaBhungane, 1 April 2016, http://amabhungane.co.za/article/2016-04-01-00-sars-krejcir-and-the-destruction-of-state-capacity, accessed 6 June 2016.

7 Ibid.

8 Julian Rademeyer, Krejcir scoffs at 'Mafia boss' claims, *Rapport*, 29 August 2010, http://www.news24.com/SouthAfrica/News/Krejcir-scoffs-at-Mafia-boss-claims-20100829, accessed 14 April 2016.

9 Henriette Geldenhuys, Sars probes fugitive Krejcir, *Cape Argus*, 29 September 2012.

10 Ibid.

11 Ibid.

12 Founding affidavit in support of an application for a preservation order as envisaged in Section 163 of the Tax Administration Act 28 of 2011. Affidavit by Johann van Loggerenberg. The Commissioner for the South African Revenue Service versus Radovan Krejcir and the individuals, close corporations, companies and trusts listed in schedule A.

13 Ibid.
14 Ibid.
15 Zelda Venter, Krejcir to lose all his assets, *Pretoria News*, 23 May 2014.
16 Founding affidavit in support of an application for a preservation order as envisaged in Section 163 of the Tax Administration Act 28 of 2011. Affidavit by Johann van Loggerenberg. The Commissioner for the South African Revenue Service versus Radovan Krejcir and the individuals, close corporations, companies and trusts listed in schedule A.
17 Ibid.
18 Ibid.
19 Ibid.
20 Ibid.
21 Ibid.
22 Ibid.
23 Ibid.
24 Ibid.
25 Ibid.
26 Ibid.
27 Ibid.
28 Ibid.
29 Angelique Serrao, Taxman places Krejcir's houses in Bloem and Bedfordview under legal restriction, *The Star*, 15 November 2013.
30 Ibid.

CHAPTER 17

1 Shain Germaner and Theresa Taylor, Judge sends Krejcir to hospital, *Cape Times*, 26 November 2013.
2 Brendan Roane, Mpiletso Motumi and Shain Germaner, Security fears see mad crush as cops clear area ahead of closed-off hearing, *The Star*, 25 November 2013.
3 Ibid.
4 Brendan Roane, I'm not flight risk, Krejcir tells court, *The Star*, 2 December 2013.
5 Ibid.
6 Brendan Roane, Krejcir accused of torture, *The Star*, 3 December 2013.
7 Witness: Krejcir poured boiling water over me, News24, 19 May 2014, http://www.news24.com/SouthAfrica/News/Witness-Krejcir-poured-boiling-water-over-me-20140519, accessed 2 June 2016.
8 Brendan Roane, Co-accused loses bid to scrap Krejcir confession, *The Star*, 4 December 2013.
9 Brendan Roane, We were opening curio shop, says Krejcir, *The Star*, 5 December 2013.
10 Lerato Mbangeni, Krejcir kidnapping co-accused a threat to witnesses, says State, *The Star*, 7 February 2014.
11 Lebogang Seale, Krejcir faces Christmas behind bars after failed bail attempt, *The Star*, 14 December 2013.

12 Founding affidavit in support of an application for a preservation order as envisaged in Section 163 of the Tax Administration Act 28 of 2011. Affidavit by Johann van Loggerenberg. The Commissioner for the South African Revenue Service versus Radovan Krejcir and the individuals, close corporations, companies and trusts listed in schedule A.

13 Angelique Serrao, Radovan Krejcir a suitable character for jail, judge told 'no link' to death, *The Star*, 4 January 2014.

14 Ibid.

15 Ibid.

16 Ibid.

17 Krejcir right-hand man arrested, SAPA, 10 June 2014, http://m.timeslive.co.za/local/?articleId=11928554, accessed 2 June 2016.

18 Brendan Roane, If you keep me in jail I'll become poor, says Krejcir – desperate plea for bail, *The Star*, 25 February 2014.

19 Ibid.

20 Theresa Taylor, Cops nab Krejcir's wife, *The Star*, 28 February 2014.

21 Ibid.

22 Brendan Roane, Krejcir, O'Sullivan in verbal stand-off, *The Star*, 6 May 2014.

23 Ibid.

24 Brendan Roane, 'My Krejcir kidnap hell', *The Star*, 19 May 2014.

25 Ibid.

26 Ibid.

27 Ibid.

28 Ibid.

29 Ibid.

30 Brendan Roane, Testimony of man 'tortured' by Krejcir queried, *The Star*, 22 May 2014.

31 Palesa Radebe, Man in Krejcir case 'spills beans', *The Star*, 14 May 2014.

32 Ibid.

33 Boiling water poured on kidnapped man's head, SAPA, 13 May 2014.

34 Krejcir and cronies tortured man, court told, SAPA, 13 May 2014.

35 Ibid.

36 Ibid.

37 Ibid.

38 Brendan Roane, Krejcir's lawyers issue subpoena to Phiyega over Czech's arrest, *Pretoria News*, 10 June 2014.

39 Amanda Watson, Krejcir defence not allowed to access O'Sullivan phone records, *The Citizen*, 25 August 2014, http://citizen.co.za/233666/krejcir-defense-not-allowed-to-access-osullivans-phone-records/, accessed 1 June 2016.

40 Ibid.

41 Palesa Radebe, Krejcir witness tells of tik pay-off, *The Star*, 16 May 2014.

42 Brendan Roane and Shain Germaner, Knife sets Krejcir judge on edge, *The Star*, 30 July 2014.

43 Ibid.

44 Brendan Roane, Court fracas over Krejcir's meals, *The Star*, 23 July 2014.

45 Posted on Facebook page Radovan Krejcir – Official.

46 Shain Germaner, Lighter side only makes him darker, *The Star*, 30 July 2015.
47 Ibid.
48 Ibid.
49 Zelda Venter, Depressed Krejcir has list of demands, *The Star*, 14 October 2015.
50 Shain Germaner, Krejcir's court applications fail spectacularly, *Saturday Star*, 5 April 2014.
51 Shain Germaner, Conviction doesn't sit well with Krejcir, *The Star*, 12 September 2015.
52 Shain Germaner, Krejcir now officially a criminal, *The Star*, 25 August 2015.
53 Phiyega welcomes Krejcir guilty verdict, *The Citizen*, 24 August 2015, http://www.citizen.co.za/652221/phiyega-welcomes-krejcir-guilty-verdict/, accessed 1 June 2016.
54 Ibid.

CHAPTER 18

1 Angelique Serrao, Assassins thwarted, *The Star*, 10 January 2014.
2 Ibid.
3 Ibid.
4 Ibid.
5 Angelique Serrao, Four linked to Krejcir in dock over plot to kill investigators, *The Star*, 14 January 2014.
6 Ibid.
7 Shain Germaner, Krejcir-accused Serero to face a string of charges, *The Star*, 23 January 2014.
8 Krejcir co-accused had phones in cell, court hears, SAPA, 18 March 2014, https://www.highbeam.com/doc/1G1-361898592.html, accessed 4 October 2016.
9 Angelique Serrao and Solly Maphumulo, Police officer 'supplied GPS data to hitmen', *Cape Times*, 17 January 2014.
10 Ibid.
11 Ibid.
12 Graeme Hosken, Police arrest Krejcir enforcers, *The Times*, 27 May 2014, http://www.timeslive.co.za/thetimes/2014/05/27/police-arrest-krejcir-enforcers, accessed 20 June 2016.
13 Shain Germaner, Alleged Krejcir hit man confesses, *The Star*, 27 May 2014.
14 Brendan Roane and Botho Molosankwe, Cops zero in on Krejcir's money man, *The Star*, 10 June 2014.
15 Shain Germaner, Intended victim linked to Krejcir overheard plot to kill him, *The Star*, 1 February 2014.
16 Angelique Serrao and Shain Germaner, Exposed: Krejcir's alleged plot to kill 5, *The Star*, 20 May 2016.
17 Ibid.
18 Ibid.
19 Solly Maphumulo, The cripple, the debt collector, the car man – 3 hits, 3 charges, *The Star*, 17 April 2014.
20 Ibid.

21 Brendan Roane and Solly Maphumulo, Krejcir charged with murder of employee, *The Mercury*, 23 April 2014.

CHAPTER 19

1 Author's interview with Jacob Nare, 12 February 2016.
2 Ibid.
3 Transcript of meeting between state witness and the head of witness protection Adam Dawood, 24 December 2015; sworn statement by Jacob Nare, 10 February 2016; sworn statement by Jacob Nare, 3 February 2016; letter sent by Attorney Darryl Furman to Deputy National Commissioner of Police Lieutenant General J Sithole, 8 February 2016; email sent by Paul O'Sullivan to the acting police commissioner, 3 February 2016.
4 Author's interview with Jacob Nare, 12 February 2016.
5 Ibid.
6 Ibid.
7 Ibid.
8 Ibid.
9 Ibid.
10 Ibid.
11 Ibid.
12 Ibid.
13 Ibid.
14 Ibid.
15 Ibid.
16 Sworn statement by Jacob Nare, 10 February 2016.
17 Ibid.
18 Ibid.
19 Ibid.
20 Transcript of meeting between state witness and head of witness protection Adam Dawood, 24 December 2015.
21 Ibid.
22 Letter sent by Attorney Darryl Furman to Deputy National Commissioner of Police Lieutenant General J Sithole, 8 February 2016.
23 Sworn statement by Jacob Nare, 10 February 2016.
24 Author's interview with Jacob Nare, 12 February 2016.

CHAPTER 20

1 Angelique Serrao, Alleged kingpin now faces over 100 charges, *The Star*, 9 February 2015.
2 Ibid.
3 Ibid.
4 Ibid.

5 Angelique Serrao, Krejcir's dark trail of crime and deception, *The Star*, 9 February 2015.

6 Ibid.

7 Graeme Hosken, 'Krejcir hitman' falls for sting, *The Times*, 26 June 2015, http://www.timeslive.co.za/thetimes/2015/06/26/Krejcir-hitman-falls-for-sting, accessed 1 July 2016.

8 Ibid.

9 Meet Krejcir's playmate, *The Star*, 29 April 2014.

10 Shain Germaner, Krejcir uses mistress as alibi for when 'drug dealer' Issa was killed, *Pretoria News*, 9 July 2015.

11 Shain Germaner, Krejcir's 'fat roll' takes centre stage in court, *The Star*, 11 May 2016.

12 Ibid.

13 Affidavit by Lucky Kgomotso Mokwena, 4 June 2015.

14 Shain Germaner, Explosive affidavit emerges in Krejcir murder trial as link to Agliotti alleged, *The Star*, 4 May 2016.

15 Ibid.

16 Ibid.

17 Ibid.

18 Affidavit by Lucky Kgomotso Mokwena, 4 June 2015.

19 Ibid.

20 Ibid.

21 Ibid.

22 Ibid.

23 Ibid.

24 Ibid.

25 Ibid.

26 Ibid.

27 Ibid.

28 Ibid.

29 Ibid.

CHAPTER 21

1 Zelda Venter, Krejcir's son in bid to return to SA, *Pretoria News*, 26 February 2015.

2 Ibid.

3 Ibid.

4 Angelique Serrao, Another woman linked to Krejcir arrested, *The Star*, 2 November 2015.

5 Solly Maphumulo, Krejcir jailbreak – Warders' arrests imminent as shocking details of plot emerge, *The Sunday Independent*, 4 October 2015.

6 Ibid.

7 Ibid.

8 Solly Maphumulo, Krejcir's escape plan, *The Star*, 6 October 2015.

9 Ibid.

10 Ibid.
11 Ngwako Malatji, 'King of Bling' William Mbatha linked to Krejcir's escape bid, *Sunday World*, 6 October 2015, http://www.sundayworld.co.za/news/2015/10/06/king-of-bling-william-mbatha-linked-to-krejcir-s-escape-bid, accessed 19 May 2016.
12 Ibid.
13 Ibid.
14 Solly Maphumulo, Krejcir's escape plan revealed, *The Star*, 6 October 2015.
15 Shain Germaner, Saps team watching Krejcir is doubled, *Cape Times*, 13 October 2015.
16 Angelique Serrao, Cellphone found in shoe during estate agent's visit to Krejcir, *The Star*, 26 October 2015.
17 Solly Maphumulo, Krejcir in lockdown to foil escape, *The Star*, 5 January 2016.
18 Ibid.
19 Solly Maphumulo, Krejcir planning to kill judge and nemesis, *The Star*, 18 February 2016.
20 Shain Germaner, Krejcir planned war to escape prison, *The Star*, 9 May 2016.
21 Ibid.
22 Ibid.
23 Shain Germaner, No bail for Krejcir's deceitful ex-lover, *The Star*, 5 August 2016.
24 Angelique Serrao, Krejcir's Playboy mistress arrested, News24, 25 July 2016, http://www.news24.com/SouthAfrica/News/krejcirs-mistress-arrested-20160725, accessed 25 July 2016.
25 Shain Germaner, No bail for Krejcir's deceitful ex-lover, *The Star*, 5 August 2016.
26 Ibid.
27 Angelique Serrao, Krejcir's Playboy mistress arrested, News24, 25 July 2016, http://www.news24.com/SouthAfrica/News/krejcirs-mistress-arrested-20160725, accessed 25 July 2016.

CHAPTER 22

1 Radovan Krejcir's letter to the Commission on Gender Equality written from Kgosi Mampuru Prison.
2 Ibid.
3 Krejcir's exercise equipment offered to Oscar without consent, *City Press*, 13 November 2014, http://www.news24.com/Archives/City-Press/Krejcirs-equipment-offered-to-Oscar-without-consent-20150429, accessed 28 June 2016.
4 Ibid.
5 Shain Germaner and Angelique Serrao, No pay, no counsel – lawyers, *The Star*, 28 October 2015.
6 Shain Germaner, Krejcir fires lawyer in bid to save money, *The Star*, 29 October 2015.
7 Angelique Serrao and Solly Maphumulo, Fury as Krejcir sentencing delayed again, *The Star*, 18 November 2015.
8 Draft order and affidavits filed in the Johannesburg High Court in the matter between Pushpaveni Naidoo, Radovan Krejcir and Sechaba Investments, the Minister of Safety and Security and ABSA Bank Limited.

9 Shain Germaner, Court evacuated after bomb threat at Krejcir hearing, *The Star*, 23 February 2016.

10 Mzwandile Faniso and Sduduzo Dludla, Krejcir jailed for 35 years, *The Times*, 23 February 2016, http://www.timeslive.co.za/local/2016/02/23/Krejcir-jailed-for-35-years, accessed 26 June 2016.

11 Ibid.

12 Shain Germaner, Judge sentences Krejcir to 35 years in prison, *The Star*, 24 February 2016.

13 Ibid.

14 Promotions for Krejcir team, Africa News Agency, 1 October 2015.

15 Angelique Serrao, O'Sullivan is granted relaxed bail deal, *The Star*, 8 June 2016.

16 Radovan Krejcir to appeal conviction, Africa News Agency, 24 February 2016.

17 Shain Germaner, Krejcir conviction appeal under way, *The Star*, 24 May 2016.

18 Angelique Serrao, Krejcir and cronies lose their appeal, *The Star*, 21 April 2016.

19 Shain Germaner, Officials refuse to take Krejcir to court, *The Star*, 29 June 2016.

20 Ibid.

21 Shain Germaner, Krejcir extradition hearing hanging in balance, *The Star*, 4 July 2016.

22 Ibid.

23 Shain Germaner, Krejcir's mom cuts him off financially, *The Star*, 8 July 2016.

24 Shain Germaner, Krejcir appears set to negotiate plea deal, *The Star*, 21 July 2016.

25 Shain Germaner, Lawyers steer clear of Krejcir, *The Star*, 24 August 2016.

Further references

CHAPTER 2

As he ran, Radovan Krejcir. Novinky.cz, 27 April 2007, http://www.novinky.cz/krimi/114074-jak-utikal-radovan-krejcir.html, accessed 13 April 2016.

Dvořák, Martin. Krejcir left the luxury hotel three days before the journalists, iDNES.cz, 15 September 2005, http://zpravy.idnes.cz/krejcir-odjel-z-luxusniho-hotelu-tri-dny-pred-novinari-pgb-/domaci.aspx?c=A050915_154843_domaci_miz, accessed 13 April 2016.

Geldenhuys, Henriette. Prague court gives Krejcir 11-year term, *Cape Argus*, 9 December 2012.

Krejcir allegedly showed the bill CSSD 60 million. Novinky.cz, 15 May 2006, http://www.novinky.cz/krimi/85365-krejcir-ukazal-udajnou-smenku-cssd-na-60-milionu.html, accessed 13 April 2016.

Mikule, Martin. Czech multi-millionaire on the run, Radio Prague, 21 June 2005, http://www.radio.cz/en/section/curraffrs/czech-multi-millionaire-on-the-run, accessed 13 April 2016.

Radovan Krejcir. Osobnosti.cz, http://www.financnici.cz/radovan-krejcir, accessed 13 April 2016.

SAPA (South African Press Association). Krejcir used Seychelles passport to enter country, 30 November 2013.

Velinger, Jan. Football boss, associates in custody after dramatic arrests, Radio Prague, 15 November 2006, http://www.radio.cz/en/section/curraffrs/football-boss-associates-in-custody-after-dramatic-arrests, accessed 14 April 2016.

CHAPTER 3

amaBhungane. Mobster at the gates: The ugly saga of Radovan Krejcir, *Mail & Guardian*, 10 September 2010, http://mg.co.za/article/2010-09-10-mobster-at-the-gates-ugly-saga-of-radovan-krejcir, accessed 14 April 2016.

Cohen, Drew F. Asylum, shaken, not stirred, US News, 22 October 2013, http://www.usnews.com/opinion/blogs/world-report/2013/10/22/what-south-africas-james-bond-radovan-krej-reveals-about-refugees-and-asylum-seekers, accessed 14 April 2016.

ConCourt rules on M & G vs Krejcir, Politicsweb, 27 September 2013, http://www.politicsweb.co.za/news-and-analysis/concourt-rules-on-mg-vs-krejcir, accessed 19 April 2016.

De Lange, Ilse. The Constitutional Court has opened the door for the media to apply to the Refugee Appeal Board to attend the asylum hearing of controversial Czech fugitive Radovan Krejcir, *The Citizen*, 28 September 2013, http://citizen.co.za/55011/krejcir-asylum-media-ban-invalid/, accessed 14 April 2016.

Eliseev, Alex. Czech fugitive back behind bars, *The Star*, 14 June 2007.

Eliseev, Alex. Czech fugitive claims health problems, *The Star*, 8 May 2007.

Eliseev, Alex. Czech fugitive freed on legal technicality, *The Star*, 5 June 2007.

Eliseev, Alex. Czech fugitive loses battle to declare his arrest unlawful, *The Star*, 23 May 2007.

Eliseev, Alex. Legal battle looms in Czech fugitive's bail bid, *The Star*, 3 May 2007.

Eliseev, Alex. Surprise twist in the case of billionaire Czech fugitive, *The Star*, 18 May 2007.

Germaner, Shain. Krejcir extradition bid shelved for 3 months, *Pretoria News*, 13 September 2013.

Germaner, Shain. Krejcir may face extradition bid, *Pretoria News*, 31 August 2010.

Germaner, Shain and Baldwin Ndaba. Billionaire extradition case to be reopened, *The Mercury*, 2 September 2010.

Milo, Dario. Con Court rules on media access to Krejcir refugee appeal, Webber Wentzel, 21 February 2013, http://blogs.webberwentzel.com/2013/02/con-court-rules-on-media-access-to-krejcir-refugee-appeal/, accessed 14 April 2016.

O'Connor, Coilin. Fugitive Czech billionaire arrested in South Africa, Radio Prague, 24 April 2007, http://www.radio.cz/en/section/curraffrs/fugitive-czech-billionaire-arrested-in-south-africa, accessed 13 April 2016.

Pillay, Verashni. M & G leads court bid to access Krejcir asylum hearing, *Mail & Guardian*, 14 April 2011, http://mg.co.za/article/2011-04-14-mg-leads-court-bid-to-access-krejcir-asylum-hearing, accessed 14 April 2016.

Radovan Krejcir Czech-mate looms for moneyed fugitive on the run, *The Sunday Independent*, 31 October 2010.

Richter, Jan. Runaway businessman Radovan Krejcir bails out, Radio Prague, 9 July 2007, http://www.radio.cz/en/section/curraffrs/runaway-businessman-radovan-krejcir-bails-out, accessed 14 April 2016.

Serrao, Angelique. He faces 31 years' jail if he loses asylum bid, *The Star*, 25 November 2013.

Serrao, Angelique. Journalists take board 'privacy' rule to Concourt, *The Star*, 14 May 2013.

Tolsi, Niren. SALC in the News: Krejcir appeal tests rights of refugees, *Mail & Guardian*, 21 May 2013, http://www.southernafricalitigationcentre.org/2013/05/21/salc-in-the-news-krejcir-appeal-tests-rights-of-refugees/, accessed 14 April 2016.

Venter, Zelda. Krejcir hearing draws media interest, *The Star*, 16 November 2012.

Venter, Zelda. Media lose bid to attend Krejcir hearing, *The Star*, 7 December 2012.

CHAPTER 4

Rademeyer, Julian. Krejcir scoffs at 'Mafia boss' claims, *Rapport*, 29 August 2010, http://www.news24.com/SouthAfrica/News/Krejcir-scoffs-at-Mafia-boss-claims-20100829, accessed 14 April 2016.

CHAPTER 5

Affidavit of George Smith (Affidavit no. 5), 5 November 2014.

Ajam, Kashiefa. Cops are out to get me, *Pretoria News*, 7 August 2010.

Ajam, Kashiefa. Lolly at large, *Cape Argus*, 8 May 2010.

Grange, Helen. SA refuge for underworld, *Sunday Tribune*, 16 May 2010.

Hawks examine explosive O'Sullivan dossier, *The Sunday Independent*, 8 August 2010.

Hosken, Graeme. Cops aided Lolly killer to skip SA, *Pretoria News*, 6 July 2010.

Hosken, Graeme. Raids to hunt Lolly's killer, *Pretoria News*, 7 May 2010.

Hosken, Graeme. Top cops suspected of graft booted out, *Pretoria News*, 1 December 2011.

Lolly Jackson murdered, News24, http://www.news24.com/SouthAfrica/News/Lolly-Jackson-murdered-20100503, accessed 28 April 2010.

Lolly the sleaze, *Sunday Tribune*, 9 May 2010.

Lolly's unholy trinity, *The Star*, 6 May 2010.

Merten, Marianne. Cop linked to Krejcir sacked, *Cape Argus*, 8 October 2011.

Mystery veil over Lolly's killer, *The Star*, 5 May 2010.

Potgieter, De Wet. Hawks question regulars at Lolly Jackson hangout, *Cape Argus*,

16 May 2010.

Potgieter, De Wet. Interpol hunts Serbian general: Fight for sex trade control, *Sunday Tribune*, 9 May 2010.

Potgieter, De Wet. Jackson suspect linked to two more mysteries, *Cape Argus*, 6 June 2010.

Potgieter, De Wet. Mystery person at scene of Lolly Jackson murder, *Cape Argus*, 13 March 2011.

Rademeyer, Julian. Lolly turned on Krejcir – and died, *City Press*, 27 March 2011.

SAPA. Lolly Jackson shot dead, http://www.timeslive.co.za/local/2010/05/03/lolly-jackson-shot-dead, accessed 28 April 2010.

SAPA. No tease after Lolly Jackson murder, http://www.timeslive.co.za/local/2010/05/04/no-tease-after-lolly-jackson-murder, accessed 28 April 2010.

SAPA. Teazers boss Lolly Jackson murdered, http://www.moneyweb.co.za/archive/teazers-boss-lolly-jackson-murdered/, accessed 28 April 2010.

Serrao, Angelique. 'I did not kill Lolly', *The Star*, 18 April 2011.

Serrao, Angelique. Wife denies Lolly was a greedy man, *The Star*, 18 April 2011.

Serrao, Angelique and Louise Flanagan. Lolly manager held, *The Star*, 1 June 2010.

Serrao, Angelique, Shain Germaner and Kristen van Schie. Mourners bid Lolly final farewell, *The Star*, 11 May 2010.

Serrao, Angelique, Shaun Smillie and Shain Germaner. Jackson murder suspect in Cyprus, *The Star*, 6 July 2010.

Smith, Janet. Teazers don buried metres away from Hani, *The Star*, 11 May 2010.

Strip king Lolly Jackson's round-about life, *The Sunday Independent*, 9 May 2010.

Thamm, Marianne. Bad cops, assassins, Czech fugitives: The meaning of Paul O'Sullivan, *Daily Maverick*, 15 January 2014, http://www.poaa.za.com/media/bad-cops-assassins-czech-fugitives-the-meaning-of-paul-osullivan/, accessed 19 April 2016.

Wiener, Mandy. Exclusive: Lolly Jackson's widow speaks out after her husband's murder, Eyewitness news, http://ewn.co.za/2010/05/06/EXCLUSIVE-Lolly-Jacksons-widow-speaks-out-after-her-husbands-murder, accessed 28 April 2010.

CHAPTER 6

Germaner, Shain. Gemballa killer's term increased: Czech fugitive linked to case, *The Star*, 15 August 2013.

Germaner, Shain. Gemballa witness shock: Mpye perjured himself – expert, *The Star*, 7 August 2013.

Germaner, Shain. 'I know nothing about Gemballa's killing', *The Star*, 8 August 2013.

Germaner, Shain. New twist in Gemballa trial as state's star witness cries foul Krejcir link, *Pretoria News*, 7 August 2013.

Germaner, Shain. Uwe Gemballa's killer taken to another prison, *The Star*, 14 August 2013.

Mooki, Omphitlhetse. High-profile witnesses in murder case, *The Star*, 4 November 2010.

Mooki, Omphitlhetse. Trial set for three accused of kidnapping, murdering German, *The Star*, 31 August 2011.

Potgieter, De Wet. Face-off between lawyer and 'mafia boss', *Cape Argus*, 11 December 2010.

Potgieter, De Wet. Four held for Gemballa's murder, *Cape Argus*, 10 October 2010.

Potgieter, De Wet and Graeme Hosken. Sources claim slain German businessman linked to racketeering, *The Mercury*, 4 October 2010.

Uwe Gemballa's widow seeks answers, *Mail & Guardian*, http://mg.co.za/article/2013-02-22-00-uwe-gemballa-widow-seeks-answers, accessed 10 May 2016.

CHAPTER 7

Beeka murder linked to massive international crime web, *Cape Argus*, 24 March 2011.

Eggington, Shanaaz. The many faces of Cyril Beeka, Times Live, http://www.timeslive.co.za/local/2011/03/26/the-many-faces-of-cyril-beeka, accessed 23 May 2016.

Fugitive's web of crime, *The Star*, 24 March 2011.

Geldenhuys, Henriette. Beeka owed fugitive Krejcir R1,2m, *Cape Argus*, 15 January 2012.

Geldenhuys, Henriette. Gavric's status in SA reviewed, *Cape Argus*, 10 March 2012.

Geldenhuys, Henriette. How I got rich in the property market – by former murder suspect, *The Sunday Independent*, 5 February 2012.

Geldenhuys, Henriette. No proof of dealings with slain Beeka, *Cape Argus*, 13 October 2012.

Geldenhuys, Henriette. Serbian drug trafficker may be hiding in SA, *Cape Argus*, 12 February 2012.

Geldenhuys, Henriette. Squabble over Beeka's posh Plattekloof home, *Cape Argus*, 5 February 2012.

Hartley, Aziz and Quinton Mtyala, Underworld boss slain, *The Star*, 22 March 2011.

Hawks insider may have given Krejcir raid tip-off – Polela, *Cape Argus*, 24 March 2011.

'He is trying to build himself up into a boss', *Cape Times*, 24 March 2011.

Hosken, Graeme. Krejcir: Cops in firing line, *The Independent on Saturday*, 26 March 2011.

Hosken, Graeme. 'Krejcir is still dangerous', *The Star*, 26 March 2011.

Hosken, Graeme. Private eye targets Krejcir, *Pretoria News*, 25 March 2011.

Killed before he could testify, *Cape Argus*, 11 October 2013.

Krejcir denies Beeka murder claim, *Mail & Guardian*, 12 April 2011, http://www.mg.co.za/article/2011-04-12-krejcir-denies-beeka-murder-claim, accessed 23 May 2016.

Mckune, Craig and Sally Evans, Battle for control of the doors and the drugs, *Mail & Guardian*, 3 February 2012, http://mg.co.za/article/2012-02-03-battle-for-control-of-the-doors-and-drugs, accessed 23 May 2016.

Murdered kingpin's diverse shadowy dealings, *Cape Argus*, 3 April 2011.

Ncana, Nkululeko. Beeka family feud takes ugly turn, *Sunday World*, 15 September 2013, http://www.sundayworld.co.za/news/2013/09/15/beeka-family-feud-takes-ugly-turn, accessed 23 May 2016.

Potgieter, De Wet. Krejcir raid blunders taint Hawks probe, *Cape Argus*, 27 March 2011.

Potgieter, De Wet. The mark of assassins – bullet wounds close together, *The Star*, 26 March 2011.

Serrao, Angelique and Shain Germaner. Hawks uncover hit list, *The Star*, 23 March 2011.

Smillie, Shaun, Shain Germaner and Candice Bailey. New twist in Krejcir saga, *The Star*, 25 March 2011.

Sole, Sam. Krejcir, Gavric – how McMafia came to South Africa, *Mail & Guardian*, 6 January 2012, http://mg.co.za/article/2012-01-06-krejcir-gavric-how-mcmafia-came-to-south-africa, accessed 23 May 2016.

Sole, Sam, Sally Evans and Craig McKune. Underworld boss Beeka's murder mystery deepens, *Mail & Guardian*, 23 December 2011, http://mg.co.za/article/2011-12-23-beeka-mystery-deepens, accessed 23 May 2016.

Swart, Werner, Sashni Pather, Stephan Hofstatter, Mzilikazi wa Afrika and Shanaaz Eggington. Beeka exposed as SA spy, *Sunday Times*, 26 March, 2011.

CHAPTER 8

Bailey, Candice. Women take over businesses of their controversial men, *The Star*, 12 April 2011.

Businessman shot down at Cradle Restaurant, *Business Day* and SAPA, http://www.bdlive.co.za/articles/2010/10/12/businessman-gunned-down-at-cradle-restaurant, accessed 23 May 2016.

Du Preez, Yolande. Czech fugitive, two co-accused get bail, *Pretoria News*, 18 February 2012.

Du Preez, Yolande. Krejcir, co-accused in dock for robbery, *Pretoria News*, 14 February 2012.

Germaner, Shain. Krejcir elated as bail is set at R500 000, *The Independent on Saturday*, 9 April 2011.

Germaner, Shain. Krejcir fraud trial on ice for now, *The Star*, 16 April 2012.

Germaner, Shain. Krejcir in bid to reduce R500 000 bail, *The Star*, 9 July 2011.

Germaner, Shain. Magistrate rejects Krejcir's plea for court to reduce bail amount, *The Star*, 14 July 2011.

Germaner, Shain. Tight security for lawyer and accused, *Pretoria News*, 7 April 2011.

Germaner, Shain. Ugly war of words and threats in Krejcir case, *The Star*, 27 April 2011.

Hosken, Graeme. Fugitive's arrest blasted as biased, *Pretoria News*, 13 February 2012.

Hosken, Graeme. Krejcir's mother arrives amid suspicion of subterfuge, *The Star*, 7 April 2011.

Krejcir in prison mix-up, *Cape Argus*, 29 March 2011.

Maphumulo, Solly. Ambush wasn't first brush with violence, *The Star*, 13 October 2010.

Maughan, Karyn. The magical slippery man, Radovan Krejcir, *Daily Maverick*, 17 April 2012, http://dailymaverick.co.za/article/2012-04-17-the-magical-slippery-man-radovan-krejcir/#.VOLJRFUrLcs, accessed 23 May 2016.

Mooki, Omphitlhetse and Shain Germaner. Tales of hits and envy, *The Star*, 8 April 2011.

Nicholson, Zara. Beeka bodyguard is discharged, *Cape Times*, 30 March 2011.

Nicolaides, Gia. Cradle Restaurant shooting victim previously killed a robber, Eyewitness News, http://ewn.co.za/2010/10/15/Cradle-Restaurant-shooting-victim-previously-killed-a-robber, accessed 23 May 2016.

Potgieter, De Wet. 'Doctor asked me to kill Czech tycoon', *The Sunday Independent*, 10 April 2011.

Potgieter, De Wet. Top cop seeks protection, *The Independent on Saturday*, 2 April 2011.

Rademeyer, Julian. Gemballa murder fugitive claims hit, Media 24 Investigations, 16 March 2011.

SAPA. 'I have every incentive to stay in SA', 17 February 2012.

SAPA. Krejcir flew in Serbian assassins, 8 April 2011.

SAPA. Man with links to Agliotti is shot dead at wedding, http://www.sowetanlive.co.za/news/2010/10/12/man-with-links-to-agliotti-is-shot-dead-at-wedding, accessed 23 May 2016.

Swart, Werner and Sashni Pather. Krejcir: Four years of murder, sleaze and mayhem, *Sunday Times*, 26 March 2011.

Tromp, Beauregard. Doctor admits to R4m Krejcir insurance scam, *The Star*, 18 March 2011.

CHAPTER 9

Evans, Sally. Lolly's lawyer's murder rattles Jo'burg underworld, *Mail & Guardian*, 23 September 2011, http://mg.co.za/article/2011-09-23-lolly-lawyers-murder-rattles-joburg-underworld, accessed 30 May 2016.

Geldenhuys, Henriette. Lawyer murdered after rejecting estate claim, *The Star*, 13 October 2012.

Germaner, Shain. Links with Krejcir cost six their lives, *The Star*, 23 September 2011.

Germaner, Shain. Riddle of Lolly's lawyer: Dental record needed to identify charred body – Jackson's associates targeted, *Daily News*, 22 September 2011.

Krejcir debt claim 'a sham', amaBhungane, http://amabhungane.co.za/article/2012-06-15-krejcir-debt-claim-a-sham, accessed 30 May 2016.

Serrao, Angelique. Legal battle over Teazers boss Lolly's millions, *The Star*, 9 February 2012.

Serrao, Angelique. Mystery of 'missing teeth', *The Star*, 26 September 2011.

CHAPTER 10

Affidavit of George Smith (Affidavit No. 3), 5 November 2014.

Ajam, Kashiefa. Lolly extradition hearing under way, *The Star*, 12 May 2012.

Author's interviews with Owen Blumberg, 5 August 2015 and 31 August 2015, Rosebank.

Dying Louca spills beans on Lolly Jackson murder, http://www.news24.com/SouthAfrica/News/Dying-Louka-spills-beans-on-Lolly-Jackson-murder-20150421, accessed 28 April 2016.

George Louka, http://www.sabc.co.za/wps/portal/news/main/tag?tag=George%20

Louka, accessed 29 April 2016.

George Louka dies, http://www.news24.com/SouthAfrica/News/George-Louka-dies-20150511, accessed 29 April 2016.

'George Louca was not a murderer', http://ewn.co.za/2015/05/14/Dimitri-Panayiotou-George-Louca-was-not-a-murderer, accessed 29 April 2016.

Germaner, Shain. Ailing Louca to apply for release from prison before trial, *The Star*, 9 April 2015.

Germaner, Shain. Health scare lands murder accused Louca in hospital, *The Star*, 24 February 2015.

Germaner, Shain. Lolly 'killer' demands freedom, *The Star*, 7 April 2015.

Germaner, Shain. Lolly's ailing alleged killer seeking release, *The Star*, 21 April 2015.

Germaner, Shain. Louca glad to be able to tell story, *The Star*, 13 May 2015.

Germaner, Shain. Louca to appear via CCTV due to threats, *The Star*, 18 July 2014.

Germaner, Shain. Louca to try again after losing court bid to return home, *Pretoria News*, 23 April 2015.

Germaner, Shain. Louca will tell the truth, says lawyer, *Daily News*, 27 January 2015.

Germaner, Shain. State seeking to prove Louca killed Lolly Jackson, *Pretoria News*, 21 June 2014.

Germaner, Shain. Teazers murder trial delayed by illness, *The Star*, 7 March 2015.

Germaner, Shain. Will prosecution service end up in dock? *The Star*, 13 May 2015.

Germaner, Shain and Anna Cox. 'Trial dragged out so Louca would die', *Cape Times*, 13 May 2015.

Germaner, Shain and Peter Fabricius. Man wanted in SA to face Cypriot court, *The Mercury*, 27 March 2012.

Germaner, Shain, Angelique Serrao, Kevin Ritchie and Peter Fabricius. Strip club boss's suspected hitman nabbed in Cyprus, *The Star*, 27 March 2012.

Germaner, Shain and Rabbie Serumula. Lawyer says ailing Louca may not make it to court, *The Star*, 9 May 2015.

Lolly Jackson: Will we ever know?, http://citizen.co.za/281020/lolly-jackson-will-we-ever-know/, accessed 28 April 2016.

Louka has crime bosses sweating, http://www.timeslive.co.za/thetimes/2014/02/11/louka-has-crime-bosses-sweating1, accessed 29 April 2016.

Louka promised to bring down the big boys, *The Star*, 24 March 2012.

Louka remains to leave SA for Cyprus, http://www.news24.com/SouthAfrica/News/Loukas-remains-to-leave-SA-for-Cyprus-20150515, accessed 29 April 2016.

Merten, Marianne and Ivor Powell. Teazers murder man arrested, *The Independent on Saturday*, 24 March 2012.

Serrao, Angelique. Louca's tight security constrains lawyer, *The Star*, 13 May 2014.

Serrao, Angelique and Shain Germaner. Louca breakthrough in Lolly murder probe, *The Star*, 10 February 2014.

CHAPTER 11

Ajam, Kashiefa. Hawks to probe apparent hit on Czech fugitive, *The Star*, 27 July 2013.

Dolley, Caryn. Krejcir denies underworld rumours, *Cape Times*, 26 July 2013.

CHAPTER 12

Sworn statement by Paul O'Sullivan relating to his meeting with Miloslav Potiska and the whereabouts of stolen property, firearms and documentation used for criminal purposes, 30 November 2014.

Sworn statement by Miloslav Potiska on Krejcir and his link to Bassam 'Sam' Issa, 27 February 2015.

Watson, Amanda. 'Krejcir was a dangerous man' – witness, *The Citizen*, http://citizen.co.za/440701/krejcir-a-psychopath-and-a-dangerous-man-witness/, accessed 14 June 2016.

CHAPTER 13

Cox, Anna. Hawks rule out hit by police, *The Mercury*, 14 October 2013.

Dolley, Caryn. Braai-killing the latest in string of underworld hits, *Cape Times*, 16 October 2013.

Geldenhuys, Henriette. Alleged Krejcir sidekick slain, *Cape Argus*, 3 November 2013.

Krejcir's son a suspect in Issa murder, eNCA, 30 June 2015, https://www.enca.com/south-africa/krejcirs-son-suspect-issa-murder, accessed 17 June 2016.

Naik, Sameer. Murdered underworld figure couldn't keep quiet, *Pretoria News*, 9 November 2013.

Naik, Sameer. Slain 'Black Sam' Issa owed drug suppliers millions, *The Star*, 19 October 2013.

Nkosi, Bongani. Man shot was Krejcir's 'associate', *The Sunday Independent*, 3 November 2013.

Sworn statement by Jerome Safi on the threat to his life, 13 October 2013.

CHAPTER 14

Roane, Brendan. It's all hype, Krejcir's sidekick Savov tells court, *The Star*, 23 November 2013.

Roane, Brendan and Angelique Serrao. Two more appear for fraud relating to Radovan Krejcir dealings, *The Star*, 22 November 2013.

Serrao, Angelique. How did he become an SA citizen?, *The Star*, 20 November 2013.

Serrao, Angelique. Krejcir's manager in the dock on fraud rap, *The Star*, 18 November 2013.

Serrao, Angelique and Brendan Roane. Krejcir associates lie low after blast, *Cape Times*, 14 November 2013.

Van Wyk, Pauli. Bomb kills two outside Krejcir's business, *The Witness*, 13 November 2013, http://m.news24.com/news24/Archives/Witness/Bomb-kills-two-outside-Krejcirs-business-20150430, accessed 17 June 2016.

CHAPTER 15

Conway-Smith, Erin. 'All my life is like James Bond stuff. That's how I live my life', 29 November 2013, http://www.globalpost.com/dispatch/news/regions/africa/south-africa/131127/bizarre-crime-saga-czech-Radovan-Krejcir-captivates-south-africa, accessed 19 April 2016.

Roane, Brendan. Krejcir requests transfer to hospital, *The Star*, 25 November 2013.

CHAPTER 16

Ajam, Kashiefa and Sameer Naik. SARS moves in on Krejcir, *The Independent on Saturday*, 16 November 2013.

De Lange, Ilse. Krejcir's hidden millions, *The Citizen*, http://citizen.co.za/182700/krejcirs-smoke-mirrors-scheme/, accessed 6 June 2016.

Germaner, Shain. Krejcir tackles SARS in new bail bid, *The Star*, 1 April 2014.

Hosken, Graeme. Krejcir's empire in flames, *The Times*, 23 May 2014, http://www.timeslive.co.za/thetimes/2014/05/23/krejcir-s-empire-in-flames?service=print, accessed 6 June 2016.

Inside Krejcir's mansion where he partied with Playboy models and gangsters, 25 November 2015, http://www.2oceansvibe.com/2015/11/25/inside-krejcirs-mansion-where-he-partied-with-playboy-models-and-gangsters-video/, accessed 6 June 2016.

Krejcir's R100m tax bill, *City Press*, 28 July 2013, http://www.news24.com/Archives/City-Press/Krejcirs-R100m-tax-bill-20150429, accessed 6 June 2016.

Lindeque, Mia. Krejcir's JHB, Vaal properties sold for R17m, Eyewitness News, 29 November 2015, http://ewn.co.za/Topic/Czech-fugitive-Radovan-Krejcir, accessed 6 June 2016.

Maphumulo, Solly. Sars guns for Lolly, *The Star*, 10 May 2013.

Musviba, Nyasha. Czech-mate: Sars closes in on Krejcir, South African Tax Guide, 22 November 2013, http://www.sataxguide.co.za/czech-mate-sars-closes-in-on-krejcir/, accessed 6 June 2016.

Potgieter, De Wet. Krejcir ex-partner wants R36m back from SARS, *Cape Argus*, 27 March 2011.

Radovan Krejcir's pricy toys, *City Press*, 25 May 2014, http://www.news24.com/Archives/City-Press/Radovan-Krejcirs-pricy-toys-20150429, accessed 6 June 2016.

Sole, Sam and Sally Evans. SARS delivers a blow to Krejcir's assets, *Mail & Guardian*, 15 November 2013, http://mg.co.za/article/2013-11-15-sars-krejcirs-assets, accessed 6 June 2016.

Venter, Zelda. Krejcir to lose all assets, court rules, *Pretoria News*, 23 May 2014.

CHAPTER 17

Germaner, Shain. Friend links Oscar, Czech O'Sullivan's phone records 'could endanger his sources', *The Star*, 2 June 2014.

Germaner, Shain. Krejcir loses 'opportunistic' bail appeal, *Daily News*, 9 January 2014.

Germaner, Shain. No (in)mates for Czech, rules judge, *Pretoria News*, 5 April 2014.

Mailula, Naledi. Krejcir and his wife laugh at State witness's testimony, *The Star*, 17 May 2014.

Mokati, Noni. Krejcir's wife freed from jail, *The Star*, 1 March 2014.

Radebe, Palesa. Krejcir said to have turned his anger on drug runner's brother, *The Star*, 13 May 2014.

Roane, Brendan. 'Cold-hearted criminal' lashed by accused 'for torturing innocent man', *The Star*, 23 May 2014.

Roane, Brendan. 'Cops are frightened of Krejcir', *Pretoria News*, 24 May 2014.

Roane, Brendan. Hawks officer's court date with Krejcir set, *The Star*, 28 November 2013.

Roane, Brendan. Krejcir's bail bid fails on fourth time, *The Star*, 16 April 2014.

Roane, Brendan. Krejcir's legal team accused of fraud, *The Star*, 31 May 2014.

Roane, Brendan. Krejcir's manager facing extra charges involving other parties, *The Star*, 5 February 2014.

Roane, Brendan. Krejcir victim 'too weak, confused to tell cops of torture', *The Star*, 21 May 2014.

Roane, Brendan. Questions over Krejcir accused's cars, *The Star*, 12 December 2013.

Roane, Brendan. Testimony of man 'tortured' by Krejcir queried, *The Star*, 22 May 2014.

SAPA. Case on Krejcir's wife withdrawn, 11 April 2014.

SAPA. I felt no pity, Krejcir witness tells court, 15 May 2014.

SAPA. Kidnap victim tells of his injuries, 20 May 2014.

SAPA. Krejcir implicated in confession, court told, 10 December 2013.

SAPA. Krejcir's words 'seared' into kidnapped man's memory, 22 May 2014.

CHAPTER 18

Germaner, Shain. Another arrest, more charges in Krejcir case, *The Star*, 30 January 2014.

Germaner, Shain. 'Plotter' linked to slaying of Krejcir crony, *Pretoria News*, 27 May 2014.

Maphumulo, Solly. Krejcir accused of hiring hit men, *The Mercury*, 21 March 2014.

Roane, Brendan. Krejcir and three others charged with murder of debt collector, *The Star*, 22 April 2014.

Roane, Brendan. Krejcir co-accused in plot to kill investigators, swop cells, *Pretoria News*, 3 June 2014.

SAPA. Krejcir charged with debt collector's murder, 22 April 2014.

SAPA. Murder plot: Cop suspect in court, 18 January 2014.

CHAPTER 19

Evans, Sally and Sam Sole. Key witness fears Krejcir's reach, *Mail & Guardian*, 12 February 2016.

Serrao, Angelique. 'I was part of Krejcir's evil world', *The Star*, 19 February 2016.

CHAPTER 20

Chernick, Ilanit. Captain threatened me, Krejcir tells court in bid to get bail, *The Star*, 30 July 2015.

Germaner, Shain. 'Hitman' in alleged Issa witnesses plot nabbed, *The Star*, 26 June 2015.

Germaner, Shain. Issa trial marked by new twists and death threat, *Pretoria News*, 1 July 2015.

Germaner, Shain. Krejcir defence accuses State of unfair trial, *The Star*, 18 May 2016.

Germaner, Shain. Krejcir falls asleep as case drags, *The Star*, 26 May 2016.

Germaner, Shain. Krejcir implicates an ex-president in bail bid, *The Star*, 9 July 2015.

Germaner, Shain. Krejcir insists it wasn't him, *The Star*, 27 August 2015.

Germaner, Shain. Krejcir team accused of fishing for evidence, *The Star*, 19 May 2016.

Germaner, Shain. Murder accused warned: Stay away from witness, *The Star*, 10 May 2016.

Germaner, Shain. 'Only weak evidence' against Krejcir, *The Star*, 21 August 2015.

Germaner, Shain. Suspected Krejcir hitman in the dock, *The Star*, 30 June 2015.

Maphumulo, Solly. Police sure of solid Krejcir case, *The Mercury*, 24 June 2014.

SAPA. Oscar trains with Krejcir in city prison, 14 November 2014.

Serrao, Angelique. Krejcir charged with Issa murder, *The Star*, 6 February 2015.

Serumula, Rabbie, Angelique Serrao and SAPA. Bail debt owed by Krejcir led to associate Issa's murder – claim, *Pretoria News*, 7 February 2015.

Venter, Zelda. No big birthday celebration in store for jailbird Oscar, *The Star*, 22 November 2014.

Watson, Amanda. 'Leak' threatens Krejcir witnesses, *The Citizen*, 2 July 2013, http://citizen.co.za/415425/leak-threatens-krejcir-witnesses/, accessed 17 June 2016.

CHAPTER 21

African News Agency. Raid on cells foils Krejcir escape plan, 29 September 2015.

Germaner, Shain. Defence pushes for release of evidence against Krejcir 'helpers' over alleged plot to escape prison, *Cape Times*, 25 April 2016.

Germaner, Shain. Jailbreak plot: Krejcir, fellow inmate and warder face charges, *The Star*, 12 April 2016.

Germaner, Shain. Krejcir escape plotters possibly caught on video, *The Star*, 25 April 2016.

Germaner, Shain. Krejcir's son implicated in escape plot, *The Star*, 20 May 2016.

Germaner, Shain. Perhaps his lighter side only makes him darker, *The Star*, 30 July 2015.

Krejcir fights his war alone, *The Citizen*, 7 July 2015, http://citizen.co.za/419148/krejcir-fights-his-war-alone-2/, accessed 19 April 2015.

Maphumulo, Solly. O'Sullivan vows to hunt down and kill Krejcir if he escapes, *The Star*, 29 September 2015.

Ndlazi, Sakhile. Krejcir 'smuggler' gets bail after shoe to-do, *The Star*, 28 October 2015.

Nkosi, Nomaswazi. Media gets rare tour of Oscar Mampuru Prison, *Cape Times*, 2 December 2015.

Serrao, Angelique. Estate funds to cover Krejcir's legal fees, *The Star*, 8 December 2015.

Serrao, Angelique. Hello, is that shoe? Krejcir footwear a talking point, *The Mercury*, 30 October 2015.

Serrao, Angelique. Woman held over Krejcir cash deals, *The Star*, 2 November 2015.

Venter, Zelda. Krejcir son in court bid to return to SA, *Pretoria News*, 23 April 2015.

CHAPTER 22

Germaner, Shain. Bomb threat and rattling chains at Krejcir trial, *The Star*, 23 February 2016.

Germaner, Shain. Judge in Krejcir case slated by lawyer, *The Star*, 19 April 2016.

Germaner, Shain. Krejcir, co-accused to know appeal fate, *Cape Times*, 20 April 2016.

Maphumulo, Solly. Krejcir moved to SA's most secure jail, *The Star*, 5 January 2016.

Maphumulo, Solly. Krejcir's 'plan to kill judge', *Cape Times*, 18 February 2016.

Mokati, Noni. Krejcir's hard-core lockdown in Kokstad, *The Star*, 23 January 2016.

Serrao, Angelique. Fans back Krejcir on Twitter, *The Star*, 18 February 2015.

Thamm, Marianne. Czech mate: Radovan Krejcir finally runs out of luck, *Daily Maverick*, 23 February 2016, http://www.dailymaverick.co.za/article/2016-02-23-czech-mate-radovan-krejcir-finally-runs-out-of-luck/#.Vw-qKVUrLcs, accessed 14 April 2016.

Index

Acknowledgements

It was early in 2016. I was at my office at *The Star*, and I had a new tip-off on another crazy Krejcir story. A new murder plot had been uncovered. Instead of going to Google to do some background research, I went into my emails to look for an affidavit I knew I had stored there. I typed in the word 'Krejcir' and more than 200 emails popped up, many with documents attached. I sat back. The amount of information glaring at me was overwhelming.

'This is a book,' I thought to myself.

And so, this journey began.

It really started in 2010 when Lolly Jackson was murdered. As a student, I had worked in a Greek restaurant in Bedfordview and I had met Jackson once or twice. I had gone to school with his daughter, Samantha. I was in an older class, but I remembered her. I didn't know the family well, but the passing connection meant that I eagerly volunteered to work on any stories that popped up when Jackson was murdered. At that stage, I had no real idea who Krejcir was but, as time went on, that would change. I wrote countless stories on him over the years.

When I looked at those emails that day, there were six years of work staring back at me. As a journalist, you often jump from story to story, and sometimes it becomes one big blur as the years go by. There are some, however, that stick to you. For me, Krejcir was one of them.

And yet, even though I knew I had a wealth of information at my fingertips, I hesitated. I had travelled this journey before and knew a book was not something you take on lightly. There is no way round it – a book is hard work. And, for someone who has young children and a stressful full-time job, it can be torturous.

For what happened next, I have to thank *The Star*'s editor, Kevin Ritchie, whom I told of my musings that I had a book lying inside my computer. He not only eagerly convinced me to go for it, but contacted publishers to get me on my way, and checked on my progress regularly. He also allowed me to use *The Star*'s archives of stories and photographs, which helped provide material for a large portion of this book. Kevin, thank you. This book would not be here without you.

In many ways, *Krejcir* is an action story. In the space of nine years, so much happened and it is easy to get caught up in the excitement of such a dramatic tale. But, sitting on my own, wrapped up in blankets early in the cold winter mornings of 2016, when I put this book together, it was more than just the freezing temperatures that chilled my bones. Many of the people in this book are no longer here to tell us their version of what happened. You only get a real picture of how many people lost their lives when you put the full story together. Unlike in a fiction story, there is no excitement about blood being spilt. It is horrible, unnatural, and leaves broken hearts and human destruction in its wake.

The people in my life took me away from those morose thoughts. My children, my husband and my brother fill my life with such happiness and joy that I can never focus on the negatives of the work I do for too long. Thank you is not strong enough a sentiment to tell you how much I love and appreciate you. No work I do can ever be achieved without you.

Then there are those who have encouraged me every step of the way. My publisher, Ester Levinrad, who always had a kind word and such good, level-headed advice, thank you for helping me on this journey. To the editor, Mark Ronan, you were so thorough and made this story flow. Your advice was invaluable.

To my new boss, Adriaan Basson, who, as soon as I joined News24 halfway through the writing, was 100 per cent on board. The big smiles and encouraging WhatsApp messages telling me he could not wait to see my book in print helped me through the tough editing process.

My colleagues and my neighbours, Adele and Kathleen, who listened patiently to all my tired whining, and brightly told me to carry on. Thank you – one needs those little pep talks along the way.

To my colleague at *The Star*, Shain Germaner, you have been more than just a friend. You have been an inspiration and I cannot thank you enough for cheering me on and for your help with content. In the last few weeks of 2016, Shain was often the only journalist still in court covering Krejcir's cases. The media got bored with the tedious postponements and coverage has withered away. But Shain is still there, keeping everyone informed. Shain, you are a great journalist and I cannot wait to read your own book one day soon, I hope.

It is a pleasure to thank those who contributed to all those hundreds of emails I had amassed on Krejcir over the years and who gave their time and effort to help me write my stories and, ultimately, this book.

Paul O'Sullivan has always given his time and information freely. Nobody knows more about Krejcir than he does. Thank you for every bit of help. Paul has put his life on the line for years on this case and his fight against Krejcir has been truly heroic.

To Chad Thomas, who has shared his memories of Cyril Beeka and Sam Issa, and who has also sent every bit of information he has gathered over the years to me, a big thank you. Your help has been invaluable.

To the police and the NPA, who have worked tirelessly to bring Krejcir to justice, thank you. Society owes you an enormous debt of gratitude. You have turned around the perception that all police are corrupt.

There are many others who helped me with this story: police officers, attorneys and members of Krejcir's inner circle. I cannot name you here, but please know how thankful I am for all the information you have shared with me over the years.

And, finally, to you, the reader. I hope you enjoy what I have written here. It was a hard journey, but I trust you will find it was worth it.

Angelique Serrao